EU Framework for Foreign Direct Investment Control

European Monographs Series Set

VOLUME 111

Editor

Prof. Andrea Biondi is Professor of European Law and Director of the Centre of European Law at King's College London

Introduction & Contents/Subjects

As the process of European integration assumes an increasingly complex character, the EU legal system continues to undergo sweeping changes. The European Monographs series offers a voice to thoughtful, knowledgeable, cutting edge legal commentary on the now unlimited field of European law. Its emphasis on focal and topical issues makes the series an invaluable tool for scholars, practitioners, and policymakers specializing or simply interested in EU law.

Objective

The aim is to publish innovative work appealing to academics and practitioners alike. The result is an original and ongoing library of detailed analyses, theories, commentaries, practical guides, and proposals, each of which furthers the cause of meaningful European integration. Cumulatively, the series may be regarded as a 'work in progress' engaged in building a sharply defined representation of law in Europe.

Readership

Academics and practitioners dealing with EU law.

The titles published in this series are listed at the end of this volume.

EU Framework for Foreign Direct Investment Control

Edited by

Jacques H.J. Bourgeois

Wolters Kluwer

Published by:
Kluwer Law International B.V.
PO Box 316
2400 AH Alphen aan den Rijn
The Netherlands
E-mail: international-sales@wolterskluwer.com
Website: lrus.wolterskluwer.com

Sold and distributed in North, Central and South America by:
Wolters Kluwer Legal & Regulatory U.S.
7201 McKinney Circle
Frederick, MD 21704
United States of America
Email: customer.service@wolterskluwer.com

Sold and distributed in all other countries by:
Air Business Subscriptions
Rockwood House
Haywards Heath
West Sussex
RH16 3DH
United Kingdom
Email: international-customerservice@wolterskluwer.com

ISBN 978-94-035-1883-1

e-Book: ISBN 978-94-035-1921-0
web-PDF: ISBN 978-94-035-1930-2

Editor

Bourgeois, Jacques H.J., Professor at the College of Europe, Senior Advisor, Sidley Austin LLP, Brussels, Belgium.

Contributors

Bismuth, Régis, Professor at the Sciences Po Law School, Paris, France.

Bourgeois, Jacques H.J., Professor at the College of Europe, Senior advisor, Sidley Austin LLP, Brussels, Belgium

Cremona, Marise, Professor Emeritus at the European University Institute, Firenze, Italy.

Fassion, Justine, Associate, Sidley Austin LLP, Brussels, Belgium.

Henriksen, Jonas Juul, PhD, Economist, Copenhagen Economics, Copenhagen, Denmark.

Krause, Hartmut, Rechtsanwalt, Partner of Allen & Overy, Frankfurt am Main, Germany.

Lavranos, Nikos, Secretary-General EFILA, Guest Professor at the Vrije Universiteit Brussels, Belgium.

Malathouni, Eliza, PhD candidate, University of Maastricht, the Netherlands.

Martin-Prat, Maria, Director at the Directorate-General for Trade, European Commission, Brussels, Belgium.

Mendenhall, James, Attorney, Partner of Sidley Austin LLP, Washington DC, USA.

Natens, Bregt, PhD, Associate of Sidley Austin LLP, Brussels, Belgium.

Neergaard, Anders, Lawyer Manager, European Parliament, Brussels, Belgium.

Rytter Sunesen, Eva, PhD, Economist, Copenhagen Economics, Copenhagen, Denmark.

Schaake, Marietje, MEP ALDE/D66, Brussels, Belgium.

Schekulin, Manfred, Deputy Director General Trade Policy and European Integration, Federal Ministry of Science, Research and Economy, Vienna, Austria.

Schill, Stephan, Professor, University of Amsterdam, the Netherlands.

Terney, Riana, Associate, Sidley Austin LLP, Washington DC, USA.

van der Marel, Erik, Associate Lecturer Université Libre de Bruxelles, Senior Economist ECIPE, Brussels, Belgium.

Summary of Contents

Table of Contents

Preface

This book results from a conference organized in 2018 at the College of Europe during which papers were submitted and discussed and subsequently peer-reviewed. The topic of the conference was the European Commission proposal on foreign direct investment (FDI) screening. Following the adoption of the Regulation, contributions were added analysing that Regulation.

Part I consists of two chapters.

In Chapter 1, Ms Rytter and Mr Henriksen, two economists, review the role of FDI in the EU since 2003. They identify the main sectors (manufacturing, information and communication, finance and insurance), the main host EU Member States (Germany, France, Italy, the Netherlands and the UK) and the home countries of the investors (Bermuda (sic), Canada, Norway, Switzerland and the US). In their concluding remarks they note, *inter alia*, the increased average value of FDI in (potentially) sensitive sectors and over-representation of State-Owned Enterprises.

Commenting on the Rytter/Henriksen's chapter, Prof. van der Marel notes that today's economies are becoming increasingly tangible economies. Policy-makers should take account of certain features of such economies ('low footprint', seeking knowledge and finance, extreme mobility, positive spill-over effects).

In Chapter 2, Prof. Cremona addresses three legal questions raised by the EU regulation concerning FDI in the EU: whether the EU's common commercial policy powers cover regulation of FDI, what relation exists with the EU internal market powers and rules, why EU rather than Member States action.

Prof. Cremona concludes that the EU founding treaties leave the EU political institutions with a great deal of discretion in determining their policy priorities for the common commercial policy including the degree of liberalization. However, action under the EU common commercial policy powers relating to FDI is subject to the freedom of capital movement which also applies between the EU and third states. Any derogation from that freedom must be justified according to the EU treaties' rules as well as be compliant with the EU's international obligations.

In his comments on Chapter 2, Prof. Schill defends the view that the regulation proposed by the European Commission has a tangible external economic policy justification. It creates the otherwise missing possibilities to limit FDI into the EU that can be used as a bargaining chip to achieve better access of EU investors in negotiations with economically powerful countries. Paradoxically, notes Prof. Schill, introducing screening on inward FDI can serve the EU's constitutionally enshrined goal of further investment liberalisation.

As to Part II, bearing in mind that topic is the EU framework for FDI screening, rather than FDI screening by EU Member States, no attempt has been made to describe the diverse existing Member-States' systems of FDI control. Such description is available, *inter alia*, in the E.P. Briefing on foreign direct investment screening (PE 603.941) and in the European Commission Staff Working Document (SWD (2017) 297) and in Seamon, Huotari, Otero-Iglesias (eds), *Chinese Investments in Europe* (ETCN Report, December 2017).

Instead, this part contains a chapter by Dr Krause on a practitioner's experience of FDI control in Germany. He examines the filings, the required ones and the optional ones, which allow to proceed without clearance. Interestingly, he doubts whether effective legal protection is possible.

It also contains a chapter by Mr Schekulin describing the Austrian FDI screening mechanism, its scope and relevant sectors, the 'controlling influence' and the 25% of voting rights thresholds, the ex ante approval and the ex officio review.

Part III provides comments on the European Commission proposal.

Ms Martin-Prat in Chapter 5 refers to the overall context marked by a shift away from the EU's traditional investment partners to the benefit of emerging partners, such as Brazil, China and Russia, and by a changing world in which the role of the state in the economy of some third countries is increasing. This raises questions about the nature of such FDIs. The increasingly interlinked economies share not only opportunities but also threats. After describing briefly the content of the Proposed Regulation, Ms Martin-Prat stresses that it addresses issues of security and public order, which are legitimate exceptions to the EU's multilateral and bilateral commitments.

Ms Schaake in Chapter 6 draws the attention to the broader context that forms the frame of reference for the European Parliament on FDI screening but also on other trade measures. Part of that context is the broader strategy which China seems to be pushing for more political influence globally. This analysis seems to be confirmed by China buying up strategic assets in the EU. Ms Schaake too underlines that in the EU internal market it makes sense to have similar criteria of FDI screening between Member States. According to this MEP, a number of EU measures cannot adequately address the challenges the EU faces in today's intertwined global economy, especially in relation to China, if they are not placed within an overall strategy. The EU should see all the factors for what they are and then make a decision: that cannot be seen as a form of veiled protectionism.

In Chapter 7, Prof. Bismuth notes what he calls the 'cautious protective narrative' of the proposed regulation. On the one hand, it includes provisions concerning the screening of investments in strategic sectors; on the other hand, it does not deal with reciprocity and does not clearly address the anti-competitive effects of subsidized acquisitions. He questions the reliance on Article 207 TFEU as a legal basis. He perceives 'an implied obligation' for Member States to establish FDI screening mechanisms and 'a soft blocking power' of the European Commission. The proposed regulation is a missed opportunity to address reciprocity and level playing field issues.

This part concludes with a discussion of a panel consisting of two diplomats, an academic, a journalist, the general counsel of a multinational company and a consultant. The panel was chaired by Prof. Lavranos, who provides a summary of the discussion in Chapter 8.

Part IV contains two chapters on the international context of the Proposed Regulation. In their chapter, Ms Fassion and Dr Natens look at the WTO rules disciplining FDI control. They consider relevant certain WTO good governance rules which are conceptually similar to the notion of 'fair and equitable treatment' typically found in investment rules. On substance, they identify relevant provisions in the WTO Trade Related Investment Measures Agreement and in the WTO General Agreement on Trade in Services. They focus on key disciplines on non-discrimination and market access as well as on exceptions justifying departures from these disciplines. Fassion and Natens follow an interesting step-by-step analytical method to identify the issues raised by FDI control and the available exceptions. They warn that the general exceptions and the security exceptions (by the EU's own standards) will not be easy-to-reach safe havens.

Chapter 10 by Mr Mendenhall, probably the most FDI control knowledgeable US attorney, and Ms Terney provides a very instructive summary of the current laws and procedures of FDI control in the US, commonly known as CIFIUS (Committee on Foreign Investments in the United States). From an institutional point of view, there is an obvious difference between CIFIUS and what the European Commission proposed to establish. CIFIUS is exclusively federal, i.e., FDI control is centralized. What the Commission proposed is leaving matters in the hands of Member States with consultation and cooperation.

On substance, there are similarities. CIFIUS is designed to determine whether a transaction by a foreign person resulting in control of a US business poses a national security risk.

A series of factors listed in the Defence Production Act are taken into account. CIFIUS annual reports list also other factors it considered. The number of matters considered by CIFIUS as pertaining to national security appears to be increasing.

The authors also refer to judicial review. The legislation states that CIFIUS determinations are not subject to judicial review. A circuit court held in a landmark case that they are nevertheless subject to review on constitutional procedural grounds to safeguard due process.

Interesting facts and figures about the implementation are provided.

Part V contains two chapters dealing with the Regulation as adopted in March 2019. In his chapter, Mr Neergaard provides an overview of the Regulation and comments on some of the legal issues raised in the process of its adoption. He concludes that the mechanism established is likely to strengthen the capacity of the Member States to coordinate in addressing risks to security and public order.

In their contribution Jacques Bourgeois and Ms Malathouni sketched the policy aspects of the development of FDI both worldwide and from an EU perspective. In an attempt to explain the particular features of the Regulation by examining them critically, they then place the Regulation in the context of other EU tools dealing with FDI and address the question whether and to what extent these tools take account of the economic policy aspects of FDI in the EU.

We thank Sidley Austin for its generous financial assistance making it possible to organize the conference. We also thank Ms Hauspie, Secretary of the Legal Department of the College of Europe, for her constant and precious help in organizing the conference and in producing this book.

Jacques H.J. Bourgeois

PART I The Economic and EU Legal Background

CHAPTER 1

The Economics of FDI Screening

Eva Rytter Sunesen & Jonas Juul Henriksen

While foreign firms contribute to growth and job creation in the EU, foreign takeovers of strategically sensitive assets may in some cases risk compromising national security. Various screening mechanisms are increasingly being used by European Union (EU) Member States to mitigate risks of foreign direct investment (FDI) inflows. This chapter summarises some of the potential economic consequences of FDI screening and describes initiatives that can help enhance the effectiveness and efficiency of such screening mechanisms.

§1.01 LOW FDI FLOWS INTO THE EU

During 2003–2016, foreign (non-EU) firms carried out more than 55,000 FDI projects in the EU, and foreign takeovers of existing EU firms accounted for a large share of total FDI into the EU during this period. Foreign firms have a large economic footprint in the EU, and competition for global FDI is intense. In 2014, the EU received around 20% of the global FDI flows, down from 50% in 1990. Over time, low FDI inflows may harm growth and job creation in the EU.

§1.02 FOREIGN TAKEOVERS ACCOUNT FOR A LARGE SHARE OF FDI INFLOWS

During 2003–2016, foreign investors carried out around 55,400 FDI projects in the EU, amounting to a total value of more than EUR 2,500 billion, cf. Figure 1.1.[1] Close to

1. The analysis is based on a database containing all publicly recorded FDI projects into and out of Europe from 2003–2016. The database has been developed by Copenhagen Economics by combining the Bureau van Dijk Zephyr (BvD) database on M&As and the Financial Times FDI Markets database on greenfield FDI projects. Portfolio investments are excluded.

28,000 projects worth more than EUR 1,700 billion (67% of the total deal value) were mergers and acquisitions (M&As) with an average deal value of EUR 155 million. The remaining projects were greenfield investments that amounted to more than EUR 800 billion with an average deal value of EUR 30 million.

The majority of the FDI projects were in the services sectors (57%), where the average deal value of EUR 59 million was slightly smaller than the average deal value of EUR 63 million for FDI projects in the manufacturing sector. The total deal value was EUR 1,200 billion in the service sector and EUR 1,000 billion in the manufacturing sector.[2]

Figure 1.1 55,400 FDI Projects into the EU During 2003–2016

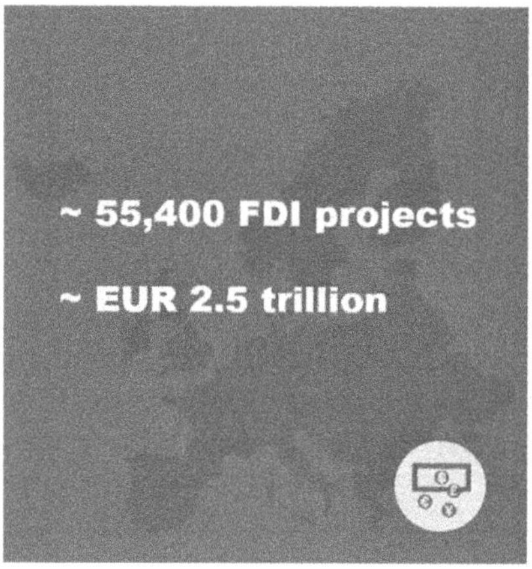

50% **M&As** ~ EUR 1,700 billion
EUR 155 million per deal

50% **greenfield investments** ~ EUR 800 billion
EUR 30 million per deal

57% in **services** ~ EUR 1,200 billion
EUR 59 million per deal

37% in **manufacturing** ~ EUR 1,000 billion
EUR 63 million per deal

3% by **public investors** ~ EUR 150 billion
EUR 497 million per deal (only M&As)

Source: Copenhagen Economics based on data from the BvD Zephyr and FT databases.

Note: Public investors include, among others, state-owned enterprises from non-EU countries. The figure is based on the report Copenhagen Economics (2017), *Screening of FDI towards the EU*. Values are in constant 2015 prices. Not all M&A deals have an associated value. The figure excludes portfolio investments, i.e., acquisitions below 10% of the stocks. Projects, primarily in the primary sector, that are neither classified as 'Services' nor 'Manufacturing' are grouped as 'Others'.

M&As by non-EU public investors amounted to EUR 150 billion and accounted for 3% of the total number of FDI projects (around 6% of the total value). These are on average larger projects with an average deal size of EUR 497 million.

2. The remaining projects (5%) are grouped as 'Others'. This group includes mainly projects in the primary sector.

While openness to foreign investment is expected to remain a key principle for the EU, there is growing concern about foreign investors, notably state-controlled or state-owned enterprises (SOEs), taking over EU companies with key technologies for strategic reasons.[3] In light of this, the European Commission has put forward a proposal for establishing a framework for screening of FDI into the EU. The objective of the regulation is to 'establish a framework for the Member States, and in certain cases the Commission, to screen foreign direct investments in the European Union, while allowing Member States to take into account their individual situations and national circumstances'.[4]

This chapter analyses developments and patterns in foreign takeovers of EU firms, particularly in potentially sensitive sectors and takeovers by foreign SOEs.[5]

§1.03 TAKEOVERS ARE CONCENTRATED IN MATURE EU MEMBER STATES

M&As by foreign investors mainly take place in the old EU Member States with mature businesses ready for takeover, cf. Figure 1.2. The UK was the main destination, accounting for 40% of all M&As in the EU during 2003 – 2016. Germany was the second largest recipient of M&As accounting for 12%. Bulgaria is the destination among the new Member States that attracts the largest share of M&As (2% of the total number of M&As in the EU). Top six EU Member States accounted for 76% of M&As by foreign investors into the EU. Hence, the remaining twenty-two Member States accounted for 24% of M&As by foreign investors in the EU.

3. European Commission (2017), *Harnessing Globalisation*. This was also reflected in a common letter from the German, French and Italian governments to Trade Commissioner Malmström.
4. European Commission (2017), *Proposal for a Regulation of the European Parliament and of the Council establishing a framework for screening foreign direct investments into the European Union* (SWD (2017) 297 final).
5. Focus in this chapter is on M&As as foreign takeovers are the main focus of the Commission's proposal on FDI screening (excluding portfolio investments). Certain greenfield investments can also be prone to screening under the proposal, e.g., due to their location. *See* more details in Copenhagen Economics (2017), *Screening of FDI Towards the EU*.

Figure 1.2 The UK Is the Main Destination for M&As in the EU

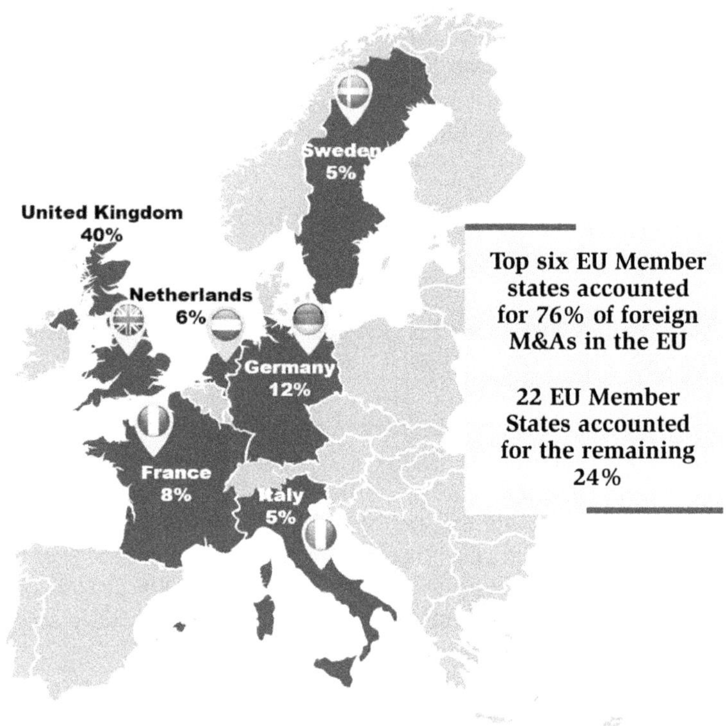

Source: Copenhagen Economics based on the BvD's Zephyr and the FT databases.

Note: The percentages are each country's respective share of total M&As by foreign investors in the EU. The period covers the years 2003–2016. Data were extracted in August 2017 and include confirmed transactions (number of M&As).

M&As in the EU during this period were undertaken by investors from 124 different countries, cf. Figure 1.3. The US accounted for more than half (51%) of the total number of M&As in the EU. The significant presence of US firms increases the exposure of the EU economy to political and economic changes in the US, and any emergence of barriers to outward FDI in the US could be a concern to EU policy-makers. Adjacent European countries, Switzerland and Norway, were the second and third largest origins of M&As in the EU.

Figure 1.3 The US Is the Main Investor in the EU

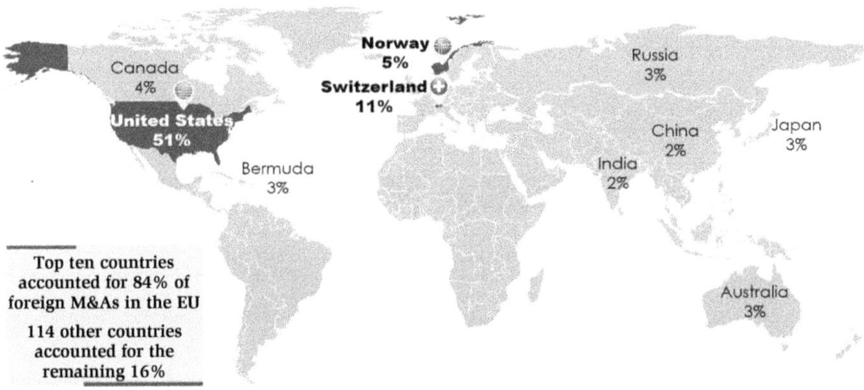

Source: Copenhagen Economics based on the BvD's Zephyr and the FT databases.

Note: The percentages are each origin country's respective share of total M&As by third-country investors into the EU Member States. The period covers the years 2003–2016. Data were extracted in August 2017 and include confirmed transactions (number of M&As).

[A] Low FDI Inflows Can Harm EU Growth and Job Creation

Foreign firms contribute substantially to the EU economy. Foreign firms accounted for approximately 1% of the total number of firms in 2014 but were responsible for an average of 5% of total employment, 11% of output and 9% of value added, cf. Figure 1.4. In addition, foreign firms accounted for a large share (7%) of investments in tangible goods, such as investments in land and other capital goods.

Foreign firms integrate in EU supply chains and support jobs through backward and forward linkages with local firms in addition to the economic activity supported directly in the foreign firms themselves. Further, foreign firms often bring important technology, know-how and management skills that can benefit local firms through productivity spillovers – this is particularly the case for small and medium sized enterprises (SMEs).[6]

6. *See* Copenhagen Economics (2018), *The World in Europe, Global FDI Flows Towards Europe: Extra-European FDI Towards Europe.*

Figure 1.4 Foreign Firms Have a Large Footprint in the EU

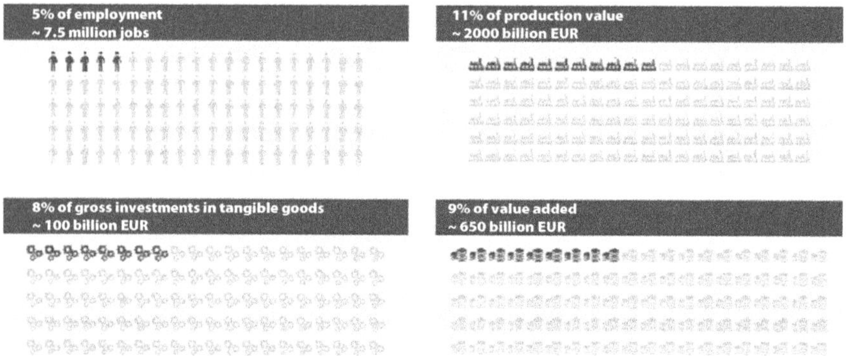

Source: Copenhagen Economics based on Eurostat's Foreign Affiliates and Structural Business Statistics.

Note: The figures show the average share of each of the four outcome measures accounted for by foreign firms (simple averages across twenty-seven EU Member States, excluding Ireland). Data are from 2014 (in cases where 2014 data is missing, data from 2013 have been used).

Competition for FDI is intense, and the EU share of global FDI flows is decreasing, cf. Figure 1.5. In 1990, the EU was the destination of around 50% of global FDI flows. This share had dropped to 20% in 2014. The same pattern can be seen in intra-EU FDI flows as EU firms also invest increasingly outside the EU. In 1994, more than 60% of EU outward FDI were targeted at another EU country. By 2012, this number had fallen to 26%. Over time, low FDI inflows may harm EU growth and job creation.

Figure 1.5 The EU Receives a Decreasing Share of Both Total EU and Global FDI Flows

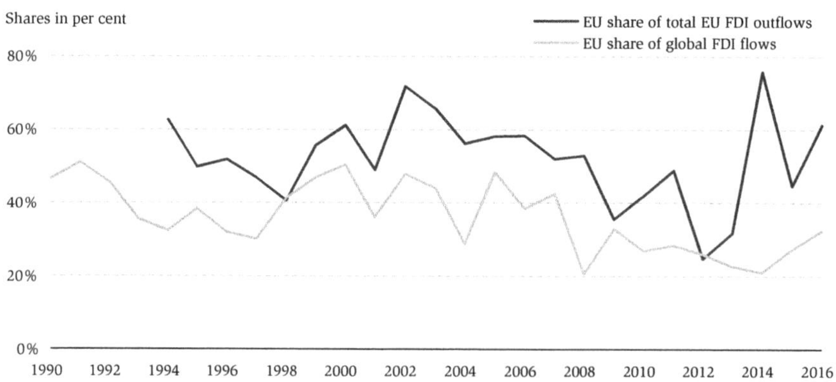

Source: Copenhagen Economics based on data from the Eurostat's Balance of Payments Statistics and WIR (2015) annex table 1.

Note: 'EU share of total EU FDI flows' is based on data from the Eurostat's Balance of Payments Statistics and EU refers to EU15 until 2012. In 2013, there is a data break and hereafter EU refers to EU28. 'EU share of global FDI flows' is based on data from WIR (2015) and EU refers to EU28.

High economic growth in the BRIC countries and other developing countries is a key driver of the shift in global FDI patterns.[7] Demand is thus the FDI driver that is most frequently used in empirical studies of global FDI (used in 115 studies), cf. Figure 1.6.

Figure 1.6 Demand Is the Most Frequently Used FDI Driver

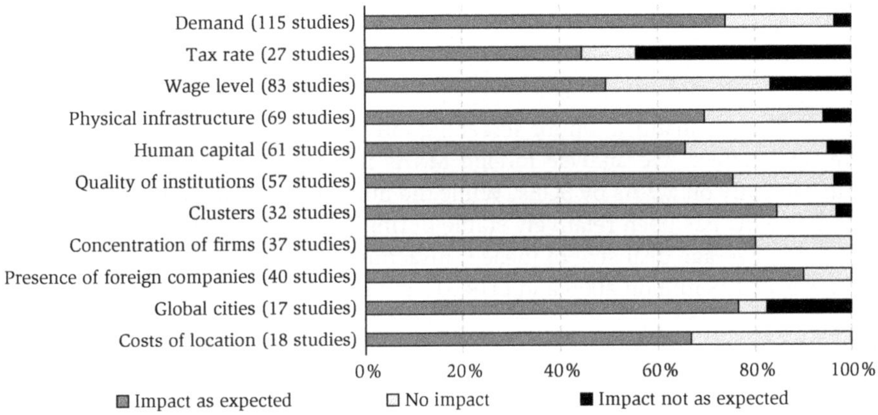

Source: Copenhagen Economics based on Nielsen, Asmussen & Weatherall (2017), 'The location choice of foreign direct investments: Empirical evidence and methodological challenges,' *Journal of World Business.*

Note: The literature survey covers 154 empirical studies of FDI location. 'Impact as expected' means that the impact quantified in the empirical study has the expected sign, 'No impact' means that the impact is not significant and 'Impact not as expected' means that the impact had the opposite sign than expected.

§1.04 THE ECONOMICS OF FDI SCREENING

FDI inflows contribute to the EU economy, but an open FDI regime may in some cases also be associated with risks. Several EU Member States already screen FDI with the aim of protecting national security,[8] and other countries are considering to amend their screening mechanisms.[9] FDI screening is typically carried out in two dimensions.

7. For further information on global FDI flows and FDI attractiveness, *see* Copenhagen Economics (2016), *Towards an FDI attractiveness Scoreboard.*
8. According to the European Commission (2017), *Foreign Direct Investment – An EU Screening Framework*, twelve EU Member States currently have screening mechanisms in place that may be used to address possible risks of FDI on the grounds of security or public order. Screening mechanisms in these countries differ widely in terms of *sectoral coverage, threshold levels*, the *origin* of the acquirer targeted by screening, and the *types of investors* prone to screening. Divergences also prevail in the design of existing screening procedures (e.g., prior authorisation mechanisms and ex-post screening mechanisms).
9. *See* Copenhagen Economics (2017), *Screening of FDI Towards the EU*, for an overview of countries where such considerations are ongoing.

First, screening can be based on characteristics of the asset, resulting in the screening of FDI in strategically important sectors. In this chapter, we define potentially sensitive sectors as utilities, defence, critical computer technology, air transport and financial services.[10]

Second, screening can be based on characteristics of the investor, resulting in predominantly screening of FDI by state-owned (or state-controlled) enterprises (SOEs). SOEs may be regarded as agents of their home country governments, pursuing political agendas and implementing government strategies beyond private business considerations.[11] Thus, if a foreign investor is directly or indirectly controlled by a government, and also receives subsidised funds or capital for the investments, there could be a stronger justification for screening foreign takeovers.[12]

In this chapter, we analyse foreign M&As in potentially sensitive sectors and zoom-in explicitly on M&As by SOEs. While the number M&As in potentially sensitive sectors in the EU has been relatively stable during 2003–2016 at around 350 projects annually, the average deal size of these transactions has increased. The average deal value was EUR 128 million 2008 and EUR 312 million in 2016. M&As by SOEs are also differently distributed across sectors compared to M&As by private investors, and investments by SOEs tend to come from non-market economies (e.g., Russia and China). This may cause concerns to EU policy-makers.

An effective screening mechanism can reduce the risk that foreign takeovers of EU firms compromise national security. In addition, initiatives to enhance the efficiency of the screening mechanism can minimise the costs and reduce the risk of unintended negative consequences of screening. Based on historical figures, it should be noted that not all EU Member States are equally exposed to FDI inflows in potentially sensitive sectors and takeovers by SOEs. This study thus supports a place-based approach to FDI screening where individual Member States adjust the scope of FDI screening to the national context.

[A] An Open FDI Regime Can Be Associated with Risks

The EU has one of the most open FDI regimes in the world, cf. Figure 1.7. In 1997, the EU and the US were almost equally restrictive to FDI. During the span of the following twenty years, the EU implemented various initiatives which lowered the regulatory restrictions on FDI. The US, on the other hand, has maintained its level of FDI restrictiveness. The lower OECD average is thus driven by lower FDI restrictiveness in the EU.

10. Potentially sensitive sectors can be defined in many ways. Copenhagen Economics (2017), *Screening of FDI towards the EU* works with three different definitions. This chapter refers to the most conservative of these where potentially sensitive sectors are defined as utilities, defence, critical computer technology, air transport and financial services.
11. Columbia Center on Sustainable Investment (2017), *Perspectives on Topical Foreign Direct Investment Issues*.
12. *See* Mannheimer Swartling (2017), *EU FDI Screening – Legal Considerations*.

Figure 1.7 The EU Is Less Restrictive to FDI than the US and OECD

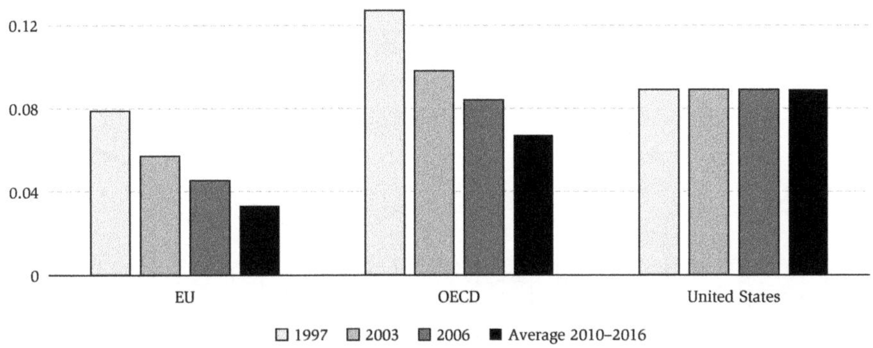

Source: Copenhagen Economics based on OECD's FDI Regulatory Restrictiveness Index.

Note: EU refers to the EU28, excluding Bulgaria, Croatia, Cyprus and Malta due to lack of data. In addition, no data were available for Latvia in 1997, for Lithuania in 1997 and 2003 and for Romania in 1997, 2003 and 2006. The FDI Regulatory Restrictiveness Index measures statutory restrictions on FDI across twenty-two economic sectors. Restrictions are evaluated on a 0 (open) to 1 (closed) scale. The values for the EU and OECD are simple averages.

An open FDI regime may be associated with risks, particularly takeovers in potentially sensitive sectors by foreign SOEs.

The number of foreign M&As in **potentially sensitive sectors** peaked in 2006, but has remained constant since at around 350 projects annually, cf. Figure 1.8. In addition, the underlying data show that the number of M&As in potentially sensitive sectors as a share of the total number of M&As has fluctuated around 20% from 2003 to 2016.[13] The average size of non-EU M&As in potentially sensitive sectors has increased since the financial crisis. The average deal size increased to EUR 312 million in 2016, up from EUR 128 million in 2008. Furthermore, the average deal size was at its all-time high in 2015 and 2016 compared to previous years. The underlying data furthermore show that the deal value of the M&As in potentially sensitive sectors reached an all-time high in 2016 at EUR 67 billion.[14] The increasing value of M&As in potentially sensitive sectors could be a concern to EU policy-makers and an argument for increased FDI screening of strategic assets and sectors.[15]

13. *See* Copenhagen Economics (2017), *Screening of FDI Towards the EU*.
14. Copenhagen Economics based on the BvD's Zephyr and the FT databases.
15. Bloomberg (2018), *How China Is Buying Its Way into Europe*, analyses Chinese FDI projects into the EU based on Bloomberg data. They conclude that the average deal value of Chinese FDI projects in Europe is declining, but that 'there is a clear upward trend in recent years' in terms of the aggregate deal value. The Bloomberg analysis differs from the one in Figure 1.4 since it does not focus on potentially sensitive sectors and investigates all FDI projects undertaken by Chinese entities.

Figure 1.8 Increasing Deal Values in Potentially Sensitive Sectors since the Financial Crisis: The Number of Projects Is Unchanged

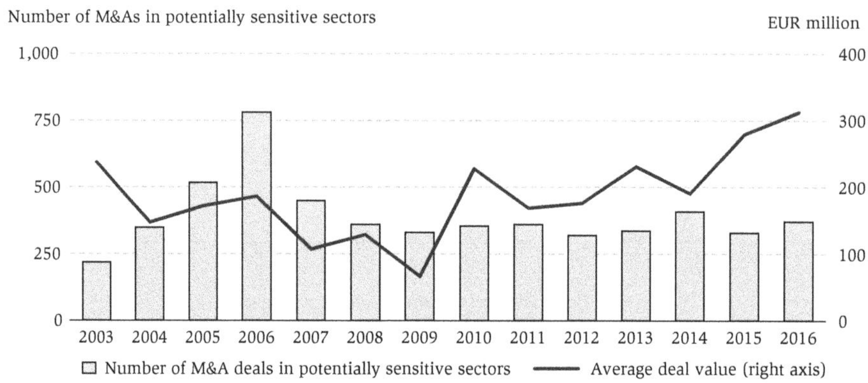

Source: Copenhagen Economics based on the BvD's Zephyr and the FT databases.

Note: Value of the projects are reported according to the price levels in 2015.

M&As by **SOEs in potentially sensitive sectors** are particularly important from a screening perspective as these may be influenced by strategic motives by home country governments. During 2003–2016, the number of M&As by SOEs in potentially sensitive sectors generally ranged from five to thirty, but peaked in 2016 with more than fifty transactions, cf. Figure 1.9.[16] From a screening perspective, the recent increase in the number of M&As undertaken by SOEs in potentially sensitive sectors could warrant special attention but it should also be kept in mind that the average value of the deals is relatively low (around EUR 100 million in 2016 on average compared to EUR 1.4 billion in 2015 and around EUR 600 million during 2003–2016).

16. Throughout the period, there are 7,408 M&As with unknown ownership, which indicates that there could be even more transactions by SOEs. In addition, it should be noted that state-subsidised firms are not recorded as SOEs.

Figure 1.9 M&As in the EU by SOEs in Potentially Sensitive Sectors

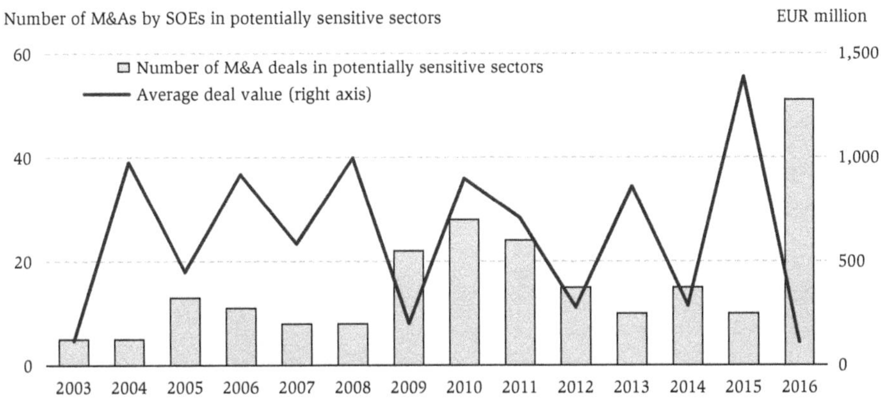

Source: Copenhagen Economics' FDI database.

Note: The period covers the years 2003–2016. Data were extracted in August 2017 and include confirmed transactions (number of M&As). There are 7,408 M&As with unknown ownership. The percentages refer to the broad scenario's share of total SOE M&As from third countries into the EU in that year.

[B] The Scope of FDI Screening Should Be Carefully Considered

Screening mechanisms already in place vary widely across countries. This is the case both in terms of the definition of potentially sensitive sectors, the focus on SOEs and the geographical coverage.

At the EU level, there are indications that SOEs have a different **sectoral investment profile** than private investors, cf. Figure 1.10. SOEs invest more in, e.g., *Mining* (13% of M&As by public investors compared to 4% for all M&As) and *Finance and insurance* (14% of M&As by public investors compared to 10% for all M&As). FDI screening could thus have a specific focus on SOEs depending on the individual Member State's definition of potentially sensitive sectors and its exposure to takeovers by public investors.

Figure 1.10 Sectoral Investment Profiles Differ for Public and Private Investors

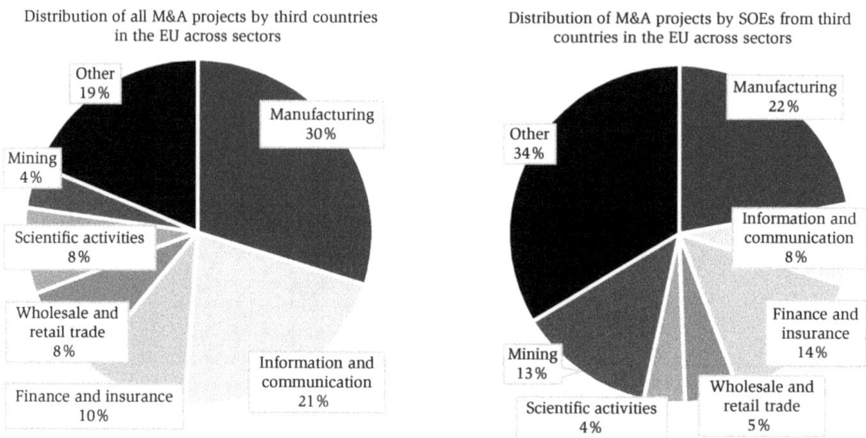

Source: Copenhagen Economics based on the BvD's Zephyr and the FT databases.

Note: The projects in the figure span the period 2003–2016. The figures are based on the number of M&As.

The **geographical coverage** of FDI screening should also be carefully considered across origin of investors. This follows by comparisons of the origin of M&As undertaken by SOEs in potentially sensitive sectors (Figure 1.11) with the origin of M&As in potentially sensitive sectors[17] and M&As in general (Figure 1.3). The US, for example, was the origin of 51% of all M&As into the EU and 46% of M&As into the EU in potentially sensitive sectors, but only 1% by SOEs in potentially sensitive sectors.

Russia, Kazakhstan, Switzerland and Norway are the four largest origin countries in terms of M&As by SOEs in potentially sensitive sectors in the EU. Whereas Russia was the origin of 3% of all foreign M&As in the EU and 5% of M&As in the EU in potentially sensitive sectors, it is the origin of 22% of the M&As by SOEs in potentially sensitive sectors in the EU.

Although FDI inflows from China have increased, China only accounts for 7% of M&As in potentially sensitive sectors by SOEs. Nevertheless, Chinese takeovers of EU firms are being heavily debated, whereas, e.g., Russian investments seem to go more unnoticed. As the origin of M&As in potentially sensitive sectors and M&As by SOEs come from a wide range of countries that may be changing over time, this speaks in favour of a country-neutral approach to FDI screening.

17. Copenhagen Economics based on the BvD's Zephyr and the FT databases.

Figure 1.11 Russia Accounted for 22% of M&As (49 Deals) by SOEs from Third Countries in Potentially Sensitive Sectors in the EU

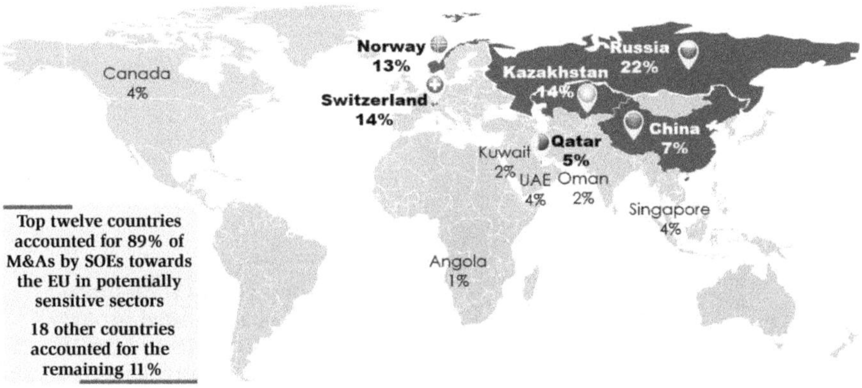

Source: Copenhagen Economics based on the BvD's Zephyr and the FT databases.

Note: The period covers the years 2003–2016. Data were extracted in August 2017 and include confirmed transactions (number of M&As). The figure reports shares in terms of number of M&A deals. The many Kazakhstani M&As were predominantly undertaken in 2016 and reflect minority investments in Dutch oil firms.

[C] Not All Countries Are Equally Exposed

M&As by foreign SOEs in potentially sensitive sectors are centred in the Netherlands (20%), the UK (15%) and Germany (11%), cf. Figure 1.12.

The number of M&As by foreign SOEs in potentially sensitive sectors into the Netherlands is disproportionately high. The Netherlands only accounted for around 6% of the total number of M&As in the EU and 6% of M&As in potentially sensitive sectors, but 20% of the number of M&As by SOEs in potentially sensitive sectors. A similar pattern is observed for Cyprus (1% of all M&As and 3% of M&As in potentially sensitive sectors but 7% of M&As by SOEs in potentially sensitive sectors). These figures suggest that effective FDI screening procedures should have anti-circumvention rules in place to take account of foreign takeovers through holding companies and other financial institutions in the EU.

Figure 1.12 The Netherlands Accounted for 20% of M&As by SOEs in Potentially Sensitive Sectors in the EU

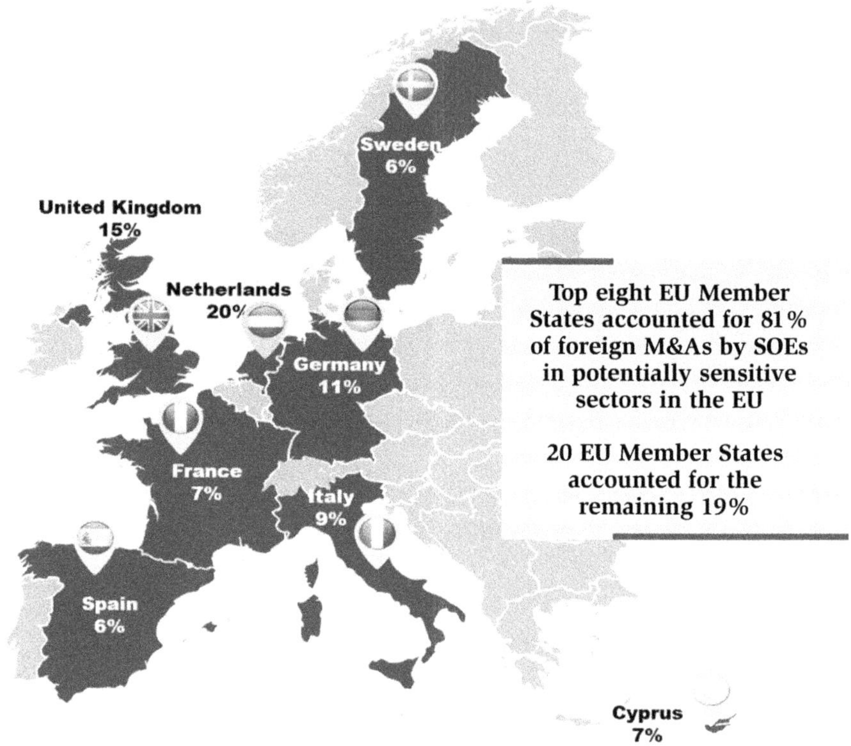

Source: Copenhagen Economics based on the BvD's Zephyr and the FT databases.

Note: The percentages are each country's respective share of total number of M&As by foreign SOEs in potentially sensitive sectors across EU Member States. The period covers the years 2003–2016. Data were extracted in August 2017 and include confirmed transactions (number of M&As). The large number of M&As in the Netherlands can partly be explained by a large number of minority investments in Dutch oil firms by SOEs from Kazakhstan.

The distribution of M&As by third-country SOEs in potentially sensitive sectors shows that some countries are prime destinations of these projects. However, it is silent on the share of total M&As in a country that is undertaken by foreign SOEs in potentially sensitive sectors.

As an example, the UK accounted for 15% of the M&As by foreign SOEs in potentially sensitive sectors. However, this only corresponds to 0.3% of the total number of M&As in the UK, cf. Figure 1.13. Cyprus, Portugal, Austria and the Netherlands are the four countries where SOEs in potentially sensitive sectors comprise the largest share of the total number of M&As from foreign investors. In Cyprus and

Portugal, almost 5% of the total number of M&As were undertaken by SOEs in potentially sensitive sectors.

Figure 1.13 Close to 5% of All M&As in Cyprus and Portugal Are Undertaken by SOEs in Potentially Sensitive Sectors

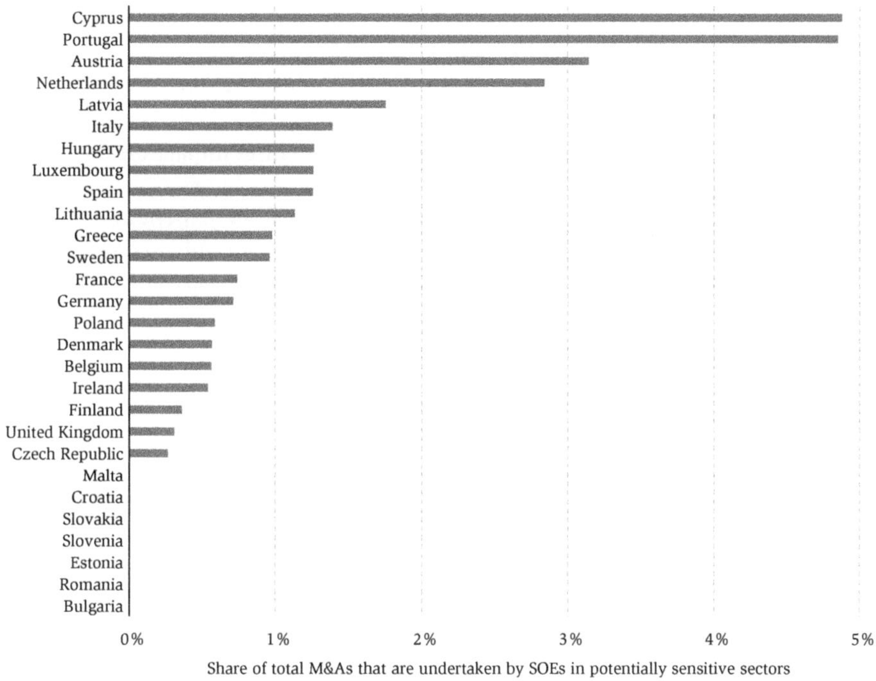

Source: Copenhagen Economics based on the BvD's Zephyr and the FT databases.

Note: Seven EU Member States did not receive any M&As by SOEs in potentially sensitive sectors.

[D] Increased Screening Can Be Associated with Costs

There is very limited knowledge about the magnitude of the economic costs of FDI screening. Nevertheless, increased FDI screening has potential implications for: (1) the administrative resources required by the authorities to conduct the screening, (2) the compliance costs, uncertainty and delays experienced by the acquiring firm, and (3) FDI inflows and access to capital for domestic firms.

[E] Increased Administrative Costs for the Responsible Authority

There are around 350 M&A deals in potentially sensitive sectors annually at the EU level, cf. Figure 1.8. Increasing the scope of FDI screening will increase the administrative costs accordingly. Case studies from Germany and Finland show that the main drivers of administrative costs are:

- **Identification of cases** requires significant resources, and it is the experience in Germany that mandatory reporting of acquisitions in critical areas saves the responsible authority the administrative effort in finding the cases themselves.
- **The number of files** increases the costs whereas the deal size and sectoral affiliation of the target company appear to have little impact on the costs of screening.
- **The complexity of the screening procedure**. It is the experience that standardisation can bring down the costs per screening but only to a certain level because certain actions depend on the particular case and are decided on an ad hoc basis.
- **Lack of cooperation**. The willingness of the potential target/acquirer to cooperate and disclose the required information and documents. The involved firms are generally interested in avoiding delays, and disputes and discussions happen only rarely (particularly when specialised lawyers are involved). The screening authorities find that procedures to treat all documents carefully and confidentially can reduce concerns on the acquirer's side and speed up the process.

[F] Increased Compliance Costs, Uncertainty and Delays for the Acquirer

The broader the scope of screening, the more firms will need to apply for approval or to notify the relevant authorities, and more firms therefore carry the costs of complying with the regulation. The more complex the regulation, the larger the compliance costs levied on the firms.

Costs also materialise in terms of delays because the screening process can take several months. In Finland and Germany, screening typically takes one to three months, but the time period is extended in more complex cases. The cooperation mechanism in the proposal by the Commission may delay the acquisition even more because further data may need to be collected and documents may need to be exchanged between the responsible authorities in two or more Member States. Delays can have significant costs for the acquirer in terms of foregone business and may influence the competitiveness of the firm.

Investors may in some cases be uncertain whether they are required to notify the authorities about a new M&A. Experience from Germany and Finland shows that initiatives to make the scope for sector-specific screening clearer and more transparent have reduced uncertainty on the investor side.[18] It is also the experience that cross-sectoral screening is more blurry and more often gives rise to uncertainty.

§1.05 LOWER FDI INFLOWS AND REDUCED ACCESS TO CAPITAL

Foreign investors basically locate their investments where the risk-adjusted rate of return is the highest. If the screening mechanisms in place make M&As in a country more costly and/or uncertain, it will make the location less attractive relative to other locations, although all other factors remain unchanged.

Overall, there is very little knowledge about the impact of FDI restrictions on a country's FDI attractiveness. There appears to be very little correlation between the OECD's FDI Regulatory Restrictiveness Index (where screening and approvals enter as one component out of four) and the stock of FDI in a given country.[19] One explanation may be that other factors (e.g., the size of the market, cost levels and skills) are more important than FDI restrictions and screening.[20] Another explanation may be that FDI screening so far has been limited to certain sectors, typically related to the defence industry, which means that the impact on aggregate FDI flows will be relatively limited.

If the scope of screening increases, screening periods become lengthier and uncertainty increases, this could reduce the country's attractiveness as an FDI location and have some unintended negative impacts.

First, if foreign takeover becomes less likely it may reduce the incentive for entrepreneurs to start-up and invest in developing new products, particularly in strategic sectors. In fact, the ongoing debate in the EU may itself give rise to enough uncertainty about future screening mechanisms that FDI inflows towards the EU is already affected.

Second, lower FDI inflows may have the consequence that local firms have more limited access to capital, which may eventually reduce their competitiveness and long-term growth prospects.

[A] Initiatives Can Make Screening Mechanisms More Effective and Efficient

Screening mechanisms already in place in EU Member States differ widely in terms of *sectoral coverage, threshold levels*, the *origin* of the acquirer targeted by screening and

18. *See* OECD (2015), *Impact of Investment Restrictive Measures on Investment*. The authors conclude that impacts on FDI flows remains difficult to assess because FDI data is highly lumpy and aggregated across sectors, which makes it difficult to relate changes in FDI flows to concrete changes in restrictions.
19. OECD (2015), *Impact of Investment Restrictive Measures on Investment*. The FDI Index contains four types of measures: equity restrictions, screening and approval requirements, restrictions on foreign key personnel, and other operational restrictions (such as limits on purchase of land or on repatriation of profits and capital).
20. Deutsche Bank (2015), *Recent Trends in FDI Activity in Europe*. Due to the already high degree of openness, Deutsche Bank concludes that there is virtually no scope for the EU to increase FDI by removing discriminatory regulation. Europe must find other ways to revive interest of foreign companies.

the *types of investors* prone to screening. Divergences also prevail in the design of existing screening procedures (e.g., prior authorisation mechanisms and ex-post screening mechanisms). Irrespective of the scope of screening, it is important that the screening mechanism is as efficient as possible to minimise the costs and reduce the risk of unintended negative consequences of screening. It is also important to design the screening mechanisms as effective as possible to ensure that FDI inflows do not compromise security and public order.

Based on experience from Germany and Finland, we find that there are at least five ways to improve the effectiveness and efficiency of FDI screening:

(1) **Mandatory reporting** of acquisitions in potentially sensitive sectors can spare the responsible authority the administrative effort required to identify the cases, but this will come at a cost to the acquirer.
(2) **Long time limits** for reopening screenings can give acquirers an incentive to comply with the mandatory reporting, but high compliance may come at the cost of increased uncertainty for the acquirer due to the longer period where the file can be opened. A **clear definition of the scope** for screening (in particular cross-sectoral screening) can reduce this uncertainty.
(3) **Standardisation** can bring down costs for the responsible authority and for the firm in case the costs are charged to the acquirer. Standardisation may also reduce delays and reduce the scope for discretion, which will reduce uncertainty.
(4) **Simple, predictable and transparent screening mechanisms** can reduce uncertainty and compliance costs for the firms. In particular, rules that make it easier to communicate with the companies save costs and time on both sides.
(5) **Treating all documents carefully and confidentially** can reduce concerns on the acquirer's side and speed up the process because the acquirer becomes more willing to cooperate and convey all required documents.

§1.06 CONCLUDING REMARKS

Foreign firms are important to growth and job creation in the EU. However, an open FDI regime can be associated with risks and several EU countries have procedures in place to screen FDI inflows. The main arguments for FDI screening relate to national security, and screening procedures are typically applied to investments in strategic sectors or assets and investments by SOEs. This chapter has analysed FDI flows into the EU to draw conclusions about the relevance and design of such FDI screening mechanisms.

First, we find that the increased average value of M&As in potentially sensitive sectors (EUR 128 million in 2008 to EUR 312 million in 2016) could be an argument for increased FDI screening of M&As in sectors defined as strategically important. *Second*, over-representation of SOEs compared to private investors in certain, potentially sensitive sectors may also support a specific focus on M&As by public investors. *Third*, M&As in potentially sensitive sectors and takeovers by foreign SOEs are unequally distributed across EU Member States, which means that the scope of FDI screening should reflect the national context and sensitivities. *Fourth*, M&As in potentially sensitive sectors and M&As by SOEs come from a wide range of home countries that seem to be changing over time, which speaks in favour of a country-neutral approach to FDI screening.

COMMENT ON CHAPTER 1

Comment on Copenhagen Economics Report 'Screening of FDI Towards the EU'

Erik van der Marel

Foreign Direct Investments (FDI) occupy an important value in the European Union (EU) economy. Despite a hit the value of mergers and acquisitions (M&A) experienced during the global financial crisis (GFC), M&As by third countries (i.e., from outside the EU) has seen a clear increasing trend. Foreign investments can leave a great positive impact in a country as it a source for economic activities, knowledge and job creation. Burdensome regulations with respect to investments, such as restrictive screening procedures, could potentially inhibit FDI's role as an important contributing factor to economic growth.

Generally, screening procedures are widely considered as a burdensome measure for companies and therefore form a restriction to investment and trade. For instance, the OECD's Foreign Direct Investment Restrictiveness Index assesses screening procedures as a restriction for foreign investments. As the Copenhagen Economics report 'Screening of FDI towards the EU' points out, screening is likely to be associated with negative effects such as administrative resources that are required to conduct screening, compliance costs, risk of lower FDI inflows, as well as reduced access to capital for domestic firms. Yet, the report also states that more research is needed to make any firm conclusions on the actual and potential negative effects of screening procedures. In short, more research is needed.

This note agrees but makes the case that if the European Commission (or any government) is planning to apply screening procedures or extend the application of screening procedures into other sectors, it should take note of the changing nature of the economy. Today's economies, and in particular that of many OECD countries, are shifting into an increasingly intangible one (Figure 1). Intangible economies are economies that have a high share of investments made by domestic and foreign investors in intangible assets as opposed to traditional assets such as buildings, equipment and machinery. Examples of intangible assets in industries and sectors are computerized information, (such as software and databases); innovative property (such as R&D, copyrights, designs, trademarks); and economic competencies (including brand equity, firm-specific human capital, networks joining people and know-how that increases enterprise efficiency).[1]

Figure 1 Intangibles Are Becoming Increasingly Important in the EU

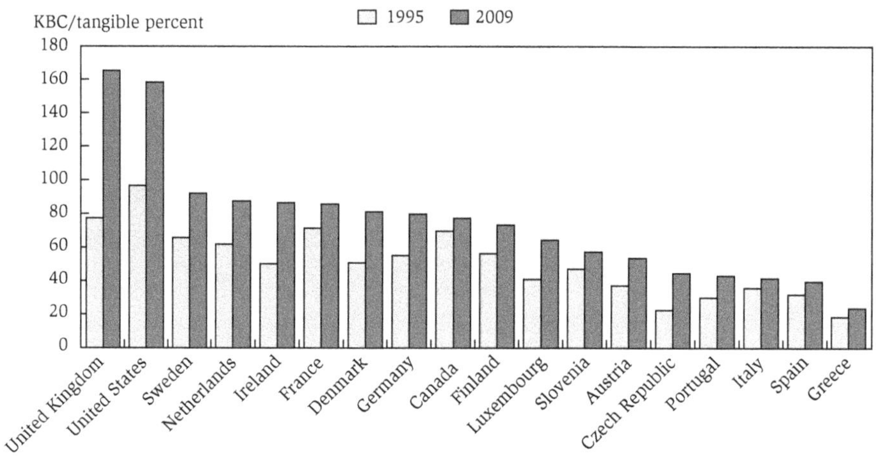

Source: OECD (2013).

Because of intangible investments, not only entirely new recently emerged sectors are part of the intangible economy, such as the data processing sector, platforms, or other digital sectors, but also traditional industries and services have become increasingly intangible, often with the help of digital tools and other ICT services, such as the use of platforms, the applications of artificial intelligence (AI) and other ICT services embedded in production processes of industries. Indeed, intangible investments made by multinational enterprises (MNEs) and the digitalization the economy appear to go hand in hand. In fact, digitalization in combination with the high proportion of services in many OECD countries (a part of the economy in itself that is highly digitalized) are often-mentioned factors that explain the shift towards a higher share of intangibles in many economies.

These developments have important implications for governments that would like to develop investment policies across intangible sectors, particularly when these policies are applied in a restrictive manner, which means that they would come along with significant costs for businesses. Many sectors are marked by a high degree of intangible assets, such as digital sectors, digital-enabled services (R&D, innovative property, etc.) and computer technologies, as well as utilities, air transport and

1. OECD (2013), 'New Sources of Growth: Knowledge-Based Capital Key Analyses and Policy Conclusions', Synthesis Report, OECD, Paris.

financial services, are known as sensitive and sometimes even strategic sectors in the EU where screening procedures could potentially apply. However, these intangible sectors have certain features that are important to mention for policy makers, namely, (a) they often leave behind a lower 'footprint', (b) they are knowledge and finance seeking, (c) they are extremely mobile, and finally (d) they create positive spill-over effects. Policy makers should be aware of these factors before developing any investment policies for the following reasons explained.

First, some sectors with high intangible investments, particularly digital investments, are known for having a lower footprint than other traditional industries. By footprint, economists usually mean that investment made by MNEs are characterized by positive contributions which are directly visible such as physical investments in infrastructure or machines and employment creation in the host country. Even though the digital MNEs create more employment as they grow compared to other traditional MNEs, they actually have a lower level of assets compared to what they earn (Figure 2). The absence of factors such as high fixed costs of entering a market, high capital expenditures and debt or even squeezed margins are often absent in digital investments[2] and therefore generate greater earnings compared to what they invest. This factor is likely to affect how digital MNEs make decisions to enter a foreign market.

Figure 2 Changing Footprints Regarding Foreign Assets and Foreign Sales of Digital MNEs

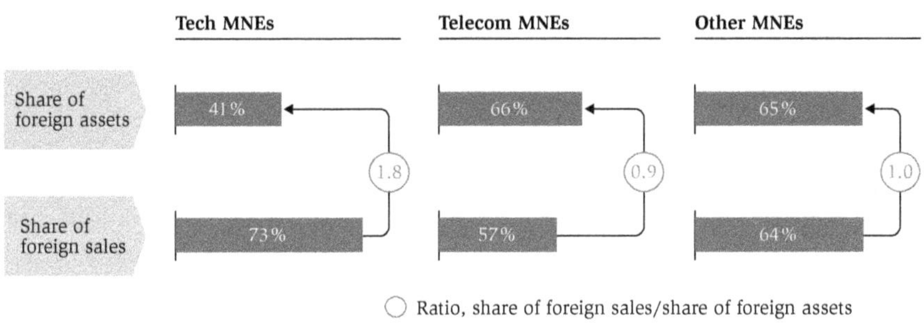

Source: UNCTAD (2017).

That is, traditionally foreign investments made in host markets would also generate higher level of assets, and along with that job creation. If digital and other intangible MNEs bring in lower levels of assets, or assets that are placed in branding, know-how and intellectual property, it would allow these firms to serve the host markets potentially without a physical presence as opposed to when investments need to be made in machineries, buildings, sites, equipment and locally sourced (tangible) inputs from domestic suppliers. The empirical trade literature has found that MNEs typically face a trade-off between serving the market locally or exporting to the host

2. UNCTAD (2017), 'World Investment Report 2017: Investment and the Digital Economy', UNCTAD, Geneva.

market at arm's length. Many factors depend on making a decision of which trade costs is a strong predictor: the higher trade costs through restrictive policies, the more a company is inclined to services markets at distance. Restrictive screening requirements in intangible sector could therefore exacerbate the lower footprint that intangible sectors already create.[3]

Second, connected to this, traditional investments are also known to be therefore 'market-seeking' behaviour. This means that they go to those markets where the foreign demands of their products or services are big enough. Even if production, and therefore investments, for whatever reason is decided to not establish in the host market, investment in a battery of other downstream activities in the supply chain could nonetheless be established in the host market such as the distribution of the good or the marketing of the good or services. That would also create economic activity and jobs. However, digital investments tend to be less market seeking. Through online connections, platforms and online collaborations over the internet, some of the traditional motivations for undertaking FDI are weakened. Instead, digital FDI can be more motivated by knowledge-seeking or finance seeking.[4] Restrictive screening procedures could distort the reasons between the two motivations for undertaking investments.

Third, investments in intangible and digital sectors are also extremely mobile. Given the fact that digital and intangible investments require a lot less investments in traditional machines and equipment, intangible MNEs have a much lower cost burden in case of leaving a host country. This makes investment made in the host country less sticky and more sensitive to policies that MNEs find too burdensome for their operations. Admittedly, screening procedures apply to MNEs once they enter a market, but in case new procedures apply in case a firm invests again, regulatory policies related to investment should ideally avoid any chilling effect.

Finally, intangible investments also generate great spill-over effects.[5] Spill-overs are an economic characteristic that makes it such that others in the economy can (also) benefit from private investments, the sheer presence of an MNE, or an idea. Often, benefits from spill-overs arise from knowledge that a certain lead company, or MNE, has and that 'spills over' to other firms that deal with the MNE in the market. As such, these other firms benefit from obtaining or implementing that know-how. Traditionally, spill-overs can take form as new inventory systems, management techniques, but intangible investment of a wider range of knowledge and ideas can now be easily transmitted to other firms in the local market. Partly this is because intangible items such as design, computerized information or networks are harder to protect. Spill-overs

3. Note, however, that this lower footprint does not necessary or by definition harm economic growth created through investments by digital and intangible MNEs. Digital and intangible investments in fact great high productivity benefits which in some cases can be higher than the traditional investments have created.
4. Some intangible MNEs tend to even have more opportunities to exploit tax-efficient corporate structures, *supra* n. 2.
5. J Haskel and S Westlake, *Capitalism Without Capital: The Rise of the Intangible Economy* (New Jersey, Princeton University Press, 2017).

create economic gains not only for the lead firm but also the wider market and therefore are an important contributor to economic growth.

However, higher restrictions regarding digital investments, including restrictive screening measures, are associated with lower spill-over effects. This is shown on the horizontal axis in Figure 3 which plots ECIPE's Digital Trade Restrictiveness Index regarding investments only for EU countries. It captures not only all sorts of investment measured in digital sectors such as equity restrictions but also screening measures. The vertical axis in the figure plots an indicator measuring the extent to which countries profit from spill-over effects resulting from FDI. Greater values of each indicator indicate higher levels of investment restrictions and greater abilities from benefiting from spill-over effects respectively. The relationship between the two measures shows a declining trend. This means that greater levels of restrictions affecting digital investments are associated with *lower* spill-over effects in the EU. In other words, countries which are more restricted with regards to investments in the digital economy benefit less from spill-over effects.

Figure 3 Relationship Between Spill-Over Effects and Investment Restrictions in Digital Sectors

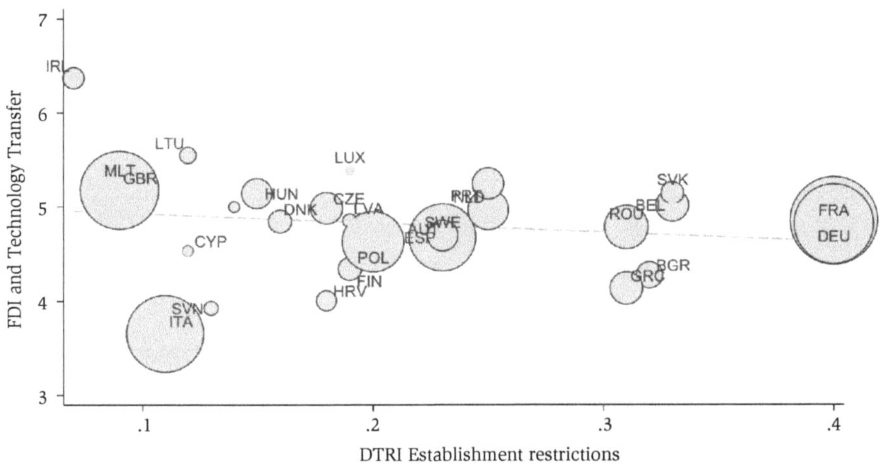

Source: ECIPE; Ferracane et al. (2018), WEF (2015).[6]

For these four reasons, policy makers of any country should be aware that introducing restrictive policies related to intangible and digital investments can have adverse economic effects for now and in the future. As the prospective economic growth in many EU countries depend on how effectively one can work with intangible

6. MF Ferracane, H Lee-Makiyama and E van der Marel, 'Digital Trade Restrictiveness Index' European Center for International Political Economy, Brussels, ECIPE (2018). WEF, 'Global Information Technology Report 2015: ICTs for Inclusive Growth', Davos, World Economic Forum (2015).

and digital investment, any restrictive policy may slow down such effective transition. However, of course much also depends on how policy measures are designed and should ideally be formulated in such a way that it avoids any unnecessary cost increase. If this is not the case, then policy measures can be considered as restrictive as it would mean that alternative policies are available against lower costs or against not costs at all – which would mean that the policy barrier would not need to be implemented at all.

Which countries are then restricted when it comes to investment policies in digital sectors? ECIPE's Digital Trade Restrictiveness Index (DTRI) can shed light on this issue as it records an array of policy measures related to investment, including screening, that specifically covers digital sectors and industries, such as telecommunications, ICT and data services, and others[7] (Figure 4). Admittedly, in this index, screening only forms one item among various others such as foreign equity restrictions and measures related to the appointment of foreign directors and managers. However, it gives a good idea of the broader trend in the EU which countries are likely to be in favour or against any new investment measures in the digital economy, including new screening measures. It also provides policy makers in these countries with a benchmark to compare their ranking with other countries and allows to investigate best practices across EU countries.

Figure 4 DTRI Establishment Restrictions in Digital Sectors in the EU

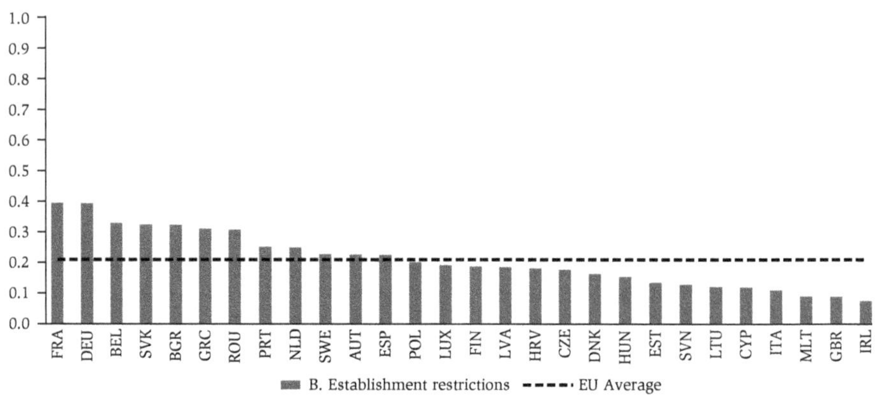

Source: ECIPE; Ferracane et al. (2018).[8]

7. More specifically, the DTRIs Cluster B is analysed which covers measures related to investment only. The full DTRI index also covers Clusters A, C and D, and includes a host of other policy restrictions related to digital trade that fall outside the scope of investments. The index ranges from 0 (completely open) to 1 (virtually restricted).
8. *Supra* n. 6.

Figure 4 shows that France and Germany are most restricted in the EU when it comes to investment restrictions in digital sectors. The two countries apply a wide range of restrictions, including screening measures. Although these screening measures are not directly applied so as to show a net economic benefit, they nonetheless have regulations in place that require screening on the basis of national security when it concerns a sensitive of strategic sector such as telecommunications (France) or that threaten the public policy or public order (Germany). Other review procedures are also in place in both countries that go beyond competition reasons and target foreign acquisition and mergers. Other countries such as not only Ireland, the UK, but also Malta and Italy can be found on the other extreme of the ranking. These countries are least restricted in the EU and show that only a few minor restrictions related to investments are in place. Overall, Figure 4 makes clear that on average the level of investment restrictions in digital sectors are fairly low in the EU, as indicated by the dashed line.

CHAPTER 2

Regulating FDI in the EU Legal Framework

Marise Cremona

§2.01 INTRODUCTION

The impetus for EU action on inward investment is politically linked to DG Trade's 2015 Strategy paper 'Trade for All',[1] European Parliament and Member State initiatives,[2] and the Commission's reflection paper on 'Harnessing Globalisation' of May 2017.[3] Legally it is linked to the expansion of the EU's trade policy competence by the Lisbon Treaty to include foreign direct investment (FDI),[4] to the consequent expansion of EU trade agreements to include investment and the implications this has for the operation of the internal market. At the same time, since 2006 the EU's trade policy has been focusing on negotiating bilateral agreements with highly developed economies

1. Communication 'Trade for all: towards a more responsible trade and investment policy', COM (2015) 497 of 14 Oct. 2015.
2. Letter to the Commission from France, Germany and Italy on 'Proposals for ensuring an improved level playing field in trade and investment', February 2017; European Parliament resolution of 5 Jul. 2017 on building an ambitious EU industrial strategy as a strategic priority for growth, employment and innovation in Europe, P8_TA(2017)0305, paras 19–20; both available at: http://www.europarl.europa.eu/legislative-train/theme-a-balanced-and-progressive-trade-policy-to-harness-globalisation/file-screening-of-foreign-direct-investment-in-strategic-sectors.
3. Reflection Paper 'Harnessing Globalisation', COM (2017) 240 of 10 May 2017. *See, e.g.*, p. 15: 'Openness to foreign investment remains a key principle for the EU and a major source of growth. However, concerns have recently been voiced about foreign investors, notably state-owned enterprises, taking over European companies with key technologies for strategic reasons. EU investors often do not enjoy the same rights to invest in the country from which the investment originates. These concerns need careful analysis and appropriate action.'
4. Article 207(1) TFEU provides that: 'The common commercial policy shall be based on uniform principles, particularly with regard to changes in tariff rates, the conclusion of tariff and trade agreements relating to trade in goods and services, and the commercial aspects of intellectual property, foreign direct investment, the achievement of uniformity in measures of liberalisation, export policy and measures to protect trade such as those to be taken in the event of dumping or subsidies.'

(Korea, the USA, Canada, Japan), agreements which create – alongside market opening opportunities for EU companies – a greater potential impact (in goods, services and direct investment) on the domestic EU market. Liberalisation and regulation go hand in hand: liberalisation creates a demand for a levelling of the playing field.[5]

The focus of this chapter is on inward FDI. We will address three related legal questions posed by the regulation of investment within the EU. First is the degree to which the EU's common commercial policy (CCP) competence covers regulation of FDI as well as liberalisation or market access. Second, especially in the context of inward investment, is the relation between the CCP and the regulatory competence derived from internal market powers. And third, is the extent to which it is necessary for action to be taken at EU as opposed to Member State level, and the degree to which EU powers leave space for Member State action. The answers to these questions have been changing: unlike the import of goods, which for many years has been covered by a general import regulation and the common customs code, the treatment of third-country investors has until now been largely left to the Member States, and regulated at EU level, if at all, via sectoral internal market legislation (such as the directives on credit institutions, air services or energy). In contrast the recent Commission proposal for a Regulation on screening FDI is for a horizontal (non-sectoral) EU initiative based on CCP (and therefore exclusive) powers.[6] Can this shift be legally justified?

To address these questions we need to look more closely at what regulation of FDI might entail, and the legal and policy context in which it takes place. EU competence and its legal basis may vary depending on whether, for example, we are talking about: applying internal legislation to foreign (third country) investors alongside EU establishments; devising internal legislation specifically applicable to foreign investors; negotiating a bilateral (trade and) investment agreement which includes provisions on regulation and investor protection alongside market access commitments; or participating in multilateral rule-making which is designed to regulate an aspect of FDI (e.g., on taxation).

When considering the balance between EU and Member State powers to regulate inward investment, it is clearly important to determine the precise scope of CCP competence, since this is an exclusive competence which does not depend on any prior

5. *See, e.g.*, European Council conclusions on trade policy, 22–23 Jun. 2017, EUCO 8/17, at paras 16–17: 'The EU will pursue a robust trade policy upholding an open and rules-based multilateral trading system, with a central role for the WTO. Firm in the belief that trade contributes to creating wealth and jobs, it will keep markets open and fight protectionism. It will actively promote an ambitious free trade agenda on the global scene. To this end, it will seek to foster a truly level playing field, while remaining vigilant concerning the respect and promotion of key standards, including social, environmental, health and consumer standards that are central to the European way of life. The European Council is convinced that trade and investment can only be free if it is also fair and mutually beneficial .... it welcomes the Commission's initiative to harness globalisation and, inter alia, to analyse investments from third countries in strategic sectors, while fully respecting Members States' competences.' *See also* European Parliament Resolution of 5 Jul. 2017, note 2, para. 16.
6. Proposal for a Regulation of the European Parliament and of the Council establishing a framework for screening of foreign direct investments into the European Union, COM (2017) 487, 13 Sept. 2017.

exercise of internal regulatory powers by the Union.[7] Although the operation of EU internal market competence and the scope of Member State's discretion is a significant element in the legal regulation of FDI, a determination that the CCP is applicable would therefore appear to close down further discussion as to the appropriate level of action.

The CCP has another significant characteristic. The Treaty does not predetermine the purposes for which CCP powers may be used. In the CCP, there is no equivalent of the internal market as a fundamental choice structurally built into Union law and policy. Certainly, liberalisation is an objective,[8] but there are other objectives which may (indeed, should) also be taken into account; as the Court pointed out in Opinion 2/15, the objective of sustainable development must now be seen as 'an integral part' of the CCP.[9] How these multiple objectives are translated into specific policy outcomes is a matter for the political institutions. And because these powers are exclusive, subsidiarity does not apply: there is no need to show that the objectives of the measure can be better achieved at EU level.[10] It is sufficient that the instrument and its objectives fall within the scope of the CCP and that there is political will to act within the Treaty-based institutional structures. In contrast, where internal market powers form the basis for EU action - whether internal or external - it must be shown that action at EU level is necessary and that action will serve the objective of achieving, or contribute to the functioning of, the internal market.[11]

Finally, we should bear in mind two features of the Court's approach to competence and choice of legal basis. First, the avoidance of legal basis redundancy: the preference where possible is for a single legal basis which reflects the instrument's predominant purpose, as opposed to an accumulation of legal bases; this reflects the function of the legal basis which is to provide the Union with a sufficient power to act rather than reflecting different facets or objectives of the measure. Second, a tendency is visible in the post-Lisbon case law on external policy to favour broadly conceived express external legal bases (such as the CCP) over external powers derived from internal competences.[12]

§2.02 REGULATING INWARD FDI: THE COMMISSION PROPOSAL

The Commission's Communication of September 2017, 'Welcoming Foreign Direct Investment while Protecting Essential Interests', while reiterating the commitment to a

7. Case 41/76 *Suzanne Criel, née Donckerwolcke and Henri Schou v. Procureur de la République*, EU:C:1976:182, para. 32.
8. Article 206 TFEU.
9. Opinion 2/15, EU:C:2017:376, para. 147. *See also* Art. 207(1) TFEU: 'The common commercial policy shall be conducted in the context of the principles and objectives of the Union's external action.'
10. Article 5(3) TEU.
11. For example, as regards capital movements and non-direct foreign investment, *see* Opinion 2/15, note 9, paras 239–242.
12. Note, for example, the structure of argument in Opinion 2/15: the Court starts with Art. 207 TFEU (the CCP) and only considers the applicability of implied powers for those parts of the agreement which are held to fall outside the CCP (transport services, non-direct foreign investment).

policy of openness to FDI, signalled the Commission's intention to adopt 'vigorous and appropriate policies':

> to first, open markets for EU companies in third countries, ensure that everyone plays by the same rules and protect EU investments in third countries, and, second, to protect assets in the EU against takeovers that could be detrimental to the essential interests of the EU or its Member States.[13]

The Working Document accompanying this Communication and the proposal for a Regulation spells out what the Commission sees as the problem:

> in exceptional cases, foreign investments are problematic when they pose a threat to security or public order .... In such circumstances, FDI may need to be assessed and/or conditioned or prohibited. This is the case where foreign investors – especially but not only when they are state owned or controlled, including through financing or other means of direction – may seek to acquire control of or influence in European undertakings whose activities have repercussions on critical technologies, infrastructure, inputs or sensitive information. Such acquisitions may allow the States in question to use these assets to the detriment not only of the EU's technological edge but also its security and public order.[14]

It is significant that the Commission here links the justification for action to the demands of security and public order, not simply to the Union's economic priorities (its 'technological edge'); this reflects the need to comply with both EU law on freedom of movement of capital and with the EU's and Member States' WTO commitments.[15] Justifying the need to act at EU level the Commission points to the fact that about half the Member States have some provision for screening of FDI, but the scope and nature of these controls varies. It argues that this divergence creates 'uncertainty for foreign investors that face different FDI screening regimes from different Member States';[16] that the absence of an EU-wide regime makes it difficult to monitor the levels and types of inward investment as well as individual Member State screening decisions, and to respond when the interests of several Member States may be affected. The Commission's proposal contains for elements:

- *Monitoring* by the Commission of FDI flows, 'especially in strategic sectors ... that may raise security or public order concerns, in particular when the investor is owned or controlled by a third country'.[17]
- *Coordination* between the Member States, 'to exchange information on FDI flows and FDI screenings and promote policy convergence on FDI screening policies'.[18]
- *An 'enabling framework' for FDI screening by Member States*, established via a Regulation which will (i) set conditions and a procedural framework for

13. COM (2017) 494 of 13 Sept. 2017, p. 5.
14. SWD (2017) 297 of 13 Sept. 2017, p. 6.
15. On the WTO, *see* further Ch. 9.
16. SWD (2017) 297 of 13 Sept. 2017, p. 8.
17. *Ibid.*, p. 8. Strategic sectors include energy, space, transport and technologies linked to these.
18. *Ibid.*, p. 9.

screening and (ii) provide for exchange of information on screening between Member States and the Commission.
- *The possibility of screening of FDI by the Commission itself*, in cases where FDI may affect 'projects or programmes of Union interest'.

The proposal is based on Article 207 TFEU, with the Commission simply stating that FDI falls within the CCP. Since this competence is exclusive, the principle of subsidiarity does not need to be addressed,[19] although as already mentioned the Commission justifies the need to EU action. In areas of exclusive competence, the Member States may act 'only if so empowered by the Union',[20] and in the case of an *a priori* exclusive competence such as the CCP this barrier to unilateral Member State action does not depend on the adoption of common rules at EU level. So, the proposed Regulation, as based on Article 207 TFEU, would appear to amount to an authorisation to the Member States to continue their screening programmes (if they have them) notwithstanding the movement of FDI into exclusive competence as a result of the Lisbon Treaty.[21] This is also suggested by the wording of Article 3(1) of the draft:

> Member States may maintain, amend or adopt mechanisms to screen foreign direct investments on the grounds of security or public order, under the conditions and in accordance with the terms set out in this Regulation.[22]

However, the choice of legal basis of this proposal and for the regulation of inward FDI more generally is not as clear-cut as this might suggest. It raises the question of the relationship (and boundary) between the CCP and other EU powers, in particular the provisions on rights of establishment and on capital movements, and how these powers interact with those of the Member States.[23] The Treaty provisions on establishment apply to intra-EU direct investment where the investor's holding is sufficient to enable him or her 'to exert a definite influence on the company's decisions and to determine its activities'.[24] Rules subjecting foreign holdings to prior authorisation or requiring specific levels of national ownership or control, that were applied to holdings by EU nationals or companies, are restrictions on the right of establishment, requiring justification under permitted derogations. However the right of establishment does not extend to non-EU investors and thus does not prevent the application of such requirements to non-EU investors.[25] EU legislation directed only at the initial

19. COM (2017) 494, p. 8 and Recital (6) of the proposed draft; Art. 5(3) TEU.
20. Article 2(1) TFEU.
21. Cf. the authorisation given, under certain conditions, to maintain and conclude BITs with third countries, until a BIT between the EU and that third country enters into force: Regulation 1219/2012/EU establishing transitional arrangements for bilateral investment agreements between Member States and third countries OJ 2012 L 351/40.
22. COM (2017) 487, Art. 3(1).
23. The Commission's proposal discusses the relationship between the proposed measure and the Merger Regulation (Regulation 139/2004), as well as sectoral regulations such as the granting of operating licences for provision of air services, the acquisition of holdings in financial institutions and security of energy supply.
24. *See, e.g.*, Case C-326/07 *Commission v. Italy*, EU:C:2009:193, para. 34.
25. Indeed, the Court has even held that 'it is important to ensure that the interpretation of Art. 63(1) TFEU as regards relations with [non-member] states does not enable economic operators who do

establishment of foreign (non-EU) investors within the EU would thus not fall within the scope of the Treaty provisions on establishment.

However direct investment also falls within the free movement of capital:

> Direct investments, that is to say, investments of any kind made by natural or legal persons which serve to establish or maintain lasting and direct links between the persons providing the capital and the undertakings to which that capital is made available in order to carry out an economic activity fall within the ambit of Article 56 EC [now Article 63 TFEU] on the free movement of capital. That object presupposes that the shares held by the shareholder enable him to participate effectively in the management of that company or in its control.[26]

This definition of direct investment, which forms the basis of the definition of FDI in the proposed Regulation,[27] was also explicitly adopted by the Court in Opinion 2/15 in order to define FDI for the purposes of Article 207 TFEU,[28] thereby ensuring a welcome consistency between the two sets of Treaty provisions. And this consistency - or overlap - extends further: unlike any of the other Treaty freedoms (including, as we have seen, the right of establishment) the free movement of capital expressly applies to movements between the EU and third states. So Article 63 TFEU establishes freedom of movement of capital to and from third countries, and capital movements encompass FDI. Despite the overlap between the two Treaty powers their legal implications are very different. The free movement of capital is a matter of shared competence, and the Treaty establishes a specific relationship, as regards movements of capital between the EU and third countries, between the principle of liberalisation and permissible restrictions (which are cast as exceptions), and between EU and Member State competence.[29] Article 207 TFEU, as we have seen, is an exclusive EU competence, and the Treaty does not dictate the degree of liberalisation to be achieved, or establish conditions for the imposition of restrictions.

The Commission's proposal itself reflects the ambiguity of the relation between the two competences. Although it is firmly based on Article 207 TFEU, it is striking that the proposal is framed as 'enabling' rather than authorising, and as 'establishing a

not fall within the territorial scope of freedom of establishment to profit from that freedom', Case C-464/14 *SECIL – Companhia Geral de Cal e Cimento SA* EU:C:2016:896, para. 42.

26. Case C-326/07 *Commission v. Italy*, note 24, para. 35. *See also* the reference to 'the movement of capital to or from third countries involving direct investment' in Art. 64(2) TFEU, as well as Annex I to Council Directive 88/361/EEC of 24 Jun. 1988, OJ 1988 L 178/5, as relied on by the Court in many cases, including, Case C-54/99 *Association Église de Scientologie de Paris, Scientology International Reserves Trust*, EU:C:2000:124; Case C-463/00 *Commission v. Spain*, EU:C:2003:272, paras 52–53.
27. '"Foreign direct investment" means investments of any kind by a foreign investor aiming to establish or to maintain lasting and direct links between the foreign investor and the entrepreneur to whom or the undertaking to which the capital is made available in order to carry on an economic activity in a Member State, including investments which enable effective participation in the management or control of a company carrying out an economic activity.' COM (2017) 487, Art. 2(1).
28. Opinion 2/15, note 9, para. 80, citing, *inter alia*, Case C-326/07, note 24.
29. *See, e.g.*, Art. 64(1) TFEU and its interpretation in a case such as Case C-464/14 *SECIL – Companhia Geral de Cal e Cimento SA*, note 25.

framework' for Member State screening.[30] The overall logic of the proposal is more consistent with a minimal approach to harmonising the operation of Member State's discretion in a field of shared competence.[31] And indeed, since freedom of movement of capital between the EU and third countries is established as a principle in Article 63 TFEU, and the kind of screening proposed would amount to a restriction on FDI and therefore on the movement of capital, a justification for the restriction needs to be based in the Treaties.[32] Such justification may be found in Article 65 TFEU, which refers to the possibility of the Member States taking measures justified on grounds of public policy or public security, and the Commission duly refers to this.[33] However, this justification is not attached to Article 207 TFEU but to the movement of capital under Article 63 TFEU which is a matter of shared, not exclusive, competence,[34] and Article 65 TFEU refers to action by the Member States, not by the EU.

There is no doubt that the Member States, when acting within a public policy / public security justification, do not possess complete freedom of action. They are bound by certain principles of EU law:

> It should be observed, first, that while Member States are still, in principle, free to determine the requirements of public policy and public security in the light of their national needs, those grounds must, in the Community context and, in particular, as derogations from the fundamental principle of free movement of capital, be interpreted strictly, so that their scope cannot be determined unilaterally by each Member State without any control by the Community institutions. ... Thus, public policy and public security may be relied on only if there is a genuine and sufficiently serious threat to a fundamental interest of society ... . Moreover, those derogations must not be misapplied so as, in fact, to serve purely economic ends ... . Further, any person affected by a restrictive measure based on such a derogation must have access to legal redress ... .[35]

There is also no doubt that the EU has the competence to establish both procedural and substantive conditions for the use of the public policy / public security justification, as it has done, for example, in the case of free movement of persons.[36] However the obvious legal basis for such a measure circumscribing the Member States' powers would then be the movement of capital provisions of the Treaty, not the CCP, since the derogation in question is a derogation from the freedom of movement of capital. The legal basis would be Article 64(2) TFEU which applies to 'measures on the movement of capital to or from third countries involving direct investment', although it could be argued that in establishing an 'enabling framework' for screening (even if

30. COM (2017) 487 final, p. 2.
31. Editorial comments, 'Playing by the Rules – Free and Fair Trade', (2018) 55 Common Market Law Review p. 1 at pp. 7–8.
32. *See, e.g.*, Case C-54/99 *Association Église de Scientologie de Paris, Scientology International Reserves Trust*, note 26, para. 14.
33. Article 65(1)(b) TFEU; COM (2017) 487, p. 4.
34. Opinion 2/15, paras 227–242.
35. Case C-54/99 *Association Église de Scientologie de Paris, Scientology International Reserves Trust*, note 26, para. 17 (references omitted). In addition, according to Art. 65(3) TFEU, the measures 'shall not constitute a means of arbitrary discrimination or a disguised restriction on the free movement of capital and payments as defined in Article 63'.
36. Directive 2004/38, Arts 27–33.

screening by Member States is not made compulsory) the EU would be adopting a measure 'which constitute[s] a step backwards in Union law as regards the liberalisation of the movement of capital to or from third countries', for which a special procedure is required under Article 64(3) TFEU. It is notable that although the Commission's explanatory memorandum mentions Articles 63–65 TFEU, this is to demonstrate compliance; they are not presented as a legal basis for the action proposed, and there is no mention of these provisions in the Preamble of the proposed Regulation. The Commission appears to rely simultaneously on exclusive EU competence under Article 207 TFEU and on the Treaty-preserved Member State power to derogate from free movement rules on public policy / public security grounds.

Although the above might suggest that Articles 64–65 TFEU offer a more appropriate legal basis for the proposal, we need also to look at Opinion 2/15 which may provide a justification, or at least a precedent, for using Article 207 TFEU. After all, in that case the Court considered, *inter alia*, provisions which were intended to circumscribe Member States' public policy / public security discretion. There is also the question of whether Article 207 TFEU (or indeed Article 64 or 65 TFEU) can ground a competence granting the *Commission* – as opposed to the Member States – the power to screen FDI. This requires us to look more closely at the extent to which Article 207 TFEU can provide a basis for adopting regulatory measures, and in particular the regulation of FDI.

§2.03 REGULATING INWARD FDI: PART OF THE CCP?

In its Communication of September 2017 on inward investment,[37] the Commission reiterates both its support for 'an open, sustainable, fair and rules-based global trade order' and the need to act against 'unfair practices' or in response to security or public order concerns, stating that: 'These principles apply fully to foreign direct investment from third countries, which forms part of the EU's common commercial policy.' It is tempting after Opinion 2/15 to argue that all regulation of FDI falls within the CCP, but the Court's position was more nuanced. It is certainly true that FDI is now included in the EU's CCP, but this does not mean that *any* regulation concerned with direct investment falls within the CCP; regulation of FDI, like product or services regulation, will need to satisfy the criteria established by the Court over a series of judgments, including Opinion 2/15.[38]

First, the CCP is concerned with international trade. 'Foreign' direct investment here means investment within the EU by non-EU investors (or by EU investors outside

37. Commission Communication, 'Welcoming Foreign Direct Investment while Protecting Essential Interests', COM (2017) 494 final of 13 Sept. 2017.
38. Among pre-Lisbon case law, *see* Opinion 1/94, EU:C:1994:384; Opinion 2/00; Case C-94/03 *Commission* v. *Council*; Case C-411/06 *Commission v. Parliament and Council*, EU:C:2009:518. For case law since the Lisbon Treaty, *see* Case C-414/11 *Daiichi Sankyo Co. Ltd*, EU:C:2013:520; Case C-137/12 *Commission v. Council*, EU:C:2013:675; Case C-389/15 *Commission v. Council*, EU:C:2017:798; Opinion 2/15, note 9; Opinion 3/15 EU:C:2017:114.

the EU).[39] We are not talking about direct investment which falls within the provisions on intra-EU establishment, i.e., direct investment by EU nationals or EU companies through setting up and managing undertakings and establishing branches and subsidiaries within the EU. Nor the regulation of companies or firms formed in accordance with the laws of a Member State, which under Article 54 TFEU are EU companies to which internal EU (and national) regulation will apply.

Second, in order to fall within the CCP, a measure must be shown not simply to have 'implications' for trade with third countries; it must '[relate] specifically to such trade in that it is essentially intended to promote, facilitate or govern such trade and has direct and immediate effects on it'.[40]

These criteria have been applied to trade in goods,[41] (since the Lisbon Treaty) to trade in services,[42] and intellectual property protection;[43] and in Opinion 2/15 they were applied for the first time to FDI. In adopting the same definition of direct investment as that used in the context of capital movements,[44] the Court argued that direct investment in this sense meets the 'direct and immediate effects on trade' criterion relevant to the CCP:

> [A]ny EU act promoting, facilitating or governing participation – by a natural or legal person of a third State in the European Union and vice versa – in the management or control of a company carrying out an economic activity is such as to have direct and immediate effects on trade between that third State and the European Union, whereas there is no specific link of that kind with trade in the case of investments which do not result in such participation.[45]

The same criterion is then used to argue that the CCP may cover not only measures concerned with market access but also those which concern post-establishment regulation, including fair and equitable treatment and protection against expropriation without compensation. Arguments that only market access falls within the CCP are rejected.[46] The provisions on investment protection 'are such as to have direct and immediate effects on that trade, since they concern the treatment of the participation of entrepreneurs of one Party in the management or control of companies carrying out economic activities in the territory of the other Party';[47] each 'contributes to the legal certainty of investors' and meets the CCP test: 'The establishment of such a legal framework is intended to promote, facilitate and govern trade between the

39. *See* Case C-414/11 *Daiichi Sankyo Co. Ltd*, note 38, para. 50 (and cited *inter alia* in Opinion 2/15, note 9, para. 35): 'the common commercial policy is within the context of "the Union's external action", [and] relates to trade with non-member countries, not to trade in the internal market.'
40. Opinion 2/15, note 9, para. 36.
41. *See, e.g.*, Case C-411/06 *Commission v. Parliament and Council*, note 38.
42. Case C-137/12 *Commission v. Council*, note 38.
43. Case C-414/11 *Daiichi Sankyo and Sanofi-Aventis Deutschland*, note 38.
44. Opinion 2/15, note 9, para. 80; *see supra* at note 26.
45. Opinion 2/15, note 9, para. 84.
46. As they had been in relation to goods in Opinion 1/78, EU:C:1979:224, and Opinion 1/94, note 38, and in relation to services in Case C-137/12 *Commission v. Council*, note 38.
47. Opinion 2/15, note 9, para. 95.

European Union and the Republic of Singapore, within the meaning of the case-law recalled in paragraph 36 of this opinion.'[48]

Opinion 2/15 therefore answers a number of questions on the scope of the CCP as regards FDI. The relatively inclusive approach is based on the 'direct and immediate effects on trade' test which is now well entrenched. It is a test which allows the Court a great deal of room for manoeuvre in its application, as its reasoning in relation to investment demonstrates, favouring flexibility over predictability.[49] But, it does not provide a complete answer to our questions over the regulation of inward investment: when is such regulation intended to promote, facilitate and govern international trade, whether through international agreement or legislation?

§2.04 CREATING NEW REGULATORY CONTROLS

Within the internal market we find instruments of liberalisation, combined with regulation as a condition of market access; regulation at Union level may replace national regulation justified on imperative public interest grounds, thereby helping to secure free movement. Although the provisions on the CCP as originally drafted centred on measures directly affecting trade flows (e.g., tariffs and quotas) and did not contain any explicit provision for the adoption of regulatory measures affecting external trade, since Opinion 1/78 it has been recognised that an external regulatory competence needs to accompany liberalisation if the Union is to carry on an effective commercial policy.[50] However some uncertainty remains about the precise boundary between Article 207 TFEU and other 'internal' legal bases for regulatory measures: on the one hand, FDI within the meaning of Article 207(1) TFEU clearly covers inward as well as outward investment; on the other hand, establishing a regulatory framework for activities within the internal market would normally be seen as an internal competence. It is clear that the drafters of Article 207 TFEU wished to prevent CCP powers being used as a way of bypassing limits on internal legislative competence and internal legislative procedures. As the Court has said in the case law above mentioned, the CCP is concerned with international trade, not trade between the EU Member States.[51] The 'context' of the rules established by an agreement concluded under Article 207 TFEU is 'the liberalisation of international trade, not the harmonisation of the laws of the Member States of the European Union'.[52] Further, according to Article 207(6) TFEU, 'The exercise of the competences conferred by this Article in the field of the common commercial policy shall not affect the delimitation of competences between the Union and the Member States ... .' Despite its less-than-transparent wording, this

48. Opinion 2/15, note 9, para. 94; for para. 36, *see supra* at note 40.
49. D Kleimann, 'Reading Opinion 2/15: Standards of Analysis, the Court's Discretion, and the Legal View of the Advocate General' [2017] EUI RSCAS Working Paper 2017/23; M Cremona, 'Shaping EU Trade Policy post-Lisbon: ECJ, 16 May 2017, Opinion 2/15 Free Trade Agreement with Singapore' (2018) 14 *European Constitutional Law Review*, 231.
50. Opinion 1/78, note 46. *See also* Opinion 1/94, note 38.
51. Case C-414/11 *Daiichi Sankyo Co. Ltd*, note 38, para. 50; Case C-137/12 *Commission v. Council*, note 38, para. 56.
52. Case C-414/11 *Daiichi Sankyo Co. Ltd*, note 38, para. 60.

provision prevents the exercise of CCP competence by the EU externally from having a pre-emptive effect on shared regulatory competence within the internal market.[53] In order to attempt some clarification of how these principles may apply to the regulation of inward FDI, we need to unpack the different types of regulatory instrument in question.

[A] Referencing Existing International Agreements

The CCP may encompass clauses which refer to existing standards established in international agreements binding the EU. Where an EU trade agreement does not create new regulatory norms but instead commits the parties, in giving effect to the liberalisation envisaged in the agreement, to respect those contained in other international agreements already binding on the EU, no separate legal basis is required. Such clauses, according to the Court, do not create new obligations but simply preserve the right of the parties to set their own standards in conformity with their international obligations, and in accordance with their own internal legislative procedures.[54] We should note here the Court's care to ensure that 'internal legislative procedures' are not compromised; we will return to this point.

[B] Extending Existing Regulation to Third Countries

The CCP can be used in order to extend to third countries standards applicable within the EU as a result of existing internal market legislation. At the time of the conclusion of the GATT Tokyo Round Agreements, legislation on the application of technical regulations and standards to third-country goods was adopted on the basis of CCP powers. This provided that harmonised standards would apply equally to goods of non-EU origin, and where standards have not been harmonised at Union level, the Member States are to apply national standards on a national treatment basis.[55] The principle that CCP powers may be used to adopt measures extending internal market regulation to third countries also formed the basis of the Court's judgment in the much more recent *Conditional access services* case, in which the CCP was held to be the correct legal basis for the signature of a Convention which would 'extend beyond the European Union the legal protection introduced by Directive 98/84'.[56] The internal EU rules had already been adopted under internal market powers, and the Court held that

53. *See, e.g.*, Case C-414/11 *Daiichi Sankyo Co. Ltd*, note 38, para. 59; M Cremona, 'EU External Competence – Rationales for Exclusivity' in S Garben and I Govaere (eds), *The Division of Competences between the European Union and its Member States: Reflections on the Past, Present and Future*, Hart Publishing 2017, 133 at 140–141. *See further* below.
54. Opinion 2/15, note 9, para. 165; Case C-414/11 *Daiichi Sankyo Co. Ltd*, note 38, paras 59–60.
55. Decision 80/45/EEC laying down provisions on the introduction and implementation of technical regulations and standards, OJ 1980 L 14/36. The Decision is still in force. Where the EU establishes only minimum harmonisation, direct imports from third countries will be subject to the relevant national regulations, which may exceed the minimum; the right of market access on the basis of the EU minimum standards is applicable only to third-country goods already in free circulation.
56. Case C-137/12 *Commission v. Council*, note 38, para. 61.

the aim of the projected agreement was not to harmonise internal EU rules, rather, it was to extend them to third countries:

Article 11(4) of the Convention (a disconnection clause[57]) confirms that, since the approximation of the legislation of Member States in the field concerned has already been largely achieved by Directive 98/84, the primary objective of the Convention is not to improve the functioning of the internal market, but to extend legal protection of the relevant services beyond the territory of the European Union and thereby to promote international trade in those services.[58]

Thus, there may be a difference between the (internal market) competence basis of the internal legislation and the CCP legal basis of the act (legislation or international agreement) which applies it to third-country investors or service providers.

[C] Governing the Adoption and Application of Regulatory Measures

The CCP can be used to adopt rules which facilitate the application of EU regulations, or which impose conditions on the application of Member State regulations, in international trade relations. In relation to trade in goods, the WTO agreements on sanitary and technical standards and regulations (SPS and TBT) were concluded under CCP powers, the Court finding that the SPS was intended to establish rules and disciplines to 'guide the development, adoption and enforcement' of measures so as to 'minimise their negative effects on trade', and the TBT is designed 'merely' to ensure that technical regulations and standards do not create unnecessary obstacles to trade.[59] Neither of these agreements actually establishes harmonised standards; they establish a framework of rules for their adoption and application. In the case of intellectual property, it is harder to maintain a distinction between the creation or harmonisation of rights and the adoption of 'homogeneous standards of protection' which are not (according to the Court) an end in themselves but 'a means to the end of developing trade between the contracting parties in a fair manner'.[60] However in the discussion of intellectual property protection in the post-Lisbon case law (which we will not explore further here) the Court does try to walk this tightrope.[61]

In the context of FDI, the Court in Opinion 2/15 applied this reasoning to the fair and equitable treatment obligation in the investment protection chapter of the EU - Singapore free trade agreement. Thus, for example:

> [the provision] does not contain any commitment for the Member States relating to their criminal law, tax law or social security, but in essence merely provides that,

57. A disconnection clause provides that in their mutual relations the EU Member States will apply EU rules and not the rules established by the Convention, except where there is no EU rule governing the matter in question. On such clauses, *see further*, M. Cremona, 'Disconnection Clauses in EC Law and Practice' in C Hillion and P Koutrakos (eds) *Mixed Agreements Revisited - The EU and Its Member States in the World*, Hart Publishing 2010.
58. Case C-137/12 *Commission v. Council*, note 38, para. 67.
59. Opinion 1/94, note 38, paras 30–33.
60. Case C-389/15 *Commission v. Council*, note 38, para. 60.
61. *See, e.g.*, Opinion 2/15, note 9, paras 122–126. *See also* Case C-414/11 *Daiichi Sankyo Co. Ltd*, note 38, paras 58–60.

> in the European Union or Singapore, relevant legislation must in each case be applied to an investor of the other Party 'in an equitable and non-discriminatory manner' ...[62]

So clauses in agreements (or legislation) which are concerned not with establishing or harmonising regulation, but with its operation via mutual recognition, regulatory cooperation or non-discrimination requirements, can be based upon CCP powers, even where the regulations in question have not been harmonised at EU level but derive from Member State's powers (e.g., in fields such as criminal law or taxation).[63] Similarly, the investment protection measures in the EU-Singapore agreement (like Article 65 TFEU) envisage derogations on grounds of public order or public security. Although these were argued to fall within Member State's powers, the Court held that the agreement 'does not establish any international commitment concerning public order, public security or other public interests',[64] but deals rather with *how those powers are exercised* in relation to third country direct investment. The provision in question, therefore 'does not encroach upon the competences of the Member States regarding public order, public security and other public interests, but obliges the Member States to exercise those competences in a manner which does not render the trade commitments entered into by the European Union ... redundant'.[65]

According to Opinion 2/15, then, the EU has the power on the basis of Article 207 TFEU to enter into agreements with third countries which commit to the EU and its Member States as to how its regulations (whether national or EU in origin) will be applied to third-country nationals and undertakings, as long as such commitments will facilitate international trade.

The Commission's screening proposal seems to fall within the scope of this ruling (albeit in the form of an internal legislative measure rather than an international agreement) and thus within the scope of Article 207 TFEU. Here, we have provisions designed to ensure that Member State pre-establishment screening measures, adopted for public policy / public security reasons, meet EU-imposed procedural standards. Let us return to the proposal from this perspective, to assess whether it meets the criteria for the use of Article 207 TFEU.

Does it (aim to) facilitate international trade? The Commission has pointed to the 'heightened uncertainty for foreign investors that face different FDI screening regimes from different Member States'.[66] Around half the Member States have screening mechanisms, and they vary considerably in terms of scope, criteria applied and procedure (e.g., pre- or post-establishment). The proposal would not require Member States to introduce screening; so, some disparity would continue, but it would impose a degree of substantive and procedural standardisation and transparency, as well as

62. Opinion 2/15, note 9, para. 108.
63. Likewise, a provision on expropriation would not impinge on Member State powers as regards property ownership since Member States are free to exercise those competences, as long as they do so 'in compliance with general principles and fundamental rights, in particular with the principle of non-discrimination'. Opinion 2/15, note 9, para. 107.
64. Opinion 2/15, note 9, para. 101.
65. Opinion 2/15, note 9, para. 103.
66. SWD (2017) 297, p. 8.

provision for judicial redress.[67] None of the objectives mentioned in the Commission Communication as justifying the measure are expressly concerned with promoting, facilitating or governing international trade; they are concerned with the enhancing the effectiveness of the screening process with regard to its public security / public policy objectives.[68] The reference to legal certainty in the proposal seems to refer mainly to the needs of the Member States, given that FDI is now covered by exclusive EU competence.[69] But to the extent that the proposed regime would ensure that inward direct investment into the EU is subject to an aligned screening procedure that complies with minimum procedural standards it could be said to contribute to facilitating and governing trade and to have immediate and direct effects on trade. The Court, indeed, as we have already seen, took a broad view of what may have an immediate and direct effect on trade in the field of investment: 'any EU act promoting, facilitating or governing participation – by a natural or legal person of a third State in the European Union and vice versa – in the management or control of a company carrying out an economic activity is such as to have direct and immediate effects on trade between that third State and the European Union'.[70] The screening proposal appears to meet this criterion.

By preserving Member State's discretion over introducing FDI screening, the proposal seems to avoid the charge to create new regulatory controls. It is certainly in part designed to ensure, like the provisions in the EU-Singapore agreement, that the relevant (national) legislation 'is applied in an equitable and non-discriminatory manner'. It lists the factors that 'may' be taken into account in a non-exhaustive list. It establishes that screening must not discriminate between third countries, and that the procedure, including the timescale for taking a decision, must be transparent. But, it does neither lay down the procedure in detail, nor does it specify the form that judicial redress must take. To this extent, it seems to be ensuring that the Member State procedures conform to the requirements established by the Court in the context of restrictions on capital movements, including direct investment.[71]

It could be argued that in this light the proposed Regulation goes both too far and not far enough. Too far, in establishing a coordination and information sharing system which is directed more at serving Union objectives and protecting Union interests (and those of other Member States) than at allowing the Member States to protect their own fundamental public policy / public security interests. But not far enough, because of the open-ended nature of Regulation: the list of factors that may affect security or public order is expressly non-exhaustive.[72] The proposal therefore does not ensure that the Member States only use FDI screening to protect against 'a genuine and sufficiently serious threat to a fundamental interest of society', nor does it expressly exclude the

67. And it may be that the information and reporting requirements, applicable also to Member States without screening mechanisms, will encourage the wider adoption of screening.
68. COM (2017) 494, p. 10.
69. *See* COM (2017) 487, Recital (7).
70. Opinion 2/15, note 9, para. 84.
71. *See* note 35.
72. COM (2017) 487, Preamble para. 11 and Art. 4.

pursuit of economic objectives.[73] We will return to these objections, especially the latter, in the next section; for now we may simply note that they do not take the proposal outside the scope of the CCP as interpreted in Opinion 2/15, insofar as it concerns the regulation of FDI.

In mandating screening by the Commission, on the other hand, the proposal does appear to go beyond coordinating the exercise of Member State's discretion. This Commission screening will take place avowedly in the Union interest (it would be possible where FDI is 'likely to affect projects or programmes of Union interest on the grounds of security or public order'[74]). It is not presented simply as a Commission input into the Member State screening process, since all Member States, even those with no screening mechanism, would be obliged to 'take utmost account of the Commission's opinion and provide an explanation to the Commission in case its opinion is not followed'.[75] The proposal makes a distinction between the Commission's opinion on screening initiated by a Member State,[76] and a case where the Commission initiates the screening process,[77] albeit in both cases the ultimate decision is taken by the Member State. It can therefore be argued that this part of the proposal does in effect introduce a new regulatory control on FDI, and is thus the most questionable insofar as the use of Article 207 TFEU is concerned.

[D] Establishing New Regulatory Controls on Direct Investment

Let us now move beyond the current screening proposal and turn to the conclusion of international agreements (or adoption of legislation) designed to establish harmonised standards or new regulatory controls, going beyond mutual recognition, regulatory cooperation or ensuring non-discriminatory application of domestic standards. In principle the choice of legal basis (CCP and/or internal market) in such cases should be governed by the primary or predominant purpose of the legislation. A regulatory measure may be adopted on an internal market legal basis if the regulation of external trade is ancillary to the main internal market objective; the fact that third-country enterprises are covered by an EU regulatory measure does not necessarily require the use of Article 207 TFEU. Where non-EU enterprises, or services offered by external providers, or imports or exports of goods from or to third countries, are only affected incidentally by a regulatory measure directed primarily at the internal market then an internal legal basis should be used.

---

73. In several cases, the Court has been critical of (Member State) prior authorisation mechanisms which allow too much discretion to the national authorities. *See, e.g.*, Case C-326/07 *Commission v. Italy*, note 24, para. 52: 'Even if the criteria at issue concern different kinds of public interests, they are formulated in a general and imprecise manner. What is more, the lack of any connection between the criteria and the special powers to which they relate increases the uncertainty surrounding the circumstances in which those powers may be exercised and gives them a discretionary nature, having regard to the latitude enjoyed by the national authorities in making use of them. Such latitude is disproportionate in relation to the objectives pursued.'
74. COM (2017) 487, Art. 3(2).
75. COM (2017) 487, Art. 9(5).
76. COM (2017) 487, Art. 8(3) and (6).
77. COM (2017) 487, Art. 3(2)–(3) and Art. 9.

So, for example, although Directive 2001/37 on the production, marketing and labelling of tobacco products had been adopted on the joint basis of internal market and CCP powers,[78] the Court held that the CCP legal basis was unnecessary and should not have been used. The prohibition on manufacture of non-compliant products did affect products designed for the export market but its main objective was the protection of the internal market from illegal reimports, and it was held that Article 95 EC (now Article 114 TFEU) was the appropriate legal basis.[79] Likewise, Regulation 1007/2009 on trade in seal products was based on Article 95 EC only and was framed as essentially an internal market measure, applying to seal products imported from third countries '[i]n order to ensure that the harmonised rules provided for in this Regulation are fully effective'.[80]

Where, on the other hand, a measure involves the regulation of international trade as well as trade within the internal market, a dual legal basis may be appropriate. The decision concluding the WHO Convention on tobacco control, for example, which establishes harmonised rules on the packaging and labelling of tobacco as well as containing provisions on trade in tobacco products, was based on Articles 95 and 133 EC (now Articles 114 and 207 TFEU).[81] The dual legal basis, which was not challenged, can be justified on the ground that the Convention is equally concerned with trade and with product regulation for purposes of public health.[82]

In the field of services, Directive 2013/36/EU on the authorisation and supervision of credit institutions is based on Article 53 TFEU (an internal market legal basis) and contains a title on relations with third countries, including the establishment of third-country banks in the EU and envisaging the possibility of agreements with third countries on both authorisation and consolidated supervision of credit institutions.[83] Other recent legislation regulating the financial services sector and adopted on an

78. Directive 2001/37/EC Directive 2001/37/EC on the approximation of the laws, regulations and administrative provisions of the Member States concerning the manufacture, presentation and sale of tobacco products, OJ 2001 L 194/26, was adopted on a joint legal basis of Arts 95 and 113 EC. Its predecessors had been based on an internal market legal basis alone but since Directive 2001/37 also covered tobacco products to be exported from the EU the CCP legal basis was added: *see* Recital 11, and Art. 3 which sets maximum tar, carbon monoxide and nicotine yields for all cigarettes manufactured in the EU whatever their destination.
79. Case Case C-491/01 *The Queen v. Secretary of State for Health, ex parte: British American Tobacco (Investments) Ltd and Imperial Tobacco Ltd*, EU:C:2002:741, paras 81–91. The Court went on to find, however, that since the co-decision procedure required by Art. 95 EC had in fact been used, the addition of Art. 133 EC as a legal basis did not invalidate the directive.
80. Regulation 1007/2009/EC on trade in seal products OJ 2009 L 286/3, Recital 13. For a discussion critiquing the legal basis to the Regulation, *see* T Perišin, 'Is the EU Seal Products Regulation a Sealed Deal? EU and WTO Challenges' (2013) 62 *International and Comparative Law Quarterly* 373 at 381–387.
81. Council Decision 2004/513/EC of 2 Jun. 2004 concerning the conclusion of the WHO Framework Convention on Tobacco Control OJ 2004 L 213/8. All EU Member States are also parties.
82. Cf. Case Case C-94/03 *Commission v. Council*, EU:C:2006:2, holding that a dual legal basis (environment and trade) should have been used to conclude the Rotterdam Convention on the Prior Informed Consent Procedure for certain hazardous chemicals and pesticides in international trade.
83. Directive 2013/36/EU on access to the activity of credit institutions and the prudential supervision of credit institutions and investment firms, OJ 2013 L 176/338; for the provisions on relations with third countries, *see* Title VI, Arts 47–48.

internal market legal basis also covers institutions established in third countries and offering services in the EU. For example, Regulation 513/2011/EU on the supervision of credit rating agencies by ESMA is based on Article 114 TFEU and contains provisions on the activities in the EU of credit rating agencies established in third countries, as well as regulatory cooperation between ESMA and the supervisory authorities of third countries.[84] Directive 2011/61/EU on the authorisation and supervision of alternative investment fund managers (AIFMs) is based on Article 53 TFEU and covers those which have their registered office in a Member State (EU AIFMs) and those which have their registered office in a third country (non-EU AIFMs).[85]

In the nature of things, for both practical and legal reasons, including compliance with WTO and bilateral treaty obligations, post-establishment regulation will generally be designed to apply both to domestic and foreign investors, and the use of an internal legal basis – as in the examples above – reflects its predominant purpose. The Merger Regulation, for example, (based on what are now Articles 103 and 352 TFEU) applies also to mergers and acquisitions by third-country investors.[86] Regulation 1008/2008 on the provision of air services in the EU, based on what is now Article 100(2) TFEU, imposes conditions for the grant of an operating licence which include minimum ownership and control conditions.[87] The Commission Communication gives other examples of prior authorisation and foreign (third state) ownership rules in EU legislation, such as those applying to gas and electricity,[88] and the exploration of hydrocarbons,[89] all of which have internal market legal bases.[90]

What of measures which have a primarily external focus? We have already seen that CCP powers can be used to extend to third countries existing regulatory measures adopted within the internal market.[91] Where a trade agreement includes provisions establishing new harmonised standards or post-establishment regulatory controls, should they also be regarded as falling within the scope of the CCP? Or should they be seen rather as the external dimension of the internal regulatory competence, requiring an internal market legal basis? First we may note that Article 207(6) TFEU provides that the exercise of the competence conferred by Article 207 'shall not lead to harmonisation of legislative or regulatory provisions of the Member States insofar as the Treaties exclude such harmonisation'. Harmonisation is excluded, for example, in relation to

84. Regulation 513/2011/EU, OJ 2011 L 145/30.
85. Directive 2011/61/EU, OJ 2011 L 174/1.
86. Council Regulation 139/2004 of 20 Jan. 2004 on the control of concentrations between undertakings OJ L 24/1.
87. Regulation 1008/2008, OJ L 293/3, Art. 4. Note that transport services are in any event excluded from Art. 207 TFEU.
88. Directive 2009/72/EC concerning common rules for the internal market in electricity OJ L 211/55, Art. 11; Directive 2009/73/EC concerning common rules for the internal market in natural gas OJ L 211/94, Art. 11.
89. Directive 94/22/EC on the conditions for granting and using authorizations for the prospection, exploration and production of hydrocarbons, OJ L 164/3, Art. 2(2), 'Member States may refuse, on grounds of national security, to allow access to and exercise of these activities to any entity which is effectively controlled by third countries or third country nationals.'
90. COM (2017) 494 of 13 Sept. 2017, p. 8.
91. *See above* section 2.04[b].

public health.[92] *A contrario*, it would appear that insofar as the Treaties do *not* exclude harmonisation, Article 207 could be used as a basis for external measures involving harmonisation of Member State regulation; this would clearly apply to harmonised regulation of FDI as well as goods, services and the commercial aspects of intellectual property.

On the other hand, it is possible to argue that measures which are essentially aimed at regulatory harmonisation, or at establishing new regulatory systems, go beyond the scope of Article 207 TFEU. In pointing out that the TBT and SPS agreements were 'confined to' rules on the adoption and application of regulations (i.e., rules falling within section 2.04[C] above), Opinion 1/94 could be read as suggesting that agreements which go beyond this to include substantive harmonisation should not be based on CCP powers alone.[93] Opinion 2/15 also seems to take this position. As we have already seen, in holding that the investment protection provisions in the EU-Singapore agreement fall within the scope of the CCP the Court stressed that they do not 'encroach upon the competences of the Member States regarding public order, public security and other public interests',[94] nor do they 'contain any commitment for the Member States relating to their criminal law, tax law or social security'.[95] It also found that the provisions on intellectual property 'in no way [fall] within the scope of harmonisation of the laws of the Member States of the European Union';[96] and that the provisions on sustainable development are 'intended not to regulate the levels of social and environmental protection in the Parties' respective territory' but rather to make liberalisation of trade subject to a condition of compliance with pre-existing international obligations in these fields.[97] This form of argumentation suggests that the Court was setting boundaries to Article 207 TFEU; that it does not provide a basis for adopting measures which themselves address public order or security interests, the harmonisation of (e.g.) taxation, or for regulating the protection of social, environmental or labour standards. Such matters would fall within the relevant specific competences on intellectual property, taxation or social or environmental protection, which are not only shared competences but, which in some cases, also have different voting requirements (unanimity).[98] Applying this reasoning to the regulation of FDI, we can conclude that an international agreement (or legislation) which establishes new regulatory obligations aimed at both foreign and domestic direct investment in the EU requires an internal market legal basis. This may operate as a dual legal basis alongside

92. Article 168(5) TFEU.
93. *See above* at note 59.
94. Opinion 2/15, note 9, para. 103.
95. Opinion 2/15, note 9, para. 108.
96. Opinion 2/15, note 9, para. 126.
97. Opinion 2/15, note 9, para. 166; *see* section 2.04[a] above.
98. '[T]he exclusive competence of the European Union referred to in Art. 3(1)(e) TFEU cannot be exercised in order to regulate the levels of social and environmental protection in the Parties' respective territory. The adoption of such rules would fall within the division of competences between the European Union and the Member States that is laid down, in particular, in Article 3(1)(d) and (2) and Article 4(2)(b) and (e) TFEU.' Opinion 2/15, note 9, para. 164. Art. 3(1)(d) TFEU covers fisheries conservation (exclusive competence), Arts 4(2)(b) and (e) TFEU refer to social policy and the environment respectively, both shared competence subject to the possibility of exclusivity under Art. 3(2) TFEU.

Article 207 TFEU if there is a clear international trade dimension,[99] although as we have already seen, where the predominant purpose of the measure is not to promote, facilitate or govern international trade Article 207 TFEU will not be needed as a legal basis.

In making this argument on the limits to Article 207 TFEU, the Court cites Article 207(6), which provides that '[t]he exercise of the competences conferred by this Article in the field of the common commercial policy shall not affect the delimitation of competences between the Union and the Member States'. The meaning of this provision has given rise to debate, given that the 'delimitation of competence' in the field of the CCP has been fixed by Article 3(1) TFEU.[100] In Opinion 2/15, the Court uses the provision as a rhetorical device, to support its identification of some limits to the scope of Article 207 TFEU, given its expansive approach to the ways in which regulation may have direct and immediate effects on trade. But Article 207(6) TFEU also helps to set limits to the CCP in a slightly different way. It is intended to ensure that the exercise of the EU's *external* powers under Article 207 TFEU in fields such as intellectual property and FDI, and the exercise of its regulatory competence in relation to goods or services in an external context, does not in itself imply exclusivity in those fields when the EU acts *internally*. Article 207(6) TFEU ensures that external (exclusive) action does not result in the displacement of Member State competence internally through pre-emption. Article 207(6) thus confirms that although exclusive competence over the CCP now extends into fields (such as services, intellectual property and direct investment) which are not entirely covered by internal EU rules, this does not mean that the Member States are automatically completely excluded from adopting internal rules over such fields, nor that internal rules adopted at EU level should necessarily be based on Article 207 TFEU.[101] An agreement concluded under Article 207 TFEU, and thus within exclusive EU competence, may contain commitments which will be implemented internally by the EU under shared (internal) powers, or even by the Member States.

Such an approach is consistent with the Court's statements in Opinion 2/15 and allows us to reconcile the grant of exclusive competence over FDI in Article 207(1) TFEU with the proviso as to the delimitation of competence between Union and Member States found in Article 207(6) TFEU. And this point is significant if we recall that since the EU's internal regulatory powers (such as Article 114 TFEU) are shared powers, the Member States retain the room to regulate insofar as the EU has not done

99. Cf. the WHO Convention on Tobacco Control, note 81 above.
100. *See, e.g.*, J Wouters, D Coppens and B De Meester, 'The European Union's External Relations after the Lisbon Treaty', in S Griller and J Ziller (eds), *The Lisbon Treaty – EU Constitutionalism Without a Constitutional Treaty?* Springer 2008; J-C Piris, *The Lisbon Treaty: A Legal and Political Analysis*, Cambridge University Press 2010, pp. 282–283; R Gosalbo Bono, 'The Organisation of the External Relations of the European Union in the Treaty of Lisbon' in P Koutrakos (ed.), *The European Union's External Relations a Year after Lisbon*, CLEER Working Paper 2011/3.
101. A Dimopoulos, 'The Effects of the Lisbon Treaty on the Principles and Objectives of the Common Commercial Policy' (2010) 15 *European Foreign Affairs Rev* 153, at 159. *See also* Case C-414/11 *Daiichi Sankyo Co. Ltd*, note 38, para. 59, and AG Sharpston in Opinion 2/15, EU:C:2016:992, paras 107–109.

so; and the Member States' regulatory powers are also preserved by the public policy / public security exceptions written into the internal market provisions. This brings us to the issue of Member State's discretion.

§2.05 WHAT REGULATORY SPACE FOR THE MEMBER STATES?

As we know, the exclusivity attached to Article 207 TFEU is not based on pre-emption (the existence of internal legislation) but operates *a priori* from the Treaty itself, and any Member State action within its scope (including measures justified on public interest grounds) require EU authorisation.[102] In the case of trade in goods, the general EU Regulations on import and export include a provision the wording of which is based on Article 36 TFEU; this allows the Member States to impose national regulations on imported or exported goods, insofar as the Union has not yet adopted harmonised rules.[103] As regards FDI, the Member States have been authorised, under certain conditions, to maintain and conclude bilateral investment treaties (BITs) with third countries, until a BIT between the EU and that third country enters into force.[104] This apart, there is no general authorisation allowing the Member States to act *externally* on FDI to protect their regulatory interests insofar as no Union measure exists (were the Commission proposal to be adopted on the basis of Article 207 TFEU, it might be another example). As we have seen, Article 207(6) preserves this power as far as *internal* regulation is concerned: the Member States' power of internal regulation is protected by Article 207(6) TFEU, subject to internal legislation adopted by the EU, but must be exercised in conformity with EU law.

This of course reflects the general position with respect to internal market regulation (including investment): where the EU has not yet acted Member States retain the power to regulate, subject to the requirement of compliance with their EU law obligations (Article 2(2) TFEU). However, the requirement that Member States must comply with their EU law obligations when exercising their retained regulatory powers may result in substantial constraint on their regulatory discretion, given the very extensive scope which has been given to the concept of a restriction on the right of establishment in cases such as *AGET Iraklis*.[105] In that case, it will be remembered, it was held that national legislation subjecting a firm's implementation of collective redundancies to the approval of a competent authority was a restriction on freedom of establishment: 'Such national legislation constitutes a significant interference in

102. Article 3(1) TFEU.
103. Regulation 2015/478 EU on common rules for imports OJ 2015 L 83/16, Art. 24(2)(a); this power is subject to the requirement already mentioned that in the non-harmonised sectors the Member States must apply national standards to third country origin goods, on the basis of national treatment. Regulation 2015/479/EU on common rules for exports OJ 2015 L 83/34, Art. 10.
104. Regulation 1219/2012/EU establishing transitional arrangements for bilateral investment agreements between Member States and third countries OJ 2012 L 351/40. *See also* Regulation 912/2014/EU establishing a framework for managing financial responsibility linked to investor-to-state dispute settlement tribunals established by international agreements to which the European Union is party OJ 2014 L 257/121.
105. Case C-201/15 *AGET Iraklis*, EU:C:2016:972.

certain freedoms which economic operators generally enjoy. Accordingly, it must be held that such national legislation is liable to constitute a serious obstacle to the exercise of freedom of establishment in Greece.'[106] Not only do such restrictions need to be justified by 'overriding reasons in the public interest';[107] the finding of a justified restriction – like the application of a public policy or public security derogation – may also establish the need for future legislation at EU level.

In a number of capital movements cases, we see the same principles applied to Member State restrictions on direct investment from third countries, such as prior authorisation systems. The Court has held that prior authorisation may be justified in some cases on grounds of public policy or public security, but rejected a system in which the risk to public policy or security was inadequately defined in advance, as being contrary to the principle of legal certainty.[108]

But the constraints imposed by EU law are not limited to the internal sphere; they also affect the Member States' external action and may impact Member State competence. In Opinion 3/15, the Court held that the *AETR* principle, as now expressed in Article 3(2) TFEU, may establish an exclusive EU external competence notwithstanding that the relevant EU internal legislation allows space for Member States' discretion.[109] The Member States' discretion operated within limits set by the EU legislation and was to be exercised without compromising its objectives: it is 'granted by the EU legislature and is highly circumscribed by the requirements of EU law'.[110] An international agreement which requires its parties to enact such measures therefore 'falls within an area that is already covered to a large extent by common EU rules and the conclusion of that treaty may thus affect those rules or alter their scope', within the meaning of Article 3(2) TFEU – leading to a finding of exclusivity as far as external competence is concerned.[111] So although EU competence in relation to the internal market, including establishment, does not preclude Member State regulation justified on grounds of public interest or public policy, and although EU legislation may leave scope for Member States' discretion, the operation of the *AETR* principle may mean that only the Union is entitled to enter into *external commitments* in relation to those areas of derogation.

It might then be argued that were the Commission's screening proposal to be adopted (whether on the basis of movement of capital or CCP powers), the discretion it leaves the Member States would (in the words of Opinion 3/15) be 'granted by the EU legislature and [be] highly circumscribed by the requirements of EU law'.[112] The Regulation may thus give rise to the operation of Article 3(2) TFEU and an exclusive EU competence if provisions on FDI screening were included in a future investment agreement.

106. Case C-201/15 *AGET Iraklis*, note 105, paras 55 and 57.
107. *See* Case C-201/15 *AGET Iraklis*, note 105, paras 61–78.
108. Case C-54/99 *Association Église de Scientologie de Paris, Scientology International Reserves Trust*, note 26. *See also* Case C-274/06 *Commission v. Spain* EU:C:2008:86.
109. Opinion 3/15, note 38.
110. *Ibid.*, para. 126.
111. *Ibid.*, para. 129.
112. *Ibid.*, para. 126.

If the regulatory space left to Member States by the Treaties or by Union legislation is subject to the constraints of EU law (such as proportionality, non-discrimination, and fundamental rights), to what extent do those constraints also apply to the Union in establishing a framework for the exercise of the Member States' public policy / public security discretion? The CCP does not mandate any specific level of liberalisation or require restrictions on external trade to be proportionate and the Court has been reluctant to write general Treaty principles such as non-discrimination into the substantive dimension of CCP policy choices.[113] It has referred to proportionality, but only where it was a question of interfering with fundamental rights.[114] On the other hand, there are both external and internal reasons for applying a requirement of proportionality. Externally, the EU must ensure that it complies with its international commitments, including those under the WTO and of course bilateral trade agreements. Internally, the free movement of capital requires that restrictions imposed by Member States are justified according to Article 65 TFEU, and this includes proportionality (and that the restrictions do not amount to 'a means of arbitrary discrimination or a disguised restriction on the free movement of capital'). Under the screening proposal, the restrictions would ultimately be imposed by the Member States although operating within an EU framework, and therefore Article 65 TFEU should apply, even though the measure is based upon the CCP. In other words, while the CCP provisions in the Treaties do not themselves lay down any constraints, to the extent to which the EU decides to authorise the Member States to act within the scope of the CCP, it cannot authorise them to depart from obligations derived from other Treaty norms. Here we return to the point made above: the proposal certainly does not require the Member States to act contrary to the constraints imposed by Article 65 TFEU or by the Court's case law on public policy justifications for restrictions on capital movements, but neither does it explicitly require them to act in compliance.[115] For example, the proposed Regulation does not explicitly prohibit the application of purely economic criteria. Nor, in the case of Member States without a screening mechanism, does it impose procedural guarantees (including provision for judicial redress) where the Member State acts to restrict a specific inward investment in response to a Commission opinion.[116] The proposal as it stands leaves considerable discretion to the Member States to assess their own public policy / public security concerns, thereby properly respecting the policy space granted to them by the Treaty. But a strong case can be made that where the Union decides to create a substantive and procedural framework for such measures, however minimal, it should build into that framework rules designed to ensure compliance with the Treaties and the Court's case law. This is, I

113. *See, e.g.*, Case 55/75 *Balkan-Import-Export*, EU:C:1976:8, para. 14, and more recently Case C-272/15 *Swiss International Airlines*, EU:C:2016:993, at para. 29: 'the institutions and agencies of the Union are relieved of any obligation to apply the principle of equal treatment to third countries, in order to maintain their internal freedom of action in terms of policy'.
114. *See, e.g.*, Case C-84/95 *Bosphorus v. Ministry of Transport, Energy and Communications*, EU:C:1996:312, paras 23–26.
115. *See above* at section 2.04[C].
116. COM (2017) 487, Art. 9(3) makes it clear that Commission screening can include investments in Member States without a screening mechanism.

would argue, especially so where the measure is cast as an authorisation to Member States in a context of exclusive EU competence: in such a case we are not in the realm of minimum harmonisation and the Member States are acting by virtue of Union authority.

§2.06 CONCLUSIONS

This chapter has examined the legal framework for the regulation of foreign direct inward investment, using the Commission's 2017 proposal for a Regulation on FDI screening as a lens through which to explore questions of competence and legal basis and the relationship between external powers – especially the CCP – and the internal regulatory competence based in the internal market. We started with three questions. The first concerned the degree to which the EU's CCP competence covers regulation of FDI as well as liberalisation or market access. We found that in principle post-establishment investment protection falls within the scope of the CCP as – according to the Court of Justice in Opinion 2/15 – it is designed to 'promote, facilitate or govern trade' with third States and is 'such as to have direct and immediate effects on that trade'. This includes measures designed to ensure that the liberalisation and regulation of investment takes place in accordance with the international commitments of the Union, for example, in relation to environmental or labour protection. It also includes measures which concern the application of regulatory measures, such as commitments on non-discrimination and constraints on the Member States' exercise of their public policy discretion intended to ensure that such derogations are necessary and not a disguised restriction on trade.

Second, we examined the relation, in the context of inward investment, between the CCP and the regulatory competence derived from internal market powers. Internal market legislation will frequently include provisions applicable to foreign investors or service suppliers; since legal basis is based on predominant purpose, an additional CCP legal basis is not normally required. Where a measure concerns both international trade or investment and trade or investment within the internal market a dual legal basis may be used. Internal market or other internal powers are necessary for the harmonisation of national law (e.g., on taxation or intellectual property rights), or for measures which themselves define Member State public order or security interests, or for regulating the protection of social, environmental or labour standards; such measures would normally be applicable to both domestic and foreign undertakings or investors. In addition, the adoption of CCP-based measures on direct investment in the context of international trade (FDI), or the conclusion of an international agreement including such provisions, does not affect the balance of competences with respect to internal legislation. The latter, as a result of Article 207(6) TFEU, will remain a matter of shared competence subject to the possibility of exclusivity under the terms of Article 3(2) TFEU (in particular, the *AETR* effect), and subject as well to any international commitments entered into under the exercise of CCP powers.

Applying these conclusions to the Commission's proposed Regulation on FDI screening, we concluded that it falls within the scope of the CCP. It would establish substantive and procedural constraints on the application of Member States' screening mechanisms and with one possible exception is not designed to create a new regulatory mechanism. The possible exception is the introduction of screening at EU level by the Commission, where FDI is 'likely to affect projects or programmes of Union interest on the grounds of security or public order'. This, it could be argued, introduces a new basis for screening (the Union interest) and a new EU-level screening mechanism, going beyond coordinating and managing Member State screening. On the basis of the current draft, this element – especially given that the ultimate decision is left with the Member State concerned – could be regarded as ancillary and subordinate to the predominant objective of the Regulation, which is directed at Member State screening. New post-establishment regulatory controls on direct investment, such as the imposition of conditions on the grant of operating licences, would fall within internal market powers. Both Member State and EU-level screenings, even where adopted under CCP powers, must comply with the Treaty provisions on capital movements.

This brings us to the third question, the degree to which EU powers leave space for Member State action, especially in the context of the public policy and public security derogations from the freedom of capital movements. These derogations do not give the Member States *carte blanche*, or create a ring-fence within which EU law does not apply; their use is subject to constraints based on the fundamental rules of EU law, including procedural rights.[117] Further, both procedural and substantive conditions for the use by Member States of the public policy / public security derogation may – as in the case of the screening proposal – be established by legislation. It would also be open to the EU to adopt harmonising legislation designed to replace national measures justified on public policy grounds with EU-level measures designed to achieve the same objectives: as argued above, such a measure should be based on the internal market legal basis (Article 64 TFEU) rather than Article 207 TFEU.[118]

If the limited screening proposal as it stands can indeed, as suggested here, be based on Article 207 TFEU, the authorisation granted to the Member States must comply with EU primary law, including the free movement of capital which applies between the EU and third States subject only to Treaty-based permissible derogations. This means that the authorisation is subject to the conditions imposed by Article 65 TFEU as it has been interpreted by the Court of Justice. The proposal as currently drafted does not prevent compliance with these conditions (and is clearly intended to comply with them), but not all are explicitly integrated into the framework created by the proposed Regulation, in particular the requirement that 'those derogations must not be misapplied so as, in fact, to serve purely economic ends'.[119] The non-exhaustive list of factors that may be taken into account in screening FDI, according to Article 4 of the proposal, may leave space for the Member States to adopt purely economic criteria,

117. *See* text at note 35.
118. It is beyond the scope of this paper to address the question of whether Art. 4(2) TEU, which provides that 'national security remains the sole responsibility of each Member State', would preclude action at EU level on grounds of public security. Certainly neither Art. 4(2) TEU nor Art. 73 TFEU preclude the adoption of EU measures addressing the internal security of the Union, such as those related to combating terrorism or organised crime.
119. *See* note 35.

although they would be acting contrary to the Treaty in so doing.[120] It can be argued that this solution respects the degree of discretion granted to Member States by Article 65 TFEU; it could also be argued that since the screening is authorised 'on the grounds of security or public order'[121] the exclusion of screening for 'purely economic ends' is implicit. However, it would be preferable in the interests of transparency for the Regulation itself to reflect fully the scope of this provision as interpreted by the Court of Justice.

The EU legal framework for regulating FDI is undeniably complex. It is not possible simply to rely on exclusive CCP powers for all dimensions of FDI regulation. Some aspects may certainly fall within the CCP if they are designed to affect trade with third States, but others will require other legal bases. The relationship between the CCP insofar as it covers FDI and the free movement of capital is especially tricky. It is argued here that although the EU Treaties leave the political institutions with a great deal of discretion in determining their policy priorities for the CCP, including the degree of liberalisation, action under the CCP relating to FDI is subject to the freedom of capital movements which also applies between the EU and third States. Thus any derogations from that freedom, including those authorised by the EU institutions, must be justified according to the Treaty rules, as well as compliant with the EU's international obligations.

120. It is no defence to a breach of EU law obligations that such conduct was purportedly authorised by EU legislation: Joined cases 80 and 81/77 *Société Les Commissionnaires Réunis SARL v. Receveur des douanes*, ECLI:EU:C:1978:87.
121. COM (2017) 487, Art. 3(1).

COMMENT ON CHAPTER 2

Foreign Direct Investment Control in the European Union: Rising Protectionism or Instrument for Further Investment Liberalization?

Stephan Schill[*]

This chapter complements Marise Cremona's analysis on the correct basis of competence for the proposal to introduce a screening mechanism for inward foreign direct investment (FDI) at Union level. It argues that 'Regulation (EU) 2019/452 of the European Parliament and of the Council of 19 March 2019 establishing a framework for screening of foreign direct investments into the Union',[1] should not be mistaken as exclusively aiming at protecting the internal market and specific Union or Member State interests. Instead, the proposal has a tangible external economic policy justification and outlook because the otherwise missing possibilities to limit inward FDI into the European Union (EU) which it creates can be used as a bargaining chip to achieve, on the basis of reciprocity, better access of EU investors in negotiations with economically powerful countries, such as the United States or China. Paradoxically, the introduction of screening powers on inward FDI can therefore also be seen as serving the EU's constitutionally enshrined goal of further investment liberalization, rather than only shielding the internal market from undesired external influence.

* Funding from the European Research Council (ERC Grant Agreement No. 313355), as part of the research project on 'Transnational Private-Public Arbitration as Global Regulatory Governance: Charting and Codifying the Lex Mercatoria Publica' (LexMercPub) is gratefully acknowledged.

1. Official Journal L 79/I 1 (21 Mar. 2019).

§2.01 THE FDI SCREENING PARADOX

The introduction of screening mechanisms for FDI, in particular those related to concerns of 'national security', is mostly considered as a restriction on international investment flows and may even be taken as an indication of mounting nationalism and protectionism in international economic relations.[2] This is so because the analysis of FDI screening mechanisms usually is based on the assumption that the regulator's motivation is to protect domestic policy concerns in concrete companies or undertakings against foreign mergers or acquisition. This inward-looking focus also explains that the introduction of a screening mechanism for inward FDI in the EU raises questions of competence. Is such a screening a matter of the internal market rules in light of the rules on free movement of capital in relation to third countries, or is it a matter of the EU's common commercial policy because the ordering of the EU's external economic relations is at stake? While the former would suggest Article 64(2) of the Treaty on the Functioning of the European Union (TFEU) as the basis of a (shared) EU competence, the latter would, as invoked by the Commission,[3] bring Article 207(1) TFEU as a basis of an (exclusive) EU competence into play.

In her chapter in the present book, Marise Cremona analyses these questions of competence in a detailed, comprehensive and highly instructive fashion, and provides convincing support that the new Regulation on inward FDI screening is correctly based on the EU's competence for the common commercial policy (Article 207(1) TFEU).[4] On substance, there is nothing I would want to criticize or disagree with. Instead, the purpose of this chapter is to complement and support Cremona's analysis on competence by developing an additional argument speaking in favour of viewing the proposal as part of the common commercial policy, rather than as regulating the free movement of inward capital. This argument relies on what can be called the 'paradoxical nature' of the Commission's proposed inward FDI screening.

What do I mean by that? In my reading, the goal of Regulation (EU) 2019/452 is not principally to protect the internal market and specific public policy interests of either the EU or its Member States. On the contrary, the tools for screening inward FDI the regulation would create have a tangible external economic policy justification and outlook. They empower the EU in its trade and investment negotiations with third countries when seeking to achieve, on the basis of reciprocity, better access of EU investors to third-country markets, in return for limiting the EU's screening powers

2. *See*, for example, the discussion in United Nations Conference on Trade and Development (UNCTAD), *World Investment Report 2018: Investment and New Industrial Policies* (United Nations 2018) 83–84.
3. *See* the first recital in the preamble of Regulation (EU) 2019/452. *See also* European Commission, 'Proposal for a Regulation of the European Parliament and of the Council Establishing a Framework for Screening of Foreign Direct Investments into the European Union' COM (2017) 487 final (13 Sept. 2017) 2 and 8.
4. *See* Marise Cremona, 'Regulating FDI in the EU Legal Framework' (in this book).

concerning inward FDI coming from its treaty partners into the EU. In that perspective, Regulation (EU) 2019/452 does not have an inward-looking objective in aiming to protect the internal market against outside interferences, nor is motivated by EU protectionism. Instead, and somewhat paradoxically, it can be a building block in the EU's broader external policy agenda, and implementation of its constitutional mandate, to achieve further liberalization of FDI flows. The screening powers created can be particularly important to strengthen the EU's bargaining power in bilateral negotiations with economically powerful countries, such as the United States or China, with whom the EU seeks to establish comprehensive treaty rules governing access for, and protection of, foreign investment.

In order to build up this argument, section 2 of this chapter puts Regulation (EU) 2019/452 into the context of the EU aiming to become a rule-maker that influences and shapes international investment law at a global level according to objectives laid down by EU constitutional law. Pursuant to Article 21 TEU, these objectives encompass achieving further investment liberalization and shaping international investment relations according to the EU's own constitutional values to promote and protect, amongst other, democracy, the rule of law, and human rights. Section 3 then addresses the obstacles EU constitutional law presents, in the form of the free movement of capital in relation to third countries, which only became part of EU with the 1993 Maastricht Treaty,[5] to the EU negotiating effectively for further investment liberalization in particular in bilateral settings with economically powerful countries as counterparts. Section 4 then compares the situation under EU constitutional law to the constitutional framework in force in Germany, which accords foreign investors in important regards a constitutional status that differs from that of nationals. This comparison reinforces the point that Regulation (EU) 2019/452 fulfils the important function of achieving one constitutional objective, i.e., strengthening the EU's external negotiation power, which is weakened by another area of EU constitutional law, namely the EU's internal market rules. Section 5 concludes.

§2.02 THE EU AS AN EMERGING RULE-MAKER IN INTERNATIONAL INVESTMENT LAW

Prior to the entry into force of the Lisbon Treaty, the EU had played only a smaller role in shaping international investment law at a global level. It had done so through its participation in the World Trade Organization (WTO) and the Organisation for Economic Co-operation and Development (OECD), both of which have created a (limited) set of rules for investment liberalization.[6] By contrast, the – in practice – most

5. *See* Art. 73(b) of the Treaty Establishing the European Community (Maastricht version) (signed 7 Feb. 1992, entered into force 1 Nov. 1993) Official Journal C 191 (29 July 1992).
6. Investment rules under the WTO framework are created mainly through the Agreement on Trade-Related Investment Measures (TRIMs) (signed 15 Apr. 1994 and entered into force 1 Jan. 1995) 1868 UNTS 186, the General Agreement on Trade in Services (GATS) (signed 15 Apr. 1994 and entered into force 1 Jan. 1995) 1869 UNTS 183, which covers trade in services via 'commercial presence' (so-called Mode 3), and the Agreement on Trade-Related Aspects of Intellectual Property Rights (TRIPS) (signed 15 Apr. 1995 and entered into force 1 Jan. 1995) 1869

important area of international investment law, namely, the law of international investment protection and investor-state dispute settlement (ISDS), has long been under the exclusive ambit of Member States who have concluded almost 1,600 international investment agreements (IIAs), both amongst themselves (intra-EU) and with third countries (extra-EU).[7]

The Lisbon Treaty has brought a major change in this respect, with Article 207(1) TFEU integrating 'FDI' into the EU's common commercial policy.[8] While the scope of this competence has, for almost a decade, remained contested, the CJEU has recently clarified in Opinion 2/15 that it encompassed both investment liberalization in the pre-establishment phase and substantive investment protection post-establishment.[9] The Court has held, however, that portfolio investment and ISDS were not covered by Article 207(1) TFEU and remained under shared competence.[10] In practice, this division of competences will have the consequence that agreements covering both foreign direct and portfolio investments and/or ISDS – at least when they allow recourse against Member States – will be concluded as mixed agreements, or will incrementally disappear because their ratification at EU and Member State levels is too cumbersome.[11] In either event, the negotiation of such agreements,

UNTS 299. Rules for investment liberalization in the OECD are mainly contained in the OECD Codes of Liberalisation of Capital Movements and Current Invisible Operations. *See* OECD, 'OECD Codes of Liberalisation: User's Guide' (2019), http://www.oecd.org/investment/investment-policy/38072327.pdf, accessed 25 Oct. 2019. *See* Matthias Ruffert, 'Capital, Free Flow of' in Rüdiger Wolfrum (ed.), *The Max Planck Encyclopedia of Public International Law* (online edition), www.mpepil.com, paras 17–19.

7. UNCTAD lists a total of 1,590 IIAs with at least one EU Member State as party, including 195 intra-EU and 1,395 extra-EU agreements. This excludes replaced and terminated treaties. *See* UNCTAD, 'International Investment Agreements Navigator: Advanced Search' (2018), http://investmentpolicyhub.unctad.org/IIA/AdvancedSearchBIT, accessed 30 Jul. 2018.
8. Comprehensively on the EU and its engagement with international investment law, *see* Angelos Dimopoulos, *EU Foreign Investment Law* (OUP 2011); Catharine Titi, 'International Investment Law and the European Union: Towards a New Generation of International Investment Agreements' (2015) 26 EJIL 639; Sophie Meunier and Jean-Frédéric Morin, 'The European Union and the Space-Time Continuum of Investment Agreements' (2017) 39 Journal of European Integration 891.
9. CJEU, Opinion 2/15, *Free Trade Agreement with Singapore* (16 May 2017) paras 78–110.
10. *Ibid.*, paras 238, 243 (non-direct investment) and 293 (ISDS).
11. *See* Hannes Lenk, 'More Trade and Less Investment for Future EU Trade and Investment Policy' (2018) 19 JWIT 305, 306 and 317–319. One of the main differences between mixed agreements and EU-only agreements concerns their conclusion and entry into force. Whereas the former also require ratification by the competent under the Member States, the latter only have to be approved by the Council and the European Parliament pursuant to Art. 218(6)(a)(v) TFEU in conjunction with Art. 207(2) TFEU. *See* further on mixed agreements and their implications, Guillaume van der Loo and Ramses A Wessel, 'The Non-Ratification of Mixed Agreements: Legal Consequences and Solutions' (2017) 54 Common Market Law Review 735; Gesa Kübek, 'The Non-Ratification Scenario: Legal and Practical Responses to Mixed Treaty Rejection by Member States' (2018) 23 European Foreign Affairs Review 21. In theory, it remains possible though that despite the shared competence, IIAs can be concluded as EU-only agreements, provided the Commission requests, and the Council agrees, to that mode of conclusion; *see* CJEU, Case C-600/14, *Germany/Council*, ECLI:EU:C:2017:935, para. 68; Hannes Lenk and Szilárd Gáspár-Szilágyi, 'Case C-600/14, Germany v Council (OTIF). More Clarity over Facultative Mixity?' (*European Law Blog*, 11 Dec. 2017), https://europeanlawblog.eu/2017/12/11/case-c-60014-germany-v-council-otif-more-clarity-over-facultative-mixity/ (accessed 30 Jul. 2018). Another way to avoid mixity of the entire agreement is to conclude two separate agreements, one

whether they are mixed or concluded as EU-only agreements, generally lies with the Commission.[12]

The Commission had already started, soon after the entry into force of the Lisbon Treaty, to fill the EU's new competence with life. It has first done so in a Communication of July 2010, in which it sketched out the contours and objectives of the EU's future international investment policy, terming it 'the new frontier for the common commercial policy'.[13] Expressing itself favourably concerning the general benefits of investment flows for economic growth, employment, and development, the Commission acknowledged the leading position of the EU to shape the law governing international investment relations. While building on 'best practices' of Member States,[14] the Commission stressed that the EU had better leverage in negotiating rules with third countries than Member States acting individually. It could thus better 'ensure that EU investors abroad enjoy a level-playing field, which assures uniform and optimal conditions for investment through the progressive abolition of restrictions on investment'.[15] The abolition of such restrictions is imperative for the EU not least because of the mounting significance of global value chains and services trade.[16]

That achieving further market access and investment liberalization were the core goals of the EU's common commercial policy was also echoed by the Council, which emphasized in its reaction to the Commission's July 2010 Communication, that EU IIAs should provide for 'effective and ambitious investment protection and market access'.[17] Similarly, the European Parliament, while stressing the need for transparency in international trade negotiations, and expressing concerns about the effect of IIAs on certain sensitive areas of public policy-making, recognized the importance of the external dimensions of investment protection and liberalization. It emphasized, *inter alia*, that 'investor protection for all EU investors must remain the first priority of investment agreements'[18] and highlighted the need to 'ensure reciprocity when

---

covering the trade aspects under the exclusive EU competence as an EU-only agreement, one covering investment rules under shared competence as a mixed agreement. This has happened, for example, in respect of the EU-Singapore free trade agreement after Opinion 2/15 was handed down. *See* European Commission, 'Guide to the EU-Singapore Free Trade Agreement and Investment Protection Agreement' (April 2018), http://trade.ec.europa.eu/doclib/docs/2018/may/tradoc_156885.pdf, accessed 30 Jul. 2018.

12. *See*, in detail, Mauro Gatti and Pietro Manzini, 'External Representation of the European Union in the Conclusion of International Agreements' (2012) 49 Common Market Law Review 1703, 1711–1720.
13. European Commission, 'Towards a Comprehensive European International Investment Policy' Communication from the Commission to the Council, the European Parliament, the European Economic and Social Committee and the Committee of the Regions (Communication), COM (2010) 343 final (7 July 2010), quote at 2.
14. *Ibid.*, 8.
15. *Ibid.*, 4–5 (quote at 4).
16. *See* European Commission, 'Trade for All: Towards a More Responsible Trade and Investment Policy' COM(2015)497 final (14 Oct. 2015) 5–6.
17. Council of the European Union, 'Conclusions on a Comprehensive European International Investment Policy' (3041st Foreign Affairs Council Meeting, Luxembourg, 25 Oct. 2010) para. 16, www.consilium.europa.eu/uedocs/cms_data/docs/pressdata/EN/foraff/117328.pdf, accessed 30 Jul. 2018.
18. European Parliament, 'Resolution of 6 April 2011 on the Future European International Investment Policy (2010/2203(INI))' [2012] OJ C 296 E/34, para. 15.

negotiating market access with its main developed trading partners and the major emerging economies'.[19]

The economic objectives of EU investment policy can therefore be summarized, as succinctly stated on the website of DG Trade,[20] as follows:

- open up foreign markets for EU companies;
- ensure EU companies are not discriminated against abroad;
- have a predictable and transparent business environment;
- attract international investment into the EU;
- make international investment rules clear and consistently enforced;
- protect the investments of EU citizens and companies abroad;
- ensure the free movement of payments, capital, and key personnel necessary for international investment.

Meanwhile, these objectives have already been translated into actual trade and investment agreements that the EU has concluded as part of its post-Lisbon common commercial policy. Thus, agreements like the EU-Canada Comprehensive Economic and Trade Agreement (CETA), as well as the free trade agreements with Vietnam and Singapore, contain investment rules with market access commitments for foreign investors that go beyond WTO law.[21]

At the same time, while incrementally replacing Member States as the main actors in international investment law,[22] the EU's ambition is not simply to continue past policies, but to engage in a comprehensive reform of this field of international law. This already transpired when the Commission stressed, in its July 2010 Communication, the need for 'balance' between investor interests and regulation in the public interest.[23] The desire for reform became acute though after public criticism of international investment law and ISDS mounted when plans to negotiate the Transatlantic Trade and Investment Partnership (TTIP) with the United States crystallized in 2014.

19. *Ibid.*, para. 21.
20. *See* European Commission, 'Investment' (2017), http://ec.europa.eu/trade/policy/accessing-markets/investment/, accessed 30 Jul. 2018.
21. *See* Comprehensive Economic and Trade Agreement (CETA) between Canada and the European Union and its Member States (signed 30 Oct. 2016, entered provisionally into force 21 Sept. 2017) [2017] OJ L 11/23, Arts 8.4, 9.6, 13.6. For the agreements between the EU, on the one hand, and Singapore and Vietnam, on the other hand, which have been split into EU-only free trade agreements and separate agreements addressing investment, *see* at https://ec.europa.eu/trade/policy/countries-and-regions/negotiations-and-agreements/ accessed 25 Oct. 2019.
22. Note that existing Member State IIAs with third countries can remain in place under the so-called grandfathering regulation. *See* Regulation (EU) No. 1219/2012 of the European Parliament and of the Council of 12 December 2012 establishing transitional arrangements for bilateral investment agreements between Member States and third countries [2012] OJ L 351/40.
23. European Commission (n. 13) 9.

Following a 'Public consultation on modalities for investment protection and ISDS in TTIP'[24] that was conducted in reaction to that criticism, the Commission formulated reform objectives for the EU's foreign investment policy and IIA practice.[25] On substance, IIAs should not negatively impact the right to regulate, *inter alia*, through clearer formulation of substantive standards of treatment, carve-outs, exception clauses, and institutional rules to control the interpretation and application of IIAs. On procedure, the Commission suggested a fundamental shift in ISDS from a reformed version of investor-state arbitration to the establishment of a permanent, two-tiered 'investment court system'. The Commission proposed this system first in the TTIP negotiations,[26] and since has managed to include it in CETA[27] and in the investment agreements with Vietnam[28] and Singapore.[29] Likewise, the free trade agreement between the EU and Mexico is to contain a version of the investment court system.[30] In parallel, the EU is also pushing for establishing a permanent international investment court at the multilateral level.[31]

Both the integration of market access and investment liberalization and the efforts to reform international investment law are not only matters of EU policy. Both aspects mirror the constitutional framework the Lisbon Treaty has set up for the EU's

24. The online questionnaire, consultation notice and consultation document are available at European Commission 'Online Public Consultation on Investment Protection and Investor-to-State Dispute Settlement (ISDS) in the Transatlantic Trade and Investment Partnership Agreement (TTIP)' (2018), trade.ec.europa.eu/consultations/index.cfm?consul_id = 179, accessed 30 Jul. 2018.
25. For the result of the public consultations, *see* European Commission, 'Report: Online Public Consultation on Investment Protection and Investor-to-State Dispute Settlement (ISDS) in the Transatlantic Trade and Investment Partnership Agreement (TTIP)' SWD(2013) 3 final (13 Jan. 2015), http://trade.ec.europa.eu/doclib/docs/2015/january/tradoc_153044.pdf, accessed 30 Jul. 2018.
26. *See* European Commission, 'Commission Draft Text TTIP: Investment' (2015), http://trade.ec.europa.eu/doclib/docs/2015/september/tradoc_153807.pdf. *See also* 'Investment in TTIP and Beyond – The Path for Reform', http://trade.ec.europa.eu/doclib/docs/2015/may/tradoc_153408.PDF, accessed 30 Jul. 2018.
27. *See* CETA (n. 21), Arts 8.18, 8.21–8.43. The investment court system was included in CETA at the stage of so-called legal scrubbing. The originally concluded, pre-scrubbing version of CETA of September 2014 still contained a reformed version of arbitration to settle investor-state disputes. *See* European Commission, 'Consolidated CETA Text' (1 Aug. 2014) Arts X.25ff, www.tagesschau.de/wirtschaft/ceta-dokument-101.pdf, accessed 30 Jul. 2018.
28. *See* EU-Vietnam Investment Protection Agreement (authentic text as of August 2018) Ch. 3 (Dispute Settlement) s. B (Resolution of Disputes between Investors and Parties) sub-s 4 (Investment Tribunal System), http://trade.ec.europa.eu/doclib/press/index.cfm?id = 1437, accessed 5 March 2019.
29. *See* EU-Singapore Investment Protection Agreement (authentic text as of April 2018) Ch. 3 (Dispute Settlement) s. A, http://trade.ec.europa.eu/doclib/docs/2018/april/tradoc_156731.pdf, accessed 30 Jul. 2018.
30. *See* the text published of the Agreement in principle: EU-Mexico Global Agreement (text as of 21 April 2018) Ch 19 (Investment Dispute Resolution) Arts 11 and 12, http://trade.ec.europa.eu/doclib/press/index.cfm?id = 1833, accessed 5 Mar. 2019.
31. *See* European Commission, 'Submission of the European Union and its Member States to UNCITRAL Working Group III' (18 Jan. 2019), http://trade.ec.europa.eu/doclib/html/157631.htm, accessed 5 Mar. 2019 (reproduced in UNCITRAL, UN Doc No A/CN.9/WG.III/WP.159/Add.1 (24 Jan. 2019)). On the mandate of the Commission, *see* Council of the European Union, 'Negotiating Directives for a Convention Establishing a Multilateral Court for the Settlement of Investment Disputes' (EU Doc No 12981/17 ADD 1) (1 Mar. 2018).

external relations, including the common commercial policy. As stated in Article 207(1) TFEU, 'the common commercial policy shall be conducted in the context of the principles and objectives of the Unions external action'. These principles, in turn, are set out in Article 21(1) and (2) TEU. Article 21(1) subparagraph 1 TEU lays out the general principles guiding EU external relations as follows:

> The Union's action on the international scene shall be guided by the principles which have inspired its own creation, development and enlargement, and which it seeks to advance in the wider world: democracy, the rule of law, the universality and indivisibility of human rights and fundamental freedoms, respect for human dignity, the principles of equality and solidarity, and respect for the principles of the United Nations Charter and international law.

These objectives, as further set out in Article 21(2) TEU, are to be translated into common policies and concrete actions and include, as relevant for international trade and investment relations, 'encourag[ing] the integration of all countries into the world economy, including through the progressive abolition of restrictions on international trade'[32] and actions that 'ensure sustainable development'[33] and 'good global governance'.[34] Article 21 TEU therefore sets out how the EU should shape the law of globalization through its external relations and the treaty frameworks in which it participates.

Meanwhile the Commission has interlaced its policy on external trade and investment with the Lisbon Treaty's constitutional foundations in a 2015 Communication entitled 'Trade for All: Towards a More Responsible Trade and Investment Policy'.[35] In it, the Commission expresses the connection between the EU's trade and investment policy and its basic constitutional values as follows:

> EU trade policy is for all. It seeks to improve conditions for citizens, consumers, workers and the self-employed, small, medium and large enterprises, and the poorest in developing countries, and addresses the concerns of those who feel they are losing out from globalisation. While trade policy must deliver growth, jobs and innovation, it must also be consistent with the principles of the European model. It must, in short, be responsible. It must be effective at actually delivering economic opportunities. It must be transparent and open to public scrutiny. It must promote and defend European values.[36]

In the Commission's view, a value-based trade and investment policy entails the promotion of a new approach to investment, not only insofar as it relates to the EU, but to the entire world. Indeed, the Commission considers that '[t]he EU is best placed – and has a special responsibility – to lead the reform of the global investment regime, as its founder and main actor'.[37] This reform, in turn, should be guided by connecting the

32. Article 21(2)(e) TEU.
33. Article 21(2)(f) TEU.
34. Article 21(2)(h) TEU.
35. *See* Commission (n. 16). For the position of the European Parliament, *see* European Parliament, 'A Forward-Looking and Innovative Future Strategy for Trade and Investment' Resolution 2015/2105(INI) (5 Jul. 2016).
36. Commission (n. 16) 3.
37. *Ibid.*, 15.

EU's trade and investment policy, in line with Article 21 TEU, to the goals of promoting sustainable development, human rights and good governance.[38]

Key in this context are the forms and fora through which to implement the EU's common commercial policy and its efforts to reform international investment law. While stressing its interest in using multilateral settings, in line with the demand in Article 21(2)(h) TEU to 'promote an international system based on stronger multilateral cooperation', the Commission also acknowledges the need to 'mov[e] forward bilateral relationships' and to determine EU 'priorities to open negotiations ... primarily based on economic criteria'.[39] This encompasses, above all, negotiations with economically particularly important actors, like the United States, with whom the EU wants to achieve 'an ambitious and balanced market access package comparable to the EU's FTA with Canada'[40] and China, where 'European participation in China's "One belt, one road" projects' is key.[41] In both cases, effective commitments to have access to US and Chinese markets is of preeminent importance for the EU.

All in all, as this section has shown, the progressive abolition of restrictions on international trade and investment constitutes a constitutional mandate for the EU's common commercial policy. Similarly, the efforts by the EU to reform international investment law correspond to the constitutional objective of the common commercial policy to promote democracy, the rule of law, human rights, sustainable development and global governance. It is this broader context in which the analysis of the new EU FDI screening framework should be placed. Once this is done, it becomes clear that that framework can be explained not only as an instrument to protect defensive EU interests but also has the function of helping to overcome obstacles that exist elsewhere in the EU's constitutional law to implementing the EU's constitutional mandate to liberalize investment flows and to reform international investment law, in particular as the need for bilateral negotiations of trade and investment agreements increases.

§2.03 EU CONSTITUTIONAL LAW AS AN OBSTACLE TO EU BARGAINING FOR INVESTMENT LIBERALIZATION IN BILATERAL NEGOTIATIONS

Notwithstanding the mandate in Article 21 TEU to shape the law of globalization in line with the EU's core constitutional values (rule of law, democracy, human rights and sustainable development), EU constitutional law creates significant obstacles for fulfilling this mandate effectively in treaty negotiations with third countries. Most importantly, the freed movement of capital in relation to third countries, which is laid down in Article 63 TFEU as part of the EU's internal market rules, puts the EU in a relatively weak negotiating position when seeking to bargain for more investment liberalization and greater access for its own investors to the markets of third countries.

38. *Ibid.*, 15–20.
39. *Ibid.*, 20ff (quote at 22).
40. *Ibid.*, 22.
41. *Ibid.*, 23. *See* further on the EU's approach vis-à-vis China, European Commission, 'EU-China – A Strategic Outlook' JOIN(2019)5 final (12 March 2019).

As I will show in this section, this internal market rule constitutes an obstacle for successful and efficient EU bargaining in particular in bilateral settings, which, even though Article 21(2)(h) TEU generally disfavours compared to multilateral ones, is becoming increasingly prevalent. The introduction of an EU framework for inward FDI screening closes this gap between external policy mandate and internal constitutional rules and brings the situation in the EU closer to that in place in the constitutional order of other economic powers whose ability to access foreign markets through trade and investment has been key for success, for example that of Germany addressed in section 4.

To start, it is important to understand how the rules on free movement of capital in the TFEU reduce the EU's bargaining power in respect of investment liberalization with third countries, in particular in light of the fact that a considerable amount of foreign investment activities that qualify as FDI from the perspective of IIAs are covered already by the freedom of capital movement under EU law. *Sedes materiae* in this respect is Article 63 TFEU which provides that 'all restrictions on the movement of capital between Member States and between Member States and third countries shall be prohibited'.

Introduced by the Treaty of Maastricht,[42] and unlike its predecessor in Article 67 of the Treaty of Rome,[43] Article 63 TFEUis the only fundamental freedom in the EU that not only applies in an intra-EU context but also applies in relation to and for the benefit of third-country nationals. Subject to a number of exceptions laid down in Article 65 TFEU, *inter alia*, to protect 'public policy or public security', Article 63 TFEU grants a right to non-discriminatory market access as a corollary of the prohibition of restrictions on the movement of capital from third countries. Its objective is, as stated in Article 64(2) TFEU, 'to achieve the objective of free movement of capital between Member States and third countries to the greatest extent possible'. Of relevance in the present context, Article 63 TFEU not only applies to portfolio investments[44] but also covers economic activities that qualify as FDI in the sense used in the context of IIAs.

In fact, pursuant to Annex I of Council Directive 88/361/EEC of 24 June 1988 for the implementation of Article 67 of the Treaty,[45] which the CJEU still consistently uses to determine the scope of application of Article 63 TFEU,[46] even though it was passed to implement the predecessor provision of Article 63 TFEU under the Treaty of Rome, the notion of 'capital movement' encompasses a list of economic activities, which includes:

42. *See supra* n. 5.
43. Treaty Establishing the European Economic Community (Treaty of Rome) (signed 25 Mar. 1957, entered into force 1 Jan. 1958) 298 UNTS 11.
44. *See* CJEU, Joined Cases C-282/04 and C-283/04, *Commission/Netherlands* [2006] ECR I-9141, para. 19 (with further references).
45. [1988] OJ L 178/5.
46. For a recent example, *see* CJEU, Joined Cases C-52/16 and C-113/16, *SEGRO and Horváth*, ECLI:EU:C:2018:157, para. 56.

I - DIRECT INVESTMENTS

1. Establishment and extension of branches or new undertakings belonging solely to the person providing the capital, and the acquisition in full of existing undertakings.
2. Participation in new or existing undertaking with a view to establishing or maintaining lasting economic links.
3. Long-term loans with a view to establishing or maintaining lasting economic links.
4. Reinvestment of profits with a view to maintaining lasting economic links.

   A - Direct investments on national territory by non-residents

   B - Direct investments abroad by residents

II - INVESTMENTS IN REAL ESTATE (not included under I)

A - Investments in real estate on national territory by non-residents

B - Investments in real estate abroad by residents

As a consequence of this wide definition of 'capital movement', many economic activities that qualify as FDI from the perspective of IIAs fall under the scope of the freedom of capital movements in Article 63 TFEU, and thus, give a right to foreign investors to market access within the limits of that fundamental freedom. Article 63 TFEU thus applies to 'investments in real estate' and constrains, *inter alia*, limitations on the acquisition of real estate by foreign investors, both in case of direct and indirect investments through a company incorporated in the host State that is foreign owned and controlled.[47] But, it also applies to all activities that qualify as 'direct investments' in the sense of Annex 1 of Directive 88/361/EEC, which includes the establishment of greenfield investment and the acquisition of brownfield investment through mergers and acquisitions. Also in those cases, the rules on free movement of capital in principle give third country investors a right to access the EU market.[48]

The only carve-out from the application of market access rights under the free movement of capital in relation to third-country investors investing in the EU, which the CJEU has recognized, concerns market access restrictions that fall under the freedom of establishment pursuant to Article 49 TFEU. In respect of such measures, the CJEU reasoned:

> Since the Treaty does not extend freedom of establishment to third countries, it is important to ensure that the interpretation of Article 63(1) TFEU as regards relations with third countries does not enable economic operators who do not fall within the limits of the territorial scope of freedom of establishment to profit from that freedom. Such a risk does not exist in a situation such as that at issue in the main proceedings. The legislation of the Member State in question does not relate to the conditions for access of a company from that Member State to the market in

47. *Ibid.*, paras 50–60.
48. *See* CJEU, Case C-47/12, *Kronos*, ECLI:EU:C:2014:2200, paras 40–42.

> a third country or of a company from a third country to the market in that Member State.[49]

According to this reasoning, market access restrictions affecting extra-EU investors that fall under Article 49 TFEU cannot be assessed under the free movement of capital as this would in effect give those investors a right of establishment in the EU, which they do not have pursuant to Article 49 TFEU.

The difficulty in respect of market access restrictions of extra-EU investment, of course, is in determining when the freedom of establishment is affected in case of direct investments. To the extent assets other than shareholdings in companies established in the host State are concerned, any restrictions concerning market access would seem to fall exclusively within the scope of application of the freedom of capital movement. Indeed, in respect of restrictions to acquire real estate in an EU Member State, the CJEU recently held:

> [W]hen the right to acquire, use or dispose of immovable property on the territory of another Member State is exercised as the corollary of the right of establishment, it generates capital movements. Thus, although that legislation is, prima facie, capable of being covered by both the fundamental freedoms mentioned by the referring court, the fact remains that, in the context of the main proceedings, any restrictions on freedom of establishment resulting from that legislation are an inevitable consequence of the restriction of the free movement of capital and, therefore, do not justify an independent examination of that legislation in the light of Article 49 TFEU.[50]

Consequently, market access restrictions that are merely consequences of regulations of capital movement, but that do not prohibit establishment in an EU Member State as such, are not to be assessed under the freedom of establishment under Article 49 TFEU. Extra-EU investors facing restrictions on investing in such assets, in turn, can challenge them by relying on the free movement of capital laid down in Article 63 TFEU.

The situation is different when the incorporation of a local company in a Member State of the EU for purposes of the establishment of a greenfield investment is concerned. Given that the incorporation of a company in a Member State other than the home State constitutes an exercise of the freedom of establishment under Article 49 TFEU,[51] third-country investors cannot invoke the free movement of capital to challenge restrictions to incorporate in the EU.

Similarly, the acquisition of brownfield investments through a share deal, that is, the merger with, or acquisition of, existing companies in an EU Member State, falls, under certain circumstances, under the freedom of establishment and cannot be challenged by reliance on the free movement of capital. If the acquisition of a shareholding in a company established in a Member State by a third-country investor

49. CJEU, Case C-35/11, *Test Claimants (II)*, ECLI:EU:C:2012:707, para. 100; similarly, CJEU, *Kronos* (n. 48) paras 53–54.
50. CJEU, *SEGRO and Horváth* (n. 46) paras 54–55 (internal references omitted).
51. CJEU, Case C-81/87, *Daily Mail*, ECR 1988, 5483, para. 17.

is at stake, the CJEU distinguishes in its jurisprudence as follows between the freedom of establishment and the free movement of capital:

> As regards the question whether national legislation falls within the scope of one or other of the freedoms of movement, it is clear from well established case-law that the purpose of the legislation concerned must be taken into consideration. National legislation intended to apply only to those shareholdings which enable the holder to exert a definite influence on a company's decisions and to determine its activities falls within the scope of Article 49 TFEU on freedom of establishment. On the other hand, national provisions which apply to shareholdings acquired solely with the intention of making a financial investment without any intention to influence the management and control of the undertaking must be examined exclusively in light of the free movement of capital.[52]

When a situation arises in which the CJEU considers that an investor can exercise 'definite influence' over a company, in turn, depends on the circumstances of each case.[53] No bright line rule exists and the spectrum is wide. While, at one end, no majority shareholding is necessary to establish 'definite influence' when other ways of exercising influence exist, at the other end, a participation of 10% will usually not suffice.[54]

Despite the uncertainty arising from the CJEU's jurisprudence on when market access restrictions for the acquisition of shareholdings in companies incorporated in Member States fall under the freedom of establishment, where they cannot be challenged by extra-EU investors, and when the free movement of capital applies, which protects extra-EU investors, there is a significant spectrum in which third-country investors already have a right to access the EU internal market under the free movement of capital and implement FDI projects including through the acquisition of shareholdings in EU companies.

Moreover, even in situations where market access restrictions only fall under the freedom of establishment, EU law arguably offers possibilities for non-EU investors to benefit from the freedom of establishment and tackle or circumvent market access restrictions, including FDI screenings that exist in some, but not all Member States.[55] Non-EU investors can, for example, incorporate in another Member State and, through that corporate vehicle, which qualifies as an EU company, claim the freedom of establishment in the Member State in which they ultimately want to acquire direct

52. CJEU, *Test Claimants (II)* (n. 49) paras 90–92 (internal references omitted).
53. *See* CJEU, *Kronos* (n. 48) para. 37; Georg Ress and Jörg Ukrow, 'Artikel 63 AEUV: Freier Kapital- und Zahlungsverkehr' in Eberhard Grabitz, Meinhard Hilf and Martin Nettesheim (eds), *Das Recht der Europäischen Union* (CH Beck 2017) paras 315–16. In the same vein, Steffen Hindelang, *The Free Movement of Capital and Foreign Direct Investment: The Scope of Protection in EU Law* (OUP 2009) 85 ('this study regards as the most appropriate approach a comprehensive overall view of the factual conditions under particular consideration of the applicable company law in the individual case.').
54. *See* CJEU, Case C-492/04, *Lasertec* [2007] ECR I-3775, paras 21ff and Joined Cases C-436/08 and C-437/08, *Haribo* [2011] ECR I-305, para. 36 (10% not sufficient). For an overview over CJEU case law, *see* Philip Strik, *Shaping the Single European Market in the Field of Foreign Direct Investment* (Hart 2014) 45–46.
55. *See* Stephan Schill, 'Der Schutz von Auslandsinvestitionen in Deutschland im Mehrebenensystem: deutsches, europäisches und internationales Recht' (2010) 135 AöR 498, 519–520.

influence over a company. Through such structuring, extra-EU investors can potentially circumvent market access restrictions and claim a right to market access even if the free movement of capital was initially not applicable.

All in all, the situation in the EU shows that third-country investors have broad opportunities to invoke internal market law and its fundamental freedoms in order to claim a right to market access without the need for a specific treaty commitment of the EU vis-à-vis the investor's home State. At the same time, the situation under primary EU law constitutes a weakness for the EU's negotiation power when seeking market access commitment with third countries in trade and investment agreements. After all, as far as the free movement of capital applies, and to the extent possibilities for foreign investors exist to use corporate structures in the EU exist to benefit from the freedom of establishment, extra-EU investors already have (*de iure* or *de facto*) a right to access the EU internal market and to challenge market access restrictions in EU courts. In such a situation, the EU's counterpart in a treaty negotiation concerning market access for FDI will have little incentive to open its own market to EU investors in return for market access commitments that already exist under EU constitutional law independently of a specific international treaty.

The ability to negotiate for investment liberalization on the basis of reciprocity – market access for EU investors abroad in return for market access for third-country investors in the EU – is therefore significantly limited because the EU's internal market rules. This situation may be less problematic in multilateral negotiations where reciprocity is not the key bargaining chip. In bilateral settings, by contrast – which are increasingly important for trade and investment liberalization, both as regards WTO + commitments and in light of the tangible risk that the WTO dispute settlement mechanism becomes defunct – it can effectively undermine the EU's negotiation position, in particular with economically powerful states, such as China or the United States. All of this shows that one branch of EU constitutional law, namely its rules on the internal market, could undermine the fulfilment of the objectives of another branch of EU constitutional law, that is, the EU common commercial policy and its objectives to achieve further investment liberalization and to reform international economic law along the lines of the constitutional values listed in Article 21 TEU.

§2.04 EU AND GERMAN CONSTITUTIONAL LAW COMPARED

The difficulties for the EU in negotiating access for its foreign investors to third-country markets, and their origin in the EU's constitutional structure, become particularly clear when comparing the situation under EU constitutional law to the one in other countries that prosper economically, and continue to do so because they rely on being embedded in an open global economy. A case in point is the situation in Germany, which grants to foreign investors less constitutional protection than it does to nationals, in particular as regards market access. This constitutional setting was crafted post-World War II by the founding fathers of the *Grundgesetz* (Basic Law), Germany's Constitution, at a time when Germany had not yet been embedded in the EU common market, precisely in order to empower the German government to negotiate, based on reciprocity, for market access for its own investors abroad in return for market access of third-country investors in Germany. A more detailed look at the constitutional situation in Germany illustrates this clearly and helps understand the constitutional law dilemma the EU finds itself in.

Although at the level of statutory protection there are few differences between the rights of foreign and of domestic investors in Germany, the Basic Law differentiates between both groups as regards their constitutional status.[56] While both foreign and domestic investors enjoy the right to property under Germany's Basic Law,[57] other constitutional rights that are key factors for economic activity only accrue to domestic, not foreign investors. This holds true, above all, for the freedom of profession guaranteed in Article 12 of the Basic Law, which protects against (certain) government restrictions of market access and is the basis for the freedom of enterprise.[58] Similarly, the freedom of assembly guaranteed in Article 9 of the Basic Law, which encompasses the right to establish corporations and the right of employers to associate themselves in employers' unions and interest associations, only applies to German nationals, not foreigners.[59] Foreigners, in turn, are relegated in terms of constitutional protection to

56. For this and the following, *ibid.*, 503ff. Differences at the statutory level concern the right of residence and, with regard to foreign legal entities who lack legal personality under German law, the right to operate a business. In few areas, such as arms legislation, nationality may be a ground to deny the issuance of the necessary operating permits. Finally, foreign investment in Germany may be subject to restrictions in order to protect public safety and order.

57. Article 14 (Property, inheritance, expropriation):

> (1) Property and the right of inheritance shall be guaranteed. Their content and limits shall be defined by the laws.
> (2) Property entails obligations. Its use shall also serve the public good.
> (3) Expropriation shall only be permissible for the public good. It may only be ordered by or pursuant to a law that determines the nature and extent of compensation. Such compensation shall be determined by establishing an equitable balance between the public interest and the interests of those affected. In case of dispute respecting the amount of compensation, recourse may be had to the ordinary courts.

Translations of the German Constitution into English are available at www.bundesregierung.de/breg-en/chancellor/basic-law-470510#doc94410bodyText2 accessed 5 Mar. 2019.

58. Article 12 (Occupational freedom; prohibition of forced labour):

> (1) All Germans shall have the right freely to choose their occupation or profession, their place of work, and their place of training. The practice of an occupation or profession may be regulated by or pursuant to a law.
> (2) No person may be required to perform work of a particular kind except within the framework of a traditional duty of community service that applies generally and equally to all.
> (3) Forced labor may be imposed only on persons deprived of their liberty by the judgment of a court.

See also Rupert Scholz, 'Artikel 12 GG' in Theodor Maunz, Günter Dürig et al. (eds), *Grundgesetz-Kommentar* vol. II (CH Beck 2018) paras 86, 87.

59. Article 9 (Freedom of association):

> (1) All Germans shall have the right to form corporations and other associations.
> (2) Associations whose aims or activities contravene the criminal laws, or that are directed against the constitutional order or the concept of international understanding, shall be prohibited.

the much weaker protections found in the general personal freedom or 'freedom of action' laid down in Article 2(1) of the Basic Law.[60]

Furthermore, the equal protection clause in Article 3 of the Basic Law, which prohibits discrimination, *inter alia,* based on race and origin, does not prohibit differential treatment on the basis of nationality alone.[61] As confirmed by the jurisprudence of the German Constitutional Court, Article 3 of the Basic Law also leaves considerable policy space to the legislator to differentiate between foreigners and nationals based on considerations of economic policy and would thus allow protectionist measures to a considerable extent.[62]

Another key provision of the German Constitution that leads to a distinction in constitutional status between foreign and domestic investors is Article 19(3) of the Basic Law. It provides that '[t]he basic rights shall also apply to domestic juridical persons to the extent that the nature of such rights permits'. This provision has the effect to limit the protection under any fundamental right granted by the Constitution, including rights that accrue to both foreign and domestic natural persons, such as the right to property, to 'domestic' juridical persons. 'Foreign' juridical persons, by contrast, are excluded from fundamental right protection under the Basic Law, and for this reason can also not have access to the German Constitutional Court to vindicate the right concerned.[63] This position has only recently been modified by the German

---

(3) The right to form associations to safeguard and improve working and economic conditions shall be guaranteed to every individual and to every occupation or profession. Agreements that restrict or seek to impair this right shall be null and void; measures directed to this end shall be unlawful. Measures taken pursuant to Article 12a, to paragraphs (2) and (3) of Article 35, to paragraph (4) of Article 87a, or to Article 91 may not be directed against industrial disputes engaged in by associations within the meaning of the first sentence of this paragraph in order to safeguard and improve working and economic conditions.

See also Matthias Cornils, 'Artikel 9 GG' in Volker Epping and Christian Hillgruber (eds), *Beck'scher Online*-Kommentar *Grundgesetz* (CH Beck 2018) paras 5–16, 44–54.

60. Article 2(1) German Basic Law reads: 'Every person shall have the right to free development of his personality insofar as he does not violate the rights of others or offend against the constitutional order or the moral law.' *See also* Udo Di Fabio, 'Artikel 2 Abs 1 GG' in Maunz/Dürig et al. (n. 58) vol. I, paras 77–81, 92–126.
61. Article 3 (Equality before the law):

(1) All persons shall be equal before the law.
(2) Men and women shall have equal rights. The state shall promote the actual implementation of equal rights for women and men and take steps to eliminate disadvantages that now exist.
(3) No person shall be favored or disfavored because of sex, parentage, race, language, homeland and origin, faith, or religious or political opinions. No person shall be disfavored because of disability.

See also Christian Langenfeld, 'Artikel 3 Abs 3 GG' in Maunz/Dürig et al. (n. 588) vol. I, para. 58: Uwe Kischel, 'Artikel 3 GG' in Epping/Hillgruber (n. 59) paras 132–135.
62. Kischel (n. 61) paras 55, 65, 135.
63. *See* BVerfGE 21, 207, 208–209 (concerning a constitutional complaint by a Delaware incorporated company with seat in New York):

Under Article 19(3) of the Basic Law, the basic rights granted to natural persons are also granted to legal persons, insofar as they are essentially applicable to them. However, this extension of the basic rights only relates to domestic legal persons by means of

Constitutional Court in respect of corporate entities of other EU Member States, which due to the non-discrimination provisions and the freedom of establishment laid down in EU law benefit from the Basic Law's fundamental rights on equal footing and can have recourse to the German Constitutional Court like any other German company.[64] Companies from outside the EU, by contrast, remain excluded from the protection of the Basic Law's fundamental rights.

Instructive, in the present context, are the reasons why the German Constitution excludes the protection of foreign juridical persons from fundamental rights protection and to reduce it in respect of foreigners who are natural persons. Notably that choice is not principally caused by a desire to take measures that actually differentiate between foreigners and nationals in internal economic regulation. On the contrary, these constitutional limits exist in order to enable the government to effectively negotiate, based on the idea of reciprocity, for better protection of German investors abroad, both in terms of the substantive protections granted to investment post-establishment and as regards investors' access to foreign markets.[65]

EU law differs from the constitutional situation in Germany in this key aspect: its rules on free movement of capital also accrue to non-EU investors, thus making, as outlined in section 3, treaty commitments by the EU to access for third-country investors to the internal market de facto worthless as a bargaining chip in EU negotiations of trade and investment agreements. One way to strengthen the EU's external negotiation power to achieve market access for EU investors in third countries, of course, would be to change Article 63 TFEU and to go back to the pre-Maastricht situation. Alternatively, one could consider whether the scope of Article 63 TFEU should not be reevaluated in light of the EU's new external competence for 'foreign direct investment' in Article 207(1) TFEU, for example by adapting Council Directive 88/361/EEC to the post-Lisbon situation.

Yet, all of these approaches would, independently of the political difficulties to implement them, send the wrong signal to the world, namely that the EU is backtracking on its commitment to free inward capital flows. These approaches would also be overreaching when the objective is primarily to strengthen the EU's negotiation position to achieve better access for its investor to foreign markets. For this purpose, it seems sufficient to signal, as the new regulation now does with its introduction of a framework for inward FDI screening, that a commitment in an international trade and investment agreement with the EU to free inward capital flows has value despite, and independently from, the EU's constitutional promise in Article 63 TFEU to allow free capital inflows from third countries.

> explicit constitutional provisions. Wording and rationale prohibit any extensive interpretation with respect to foreign legal persons. (translation by the present author)

Similarly, BVerfGE 23, 229, 236; 100, 313, 364.

64. *See* BVerfGE 129, 78, 94ff.
65. Schill (n. 55) 509, 511 ('Although this system has been criticized in policy terms, it constitutes a clear and deliberate choice by the constitutional legislator. It is based on the fact that the lack of constitutional protection of foreign legal persons goes along with additional room for foreign policy action for the Federal Republic to achieve the protection of German legal persons abroad through negotiations with other states on the basis of reciprocity.').

The new Regulation does exactly that: it signals that the EU and its Member States are in a position to put constraints on access for FDI to the EU market. For this purpose, the regulation re-delegates the authority for inward FDI screening that vests, per the Lisbon Treaty, with the EU, as part of its exclusive competence in respect of the common commercial policy under Article 207(1) TFEU, to the Member States (Article 3(1) of Regulation (EU) 2019/452). It also establishes a mechanism 'to ensure Union-wide coordination and cooperation on the screening of foreign direct investments likely to affect security or public order'.[66] Information-sharing among Member States and between Member States and the Commission is an important tool in this context (Articles 6-8 of Regulation (EU) 2019/452). The new regulation also ensures that Member States have the authority to screen for constellations where FDI screening is circumvented through structuring of investments through other Member States (Article 3(6) of Regulation (EU) 2019/452).

Finally, the authority the new regulation gives to the Commission to issue opinions addressed to Member States, '[w]here the Commission considers that a foreign direct investment is likely to affect projects or programmes of Union interest on grounds of security or public order' (Article 8(1) of Regulation (EU) 2019/452) is a forceful signal that the EU is able to put effective constraints on inward FDI that threaten its security or public order interests. Even though the Commission's opinions are not binding on Member States, they allow the Commission to accumulate clout to establish an effective FDI screening mechanism within the EU.

Still, in the reading proposed here, Regulation (EU) 2019/452 does not aim exclusively at allowing the EU to implement protectionist measures, but rather to negotiate its FDI screening powers away in return for better access for its own investors in third countries on the basis of reciprocity. The very purpose of the Regulation would then be to close the 'constitutional gap' that exists between the constitutional objective in Article 21 TEU to achieve further investment liberalization and the EU's internal market rules that reduce the EU's power to negotiate effectively for such liberalization with third countries. The Regulation therefore empowers the EU externally by making commitments to access the internal market again meaningful as a bargaining chip in treaty negotiations with third countries. The Regulation therefore approximates the constitutional setting in the EU with the one that exists, for example, in Germany and puts the EU in a stronger negotiating position in order to fulfil its constitutional mandate to achieve further investment liberalization and to ensure access to third-country markets for its own investors.

§2.05 CONCLUSION

As the preceding analysis has shown, the political branches of the EU, that is, the Commission, the Council and the European Parliament, have become well aware of the Lisbon Treaty's constitutional mandate in Article 21 TEU to use the EU's external relations power and particularly its common commercial policy to shape globalization

66. *See* Regulation (EU) 2019/452, seventh recital.

according to the constitutional values the EU subscribes to. For international investment relations, the EU's constitutional mandate entails, inter alia, an attempt to decrease barriers for market access for foreign investors through treaty negotiations with third countries.

As this chapter has argued, Regulation (EU) 2019/452 on inward FDI screening at EU level has to be seen in this context, namely, as an instrument that allows the establishment of a level-playing field between the EU and other major economic powers, such as the United States or China, in order to negotiate, on the basis of reciprocity, an opening of foreign markets for EU investors in return for treaty commitments that give foreign investors access to the EU market. Without the powers enshrined in the new Regulation, the EU's treaty partners have few incentives to agree to access of EU investors to their markets as their own investors already enjoy access to the EU market under the free movement of capital in Article 63 TFEU to a considerable extent. In that perspective, Regulation (EU) 2019/452 is an instrument that helps the EU to achieve its constitutional mandate to achieve further investment liberalization. It is not, by contrast, an instrument whose genuine purpose is to shield the EU market from foreign investment. It is against this background that additional support can be drawn for the argument presented by Marise Cremona that the EU's competence for Regulation (EU) 2019/452 lies in Article 207(1) TFEU.

Part II Two Examples of EU Member State FDI Control

CHAPTER 3

Foreign Direct Investment Control in Germany: The M&A Practitioner's Experience

Hartmut Krause

§3.01 INTRODUCTION

I would like to give you a practical perspective from the 'engine room' as to when you are affected by the screening of foreign direct investment (FDI). I am a transactional lawyer, advising clients on mergers and acquisitions (M&A transactions). For more than twenty years I have been supporting clients from all over the world – including the United States, Japan, China and the Middle East – in bidding for, and successfully purchasing, German businesses. I hope that my remarks will be heard in the discussion about the proposed European Regulation[1] and perhaps even seen as a useful contribution.

§3.02 PERSPECTIVE OF THE TRANSACTION PARTIES

The client's perspective – and my mission order – in these situations is very clear: get the deal done! From this viewpoint I can say: FDI screening can be a pain. You will see in a second why this is the case.

If you think about how businesses are being sold, they are often run as a controlled auction in which the seller attempts to find the best possible purchaser. Selection criteria are very clear: they include transaction certainty, a high purchase

1. Proposal for a Regulation of the European Parliament and of the Council establishing a framework for screening of foreign direct investments into the European Union, COM(2017) 487 final, 2017/0224(COD), 13 Sept. 2017.

price, and a good contract – in most cases in this order. Transaction certainty means, among other things, that the number of closing conditions in the share or asset purchase agreement should be as small as possible.

§3.03 CLOSING CONDITIONS

Some of you know that having closing conditions is often unavoidable. In jurisdictions where the competition laws require merger control clearance to be obtained or applicable waiting periods to lapse before you can consummate the acquisition of a business, you typically sign a share purchase agreement or an asset purchase agreement, you then file a request for clearance with the relevant competition authorities, and only after receiving green lights from all relevant authorities, you proceed with the closing. Prudent purchasers will therefore insist on having a closing condition stating that merger control clearance has been obtained. Conversely, sellers looking for transaction certainty will tend to select a bidder who will be subject to as few clearance requirements as possible and able to complete the relevant merger control proceedings in the shortest possible time.

The impact of FDI screening on M&A transactions is very similar. If you are a bidder and subject to FDI screening, you will usually seek protection in the form of a closing condition stating that you are only required to consummate the deal if your investment has been approved. For a seller, signing a deal with such a bidder usually means a lower degree of transaction certainty. Hence, being subject to FDI screening is a clear disadvantage. In addition to what was said earlier today, FDI screening is not only something that causes compliance costs, results in delays or uncertainty of approval. No, even worse – for the bidder it introduces the risk of not being selected.

§3.04 SELECTED PRACTICAL ISSUES

The German rules on FDI screening can be found in the *Außenwirtschaftsgesetz* (AWG)[2] and the *Außenwirtschaftsverordnung* (AWV), the AWV was amended in July 2017[3] and in December 2018[4]. I would like to highlight a few particularities of the new rules which are important from a practitioner's perspective.

First, the review period for a no action letter was extended – from one month to two months.[5] With this one-month period, purchasers were able to run proceedings for FDI screening in parallel with merger control proceedings. As about 95% of all M&A transactions receive unconditional merger control clearance after a first review ('phase

2. Außenwirtschaftsgesetz dated 6 June 2013, BGBl. I p. 1482, as amended.
3. Neunte Verordnung zur Änderung der Außenwirtschaftsverordnung, BAnz AT 17 July 2017 V1.
4. Zwölfte Verordnung zur Änderung der Außenwirtschaftsverordnung, BAnz AT 28 December 2018 V1.
5. § 58(2)1 AWV.

one'),[6] it was possible under the old rules for the vast majority of purchasers to complete merger control and FDI screening at about the same time. Obviously, this will not be possible any longer when FDI screening takes two months. But this is not the full story yet. What is perhaps most concerning is that it has become the rule that the Ministry of Economic Affairs (Ministry) opens formal investigations. You do not receive more than a formalistic reasoning for this decision, hence you do not know whether your case is particularly problematic or whether it is just that the increase of the workload in the Ministry means that the officials do not have time to clear easy cases early.[7] In addition, the review period for formal proceedings was extended to four months.[8] Now you may think that this extension will delay clearance decisions even more. But here I can say that this extension is not too relevant in practice; it was unpredictable under the old rules how long FDI screening would take, and it will remain the same under the new rules. Why is this? The four-month period starts running when the file is complete. The Ministry never tells you when this is the case. Should it turn out after three months and two weeks that some information is missing, the Ministry will let you know and the clock will start ticking again - once you have submitted the missing information. Hence, for all practical purposes, the period never starts running. As a result, you can be stuck in FDI proceedings for quite some time.

Second another burden is that German authorities proceed in the German language.[9] This means you have to translate everything. Those of you who know how share purchase agreements or asset purchase agreements for meaningful businesses look like will know what I mean: they are written in the English language and may comprise 100 pages or more, plus appendices. As a purchaser you will translate the entirety of the documentation, even though you may wonder whether the officials will read everything or whether it is just for the archives. Of course, the officials want to have a clean file; understandably, they do not want to be blamed for overlooking anything. But at the end of the day, you will still ask yourself why this must be done. The current generation of government officials speaks English very well. A rule permitting the filing of English language documents - similar to the rule permitting foreign issuers to make their capital markets filings in the English language[10] - would certainly ease the pain. One could also imagine a rule allowing the filing of English language originals plus a German language summary of the key terms, but currently the Ministry is not willing to proceed on this basis.

6. Allen & Overy, Global trends in merger control enforcement, February 2018, p. 20. The study analyses merger control activity in twenty-six key jurisdictions in 2017; http://www.allenovery.com/SiteCollectionDocuments/Global%20trends%20in%20merger%20control.pdf.
7. The Federal Government expected that the new rules would trigger ten additional filings per year; BT-DrS 18/13417, p. 2. It appears that this expectation was too modest.
8. § 59(1)1 AWV.
9. § 23 Verwaltungsverfahrensgesetz (VwVfG).
10. § 3b Wertpapierhandelsanzeigeverordnung (WpAV).

Finally, the new rules have introduced a number of new unclear terms.[11] One key reason is a broad cross-reference to the Federal Ordinance on Critical Infrastructure. This piece of legislation on cyber security is difficult to 'translate' when determining the reach of FDI screening. The time allowed today does not permit me to explore this further.

§3.05 FLYING BELOW THE RADAR SCREEN?

Under the old rules, purchasers may have considered to consummate a transaction without FDI clearance. Under the new rules, this approach has become much more risky.

First, this approach has never worked for transactions in the defence sector. They have always been subject to a filing requirement[12] and cannot be consummated without clearance.[13]

Second, the new rules introduced a filing requirement where the acquisition concerns critical infrastructure.[14] You are in breach of the law if you do not file. In other words: this is not an option.

Third, outside defence and critical infrastructure, one might consider whether it makes sense to close the deal without FDI screening. In certain situations this approach may make sense, but you will run the risk that the Ministry will pick up the case on its own initiative post-closing. If the Ministry does and then retroactively prohibits the deal, the contract will fall away.[15] This means you will have to unwind the transaction - an experience which no purchaser would like to endure: the money is out the door, hence you have to try to claim it back from the seller. If you bought an asset from a vehicle of a financial investor, the proceeds will have been distributed to the investors behind the fund, which means that you will never get the money back. At the same time, you may have to hand over control to a trustee, be restricted from voting your shares or, even worse, you or the trustee may be ordered to sell the business within a certain period of time.

Certainly, there may be businesses and markets where it is absolutely unimaginable that the acquisition affects the security and public order of the Federal Republic of Germany. In these situations, it may be an option to proceed without FDI clearance. However, one should know that the new rules drastically extended the period of time during which the Ministry may pick up unfiled transactions. In the past, this was possible only within three months after signing; under the new rules, the pick-up

11. For example: what is a 'network of petrol stations'? In Germany, petrol stations are usually not operated by 'big oil' but by independent franchisees. Does a 'network of petrol stations' cover all stations selling petrol under the same brand? Or only petrol stations that are connected to each other, through information technology or otherwise, so that their acquisition would have more than just a local impact?
12. § 60(3)1 AWV.
13. § 15(3) Außenwirtschaftsgesetz (AWG).
14. § 55(4) AWV.
15. § 15(2) AWG.

period ends at the later of five years after signing and three months after the Ministry becomes aware of the signing.[16]

§3.06 EFFECTIVE LEGAL PROTECTION?

We heard earlier today, from the member of the European Parliament, that the proposed Regulation[17] will permit purchasers to go to court, and allow them to challenge decisions of the FDI authorities. Two observations, based on experience with the German rules:

First, the yardstick for a prohibition is a tangible threat to the security or public order of the Federal Republic of Germany.[18] Whether or not a certain corporate acquisition constitutes such a threat is not subject to a full judicial review. The Ministry has always taken the position that it is for the government to decide what constitutes security or public order of the Federal Republic of Germany. German legal doctrine recognizes that the administration enjoys the prerogative in making assessments and that such assessments can be affected by so many factors that a court cannot decide whether a certain assessment is right or wrong. The courts can interfere only if the decision steps beyond certain boundaries where it cannot be justified at all. If this doctrine is upheld in FDI matters, the chances of success in the courts will be very slim.

Second, when the Ministry decides against a no action letter and opens formal review proceedings, you will typically get a formalistic reasoning, stating only that proceedings will commence because your case 'could' endanger security or public order. In theory, you can challenge the decision in court, but without substantive reasoning, it will not be easy to overturn it. Query also why you would want to go to court: it will take you two years or longer to get a final decision. You will not get an injunction because the injunction would pre-empt the main case. Even if the court decided in your favour, your victory would be useless. As mentioned earlier, the mission order is: get the deal done! If your client gets stuck in court proceedings, somebody else will buy the target business. Therefore, in practice, no bidder will pay the fees for a lawyer to win in the courtroom when the acquisition opportunity has been lost (unless the decision is clearly wrong and you can reasonably hope to win an action for damages).

§3.07 FINAL THOUGHTS

Bidders domiciled outside the EU or the European Free Trade Association (EFTA) need to prepare extremely carefully if they want to pursue a corporate acquisition in Germany. Unless it is crystal clear that security or public order cannot be affected, you need to have a strategy. It appears indispensable to speak with individuals in the Ministry, who are as high ranking as possible so that the tone will be set from the top.

16. § 55(3) AWV.
17. Regulation (EU) 2019/452 of the European Parliament and of the Council of 19 Mar. 2019 establishing a framework for the screening of foreign direct investments into the Union.
18. § 5(2) AWG; § 55(1)1 and § 59(1) AWV.

Be prepared for the information needs and for the translation requirements. This will be quite some work. Factor in all the time that you need to get this work done. Make sure that the seller is cooperating; the Ministry will request extensive information which you will be unable to deliver without support. You will fare better if experienced M&A practitioners support you in strategizing and with the implementation.

CHAPTER 4
FDI Control in the EU Framework: The Case of Austria

Manfred Schekulin

§4.01 LEGAL BASE AND COMPETENT AUTHORITY (CA)

The screening mechanism for Foreign Direct Investment (FDI) presently in force in Austria was first introduced in 2011. For this reason, the Foreign Commerce Act (*Außenwirtschaftsgesetz*, henceforth: AußWG) had to be amended.[1] A new Article 25a was inserted to provide for a legal basis. In 2013, the Act was amended again to ensure full compliance of the new mechanism with the EU acquis and international obligations,[2] *inter alia*, in the WTO and OECD context including the OECD Guidelines for Recipient Country Investment Policies Relating to National Security.[3] The main changes related to the scope of the screening mechanism and its compliance with international trade standards and norms.

Article 25a AußWG specifies the following requirements and applicable procedures which are dealt with in more detail below:

- authorisation requirements (paragraphs 1 and 2);
- scope and sectors covered (paragraphs 2 and 3);
- rules on controlling influence and threshold values (paragraphs 4 and 5);
- authorisation process (paragraphs 6–12);
- transparency and publication requirements (paragraph 14);

1. Federal Gazette No. 26/2011, https://www.ris.bka.gv.at/Dokument.wxe?Abfrage=Bundesnormen&Dokumentnummer=NOR40133378; for an unofficial English translation, *see* Annex 1.
2. *See* https://www.bmdw.gv.at/Aussenwirtschaft/aussenwirtschaftsrecht/Seiten/default.aspx.
3. Recommendations adopted by the OECD Council 2009, https://www.oecd.org/investment/investment-policy/43384486.pdf.

- preliminary requests (Article 62 AußWG); and
- sanctions (Article 89 paragraph 3 and Article 79 paragraphs 1 and 3 AußWG).

The FDI screening mechanism is implemented by the Federal Ministry for Digital and Economic Affairs (*Bundesministerium für Digitales und Wirtschaftsstandort*, henceforth: BMDW),[4] which is the Competent Authority (CA) according to Article 25a AußWG. The CA has the power to grant exemptions from the requirements for authorisation by adopting regulations according to Article 25a(13) AußWG.

§4.02 SCOPE AND RELEVANT SECTORS

The scope of the Austrian FDI screening mechanism is limited.

First, it only applies to the pre-authorisation of investments.

Second, it is limited to restrictions in the interest of public policy and public security within the meaning of Article 52 and Article 65(1) TFEU, including universal services and crisis prevention, and thus does not include a reciprocity requirement. More specifically, according to Article 25a(3) AußWG, advance approval of an investment is required in the following strategic sectors:

(1) 'internal and external security', in particular (hence not limited to) defence goods industry and security services'; and
(2) 'public policy and public security, including services of public interest and crisis prevention', in particular (hence not limited to) 'energy and water supply, telecommunications, transport, and infrastructure facilities in the field of education and training and in the health services'.

Third, all screening and authorisation requirements only apply insofar as they are in compliance with Austrian obligations under EU or international law (cf. Article 25a(2) and (8) AußWG).

§4.03 ACQUISITION PROCESS AND AUTHORISATION OBLIGATIONS

An investment has to be screened if the following applies:

(1) The acquisition/investment targets an undertaking with headquarters in Austria, or a share of it, and/or enables controlling influence over the undertaking.[5]
(2) The acquisition/investment has a minimum size (*see* threshold values below).

4. Formerly *Bundesministerium für Wirtschaft, Jugend und Familie.*
5. Note that according to Art. 25a(1) AußWG 'undertakings shall be deemed to mean legal entities and registered partnerships'.

(3) The Austrian undertaking is acquired by a person or a legal entity/undertaking from a third country who does not have EU citizenship or domicile in the EU, EEA or Switzerland.
(4) The undertaking conducts a business activity in a sector that affects public policy and public security within the meaning of Articles 52 and 65 TFEU.

§4.04 CONTROLLING INFLUENCE AND THRESHOLD VALUES

An authorisation is required if the investor acquires a controlling influence over the Austrian enterprise or if the acquisition exceeds the threshold value of 25 % of the total voting rights. In case of reciprocal shareholding and syndicate agreements rules for the aggregation of the joint exercise of voting rights apply.

§4.05 AUTHORISATION REQUIREMENTS AND PROCESS

Article 25a AußWG distinguishes two types of authorisation procedures, namely:[6]

(1) ex ante approval (upon request of the potential buyer); and
(2) ex officio review.

The latter applies in cases where, though a planned acquisition is below the threshold values stipulated in Article 25a AußWG and/or the acquiring person/undertaking has EU citizenship or domicile in the EU, the EEA or in Switzerland, there are reasonable grounds to suspect: (1) circumvention (e.g., because the company intending to invest is a shell company); and (2) that the acquisition will cause an actual and sufficiently serious threat to public policy and public security.

The approval procedure must not take longer than one month from the submission of the application (phase I) or, if an in-depth review is deemed necessary (phase II), an additional two months. After the receipt of the application, the CA has one month to notify the applicant of its intention to launch an in-depth review. If it does not notify the applicant within this deadline, the authorisation is deemed granted, and the applicant can request a formal confirmation. If the CA notifies the applicant of the launch of an in-depth review, it has two months to either: (1) grant the authorisation; (2) grant the authorisation subject to conditions; or (3) reject the authorisation. Again, if the CA fails to decide within this time limit, the authorisation is deemed granted. The same time limits apply, *mutatis mutandis*, to ex officio reviews, i.e., in cases where the CA acts based on a suspected circumvention of the authorisation requirements.

---

6. *See* https://www.bmdw.gv.at/Aussenwirtschaft/exportkontrolle-online/exportportal/Seiten/default.aspx.

§4.06 PRELIMINARY REQUESTS

In addition to formal applications for authorisation, Article 62 AußWG[7] provides for the possibility of 'preliminary requests' before any contractual obligations have been entered into by the parties involved. In these early stages, the potential buyer can request a clarification by the CA whether an authorisation for the planned acquisition is required. The CA has to respond to such a request and notify the applicant whether: (1) an authorisation is not required at all; (2) an authorisation is required and would be granted without or with conditions; or (3) an authorisation request would be rejected on procedural grounds. If the CA comes to the conclusion that an authorisation is required, the potential buyer has to file a formal request for authorisation following the procedure (including deadlines) described above.

§4.07 TRANSPARENCY AND PUBLICATION REQUIREMENTS

Article 25a AußWG includes provisions regarding the transparency of the decisions taken by the CA (i.e., publication on the website of the BMDW).[8] The CA has, for any application that it receives, to publish the following information: (1) the buyer, i.e., the acquiring person(s) or undertaking(s); (2) the undertaking which will be acquired; and (3) a summary of its decision.

§4.08 SANCTIONS

If the authorisation for an investment in an Austrian enterprise has not been granted in accordance with Article 25a AußWG, the transaction is deemed not concluded. In cases of infringement, national courts are entitled to impose penalties including imprisonment for up to five years, depending on the type and degree of the offence (cf. Article 79(1) and (3) AußWG). This means that for example for culpable negligence up to one year imprisonment or a fine of up to 360 daily rates can be imposed, while up to three years imprisonment are foreseen in case of intentional fraud, and six months to five years imprisonment in case of commercial and serious fraud.

§4.09 RESULTS AND EVALUATION

Since the introduction of the FDI screening mechanism in 2011, the number of applications received by the CA has been limited (Table 4.1). To date (May 2018), out of six applications, two authorisations were granted unconditionally, and in four cases, the CA decided that no authorisation was necessary. In addition, two preliminary requests have been filed so far.

7. Preliminary requests are an instrument which applies for all measures related to export control under the AußWG.
8. Details can be found at https://www.bmdw.gv.at/Aussenwirtschaft/aussenwirtschaftsrecht/Seiten/Veröffentlichungen-gemäß-§-25a-Abs.-14-AußWG-2011.aspx.

Table 4.1 Summary of Statistics on FDI Screening in Austria 2012–2018

Number of Applications	6
Authorisations granted	2
Authorisations granted on conditions	0
Authorisations deemed not necessary	4
Authorisation rejected	0
Preliminary requests	2
Informal information requests	Regularly

At the same time, the CA is facing a significant – and continuously increasing – number of informal requests for information. It can be argued that this increase reflects an increased awareness of the FDI screening mechanism among potential investors.

The text of Article 25a AußWG is as follows:

§ 25a *Außenwirtschaftsgesetz* (Foreign Commerce Act)

(*Unofficial English translation*)

Segment 4

Restriction of investments in undertakings in the interest of public policy and public security

Authorisation obligations

§ 25a. (1) Except as otherwise provided in Paras (2) through (11), the following processes concerning undertakings which are domiciled in Austria shall not be subject to any restrictions:

1. acquisition of the undertaking,
2. acquisition of a stake in such undertaking, or
3. acquisition of a controlling interest in such undertaking.

   Undertakings shall be deemed to mean legal entities and registered partnerships.

(2) Provided that European Union or international law does not conflict with the authorisation obligation, a process in the sense of Para (1) shall require the authorisation by the Federal Minister of Economy, Family and Youth if:–

1. the enterprise concerned is domiciled in Austria and is subject to the accounting standards of the Third Book of the Austrian Commercial Code UGB, German Imperial Law Gazette p. 219/1897, and
2. is active in a sector that affects public policy and public security in the sense of Articles 52 and 65 (1) of the TFEU, and
3. the acquisition is made by a natural person who is not a citizen of the European Union or a citizen of the European Economic Area or of Switzerland, or a legal entity or undertaking which is domiciled in a third country with the exception of the European Economic Area and Switzerland.

The process shall not be carried out prior to the issuance of the authorisation.

(3) Sectors in the sense of Para (2) 2 shall be:–

1. sectors of internal and external security, including, without limitations,
   a) defence goods industry, and

   b) security services,
2. sectors of public policy and public security, including services of public interest and crisis prevention, including, without limitations,
   a) energy supply,
   b) water supply,
   c) telecommunications,
   d) transport, and
   e) infrastructure facilities in the field of education and training and in the health services.

(4) No authorisation requirement under Para (2) shall apply to investments in undertakings where the voting right share of the buyer in the sense of Para (2)(3) is less than 25% after the acquisition of the stake. In computing such voting right share, the shares held in the undertaking to be acquired by other persons or undertakings in the sense of Para (2)(3) shall be added when they meet at least one of the following prerequisites:
1. the buyer holds 25% or more of the voting rights in such other person or undertaking,
2. such other person or undertaking holds 25% or more of the voting rights in the buyer,
3. another person or undertaking in the sense of Para (2)(3) holds 25% or more of the voting rights in such other person or undertaking as well as in the buyer, or
4. the buyer has entered an agreement with such other person or undertaking on the joint exercise of voting rights.

(5) The acquisition of a controlling interest shall be subject to the authorisation requirement pursuant to Para 2 if such controlling interest is exercised by the person or undertaking in the sense of Para (2)(3) on their own or jointly by several persons or undertakings of whom or which at least one person or undertaking is a person or undertaking in the sense of Para (2)(3). An acquisition in this sense shall be, without limitations:
1. two persons or undertakings in the sense of Para (2)(3) entering an agreement on the joint exercise of voting rights by which they are together entitled to at least 25% of the voting rights; or
2. the termination of an agreement on the joint exercise of voting rights entered with another person or undertaking upon which one person or undertaking in the sense of Para (2)(3) is entitled to at least 25% of the voting rights.

   In computing the voting right shares pursuant to Items 1 and 2, Para (4) shall be applied *mutatis mutandis*.

(6) If an authorisation pursuant to Para (2) is required, the buyer(s) shall submit an application for authorisation–
1. prior to entering the contract on the acquisition of the undertaking or stake or prior to entering the legal transaction(s) required for acquiring the controlling interest, or
2. in the event of a public bid prior to the publication of the decision on submitting the bid.

(7) The application for authorisation shall include, without limitations:
1. name, address and, if available, telephone number, fax number and e-mail address of the buyer in the sense of Para (2)(3);
2. name, address and, if available, telephone number, fax number and e-mail address of the undertaking which is to be acquired or invested in;
3. description of the business activities of the undertaking in terms of Para (3)(1) or (2);

4. description of the planned acquisition; and
5. naming of a person authorised to accept service in Austria.

(8) The Federal Minister of Economy, Family and Youth shall issue a notification in writing within one month of receiving the application that either:–
1. no authorisation process is commenced because of conflicting obligations under European Union or international law, or
2. there are no objections to the acquisition because there is no threat to the interests of public policy and public security in the sense of Articles 52 and 65 (1) of the TFEU including services of public interest and crisis prevention, or
2. an in-depth investigation procedure is initiated because a more exhaustive examination of the effects on such interests is required.

If no written notification is issued within this period the process shall be deemed to have been authorised.

(9) Within two months of service of the written notification to initiate an investigation procedure in the sense of Para (8)(3), a written notification shall be issued by which:–
1. the process shall be authorised if there is no threat to the interests specified in Para (8)(2), or
2. when the process is expected to constitute an actual and sufficiently serious threat to public policy and public security in the sense of Articles 52 and 65 (1) of the TFEU, including services of public interest and crisis prevention, which affects a basic interest of society:–

a) authorisation shall be granted subject to stipulations necessary to eliminate such threat, or
b) authorisation shall be refused when stipulations to eliminate such threat do not suffice.

If no written notification is issued within this period, the process shall be deemed to have been authorised.

(10) Upon application, a confirmation shall be issued concerning the fact that a process is deemed to be authorised by way of the expiry of the period defined in Para (8) or (9).

(11) The Federal Minister of Economy, Family and Youth shall be authorised to mandate *ex officio*, by way of a written notification, an authorisation requirement for the acquisition of, investment in or acquisition of a controlling interest in an undertaking domiciled in Austria if–
1. the process does not meet the requirements pursuant to Para (2)(3) and Para (4), and
2. there are reasonable grounds for the suspicion that the process is intended to circumvent an authorisation requirement, and
3. there are reasonable grounds for the suspicion that the process may endanger the interests referred to in Para (8)(2), and
4. the requirements pursuant to Para (2)(1) and (2) are met, and
5. no obligations under European Union or international law conflict with an authorisation process.

The process shall not be carried out prior to the issuance of the authorisation. In evaluating any suspicion of circumvention in the sense of Item 2 above, the true economic content and actually achieved influence on the undertaking to be acquired shall be relevant in terms of an economic consideration.

(12) The procedure pursuant to Para (11) shall be governed by Paras (9) and (10) subject to the condition that the two-month decision period commences as of the date of service of the instruction to obtain authorisation.

(13) The Federal Minister of Economy, Family and Youth shall be authorised to provide, by way of a regulation, for exemptions from the authorisation requirements for certain types of processes in the sense of Para (1) if it is clear from the start that such processes will not constitute any threat to the interests referred to in Para (8)(2).

(14) The Federal Minister of Economy, Family and Youth shall provide for the suitable publication of decisions pursuant to Para (8)(1) or (2), Para (9) or Para (12) or final decisions based on procedural grounds. Such publication shall state:

1. the buying persons or undertakings,
2. the undertaking to be bought, and
3. whether:-
   a) the process was deemed to be unobjectionable,
   a) conditions were stipulated,
   b) the process was not authorised, or
   c) the application was rejected on procedural grounds.

Part III Comments on the European Commission Proposal

CHAPTER 5

The European Commission Proposal on FDI Screening

Maria Martin-Prat

§5.01 OVERALL CONTEXT: BENEFITS OF INWARD FDI FOR THE EU ECONOMY, RECENT TRENDS AND CONCERNS

Let me start by stating the obvious: foreign direct investment (FDI) is beneficial to the EU economy in terms of growth, jobs and innovation. Six per cent of jobs in the EU are provided by companies owned by foreign investors. The EU is the biggest provider of FDI abroad but also the biggest receiver of FDI: in 2015, the stock of inward FDI in the EU stood at over EUR 5.7 trillion – compared with EUR 5.1 trillion in the US and EUR 1.1 trillion in China.

FDIs link EU companies with global value chains that drive the modern economy. It boosts productivity and makes our companies more competitive by improving resource allocation, bringing in capital, technologies and expertise, increasing competition, stimulating innovation and opening new markets for the EU's exports.

EU Member States are making huge efforts to attract foreign investors and compete against each other for FDI. Inward flows into the EU went down in the aftermath of the financial crisis but this was part of a global phenomenon. By now, growth is back in the EU and inward FDI figures reflect our dynamism and attractiveness: In 2015, inward FDI reached almost EUR 470 billion – more than in 2007, the highest level before the crisis.

There can be no doubt about the EU's openness to international investment. As consistently recognised by the OECD, the EU has one of the most liberal frameworks for FDI in the world.

For those reasons, the EU supports liberalisation of investments worldwide: opening markets, ensuring level playing field for our companies, guarantee a rule-based ecosystem.

Traditionally our investment partners have been countries that have similar economic values to us and use the same rule book. They were often members of the OECD like USA, Switzerland, Canada or Japan. Those countries are still the main investors in the EU. But, their share has been decreasing to the benefit of new emerging partners, such as Brazil, China or Russia.

The world around us is also changing. The role of the State in the economy of some third countries is increasing. This raises questions as to the final motivation of FDI - of strategic nature rather than economic rationale - especially when the investor is a state-owned enterprise or receives subsidies which give to a government influence over the investor's decision.

Concerns have been expressed by some Member States and some stakeholders that, in some cases, foreign investors might seek to acquire strategic assets that allow them to control or influence European firms whose activities are critical for our security and public order. This includes activities related to the operation or provision of critical technologies, infrastructure, inputs or sensitive information.

Acquisitions by foreign state-owned or controlled companies in these strategic areas may allow third countries to use these assets not only to the detriment of the EU's technological edge but also to put our security or public order at risk.

The same concerns have been made in many parts of the world, not only in the EU.

§5.02 EXPERIENCES WITH FDI SCREENING

Outside Europe, most of our partners now have a mechanism to screen foreign investment. We just heard about the example of CFIUS, but there are many more. This shows that screening mechanisms are rather common in the investment landscape and that companies integrate government screening into their investment processes.

In the EU itself, twelve Member States already have a screening mechanism in place and we heard about the experience of Austrian and Germany. Those systems vary in terms of scope and or processes:

- some are limited to military activities and some are broader and include for instance security of supply or critical infrastructures;
- some include a threshold in terms of shareholding above which the investment is screened;
- some are based on notification and prior approval, some can look at operations ex post.

All those mechanisms bring meaningful experience to the discussions which have only recently emerged at EU level.

[A] EU Dimension

As our economies in the EU are increasingly being interlinked, it becomes more and more obvious that we share in common not only the opportunities but also the threats.

A critical technology or infrastructure may be critical not only for one country alone but also for its neighbours and sometimes for the whole Union. Even more when we talk about projects of EU interests which benefit from EU funding and which are meant to shape our collective future – for instance, the navigation system Galileo, trans-European networks for Energy or the EU's research and innovation programme Horizon 2020.

When looking at those collective challenges, our current instruments do not seem adequate. There is a clear lack of coordination among Member States but also lack of information within the EU about who is investing and where.

This is why we have come to a proposal which aims at striking a good balance between:

- keeping an open and welcoming investment climate in the Union; and
- establishing an appropriate framework for the FDI screening procedures of Member States when they decide to do so;
- improving the coordination and the information at EU level on FDIs, when foreign acquisitions may put at risk security and public order in the EU.

[B] Content of the Commission Proposal: Four Features

First, it enables Member States to maintain or adopt FDI screening mechanisms on grounds of security and public order. The Regulation does not require Member States that do not wish to screen FDI to set up anything; rather, as FDI falls under the exclusive competence of the Union, it provides Member States wishing to do so with legal certainty in that regard.

Second, it sets out some basic requirements for FDI screening mechanisms such as transparency, judicial review as well as non-discrimination among third countries; and it gives guidance as to the screening factors.

Third, it establishes a cooperation system among the Member States and between the Member States and the Commission through which we can exchange information on incoming FDI operations that can affect security and public order.

Finally, it gives the Commission the discretion to issue an advisory opinion in two cases:

(1) in case FDI may affect security or public order in relation to a project or programme of Union interest, i.e., programmes which receive substantial EU funding, or which are covered by Union legislation regarding critical infrastructure, critical technologies or critical inputs.
(2) where the Commission considers that a foreign investment is likely to affect security or public order in one or more Member States.

This is a carefully calibrated role, based on cooperation among MS and the Commission. It also reflects a conscious decision to avoid interfering with Member States' existing review mechanisms and to avoid a heavy decision-making procedure.

We understand that concepts such as 'security' are very close to Member States' traditional realm of competence. What we all need to understand now is that security or public order has an increasingly European dimension, not only for the obvious reason that we are in an internal market, but also because of the way societies and economies are interconnected today.

[C] A Policy in the Making

Some countries have a long experience with FDI screening (e.g., the US with CFIUS), but this is rather a new policy area in the EU. Some would like us to go beyond the current proposal while others question even the rationale of FDI screening. We consider that the current proposal is proportionate and a necessary step at EU level to enhance transparency between Member States and the Commission in the area of FDI. We are in the process of working with the Member States and the European Parliament through the ordinary legislative procedure. Timing is tight, but we aim to ensure that we end up with an efficient framework which protects security and public order in the EU and does not create unnecessary new burden for companies or for administration.

We are already engaging on more debate and analysis. Alongside the proposal for Regulation, the Commission announced the launch of a coordination group on inward FDI and of further analysis on FDIs in the EU.

[D] To Be Seen in the Overall Context of What We Want to Achieve

This is not a protectionist move. The Regulation addresses issues pertaining to security and public order, which are legitimate exceptions to our multilateral and bilateral commitments. You will not find elements dealing with reciprocity or industrial policy concerns.

That does not mean that we are turning a blind eye on those questions: We have an ongoing agenda of trade and investment negotiations where we seek to address questions of investment liberalisation and investment protection, so that our companies benefit from a level playing field with our partners.

The proposal should not be seen in isolation, but with a view to the global picture, as part of the response to 'harness globalisation'.

CHAPTER 6

Comment of a Member of the European Parliament

Marietje Schaake

The foreign direct investment (FDI) screening proposal currently under discussion in the Parliament is quite technical, and it helps to occasionally zoom out a little bit. To give a broader context, as well as to see how that context creates the frame of reference for us in the European Parliament, not just on FDI screening but on other trade measures as well, we must look at the bigger geopolitical picture of the EU's competitiveness and the changing flows of not only goods and services and investment but also power relations. And let us call a spade a spade: a lot of this debate is informed about concerns with regard to China.

Let me just list a few of those concerns, not all of them are related to FDI. Corporate espionage, reliability of technology and networks, for example. Are there other back doors that are being used for other purposes? We have just heard about espionage on the African Union headquarters after it was developed by Chinese companies. This is but one example that fits in a broader strategy through which China seems to be pushing for more political influence globally. Its behaviour and its buying up of strategic projects in Europe seem to confirm that analysis. Does this strategy work? Think about Chinese investments in harbours in Greece and the Greeks' subsequently voting against calling out – in the UN – China's ongoing human rights violations. We have already had broad discussions about: dumped and subsidised goods, and discrimination; the challenges European companies face in China such as arbitrary treatment, the expansion of China's military capacities and within the WTO; China's market economy status and its commitments which only exist on paper. And now, on top of this comes the quite extraordinary rise of FDI in Europe, accompanied by concerns about the loss of competitiveness and takeovers in strategic sectors.

So, without being hysterical or naive, we are, really looking at how to strengthen not only rules but also value-based trade in Europe. This is even essential in current times, and I commend the commissioner, Commissioner Malmström, for her approach in trying to merge these two topics.

So, now zooming in on the question of FDI screening: The current FDI screening discussion perfectly fits in a broader discussion of concern about fair trade, and I was therefore not at all surprised that it was the Italian, German and French governments that urged for European action in a letter to the Commission last year. We have heard about measures to create more oversight, more sharing of information, more coordination between Member States when it comes to the screening of FDI and the considerations that governments and authorities might have when taking decisions not to accept investment.

The kind of screening that already happens on the European level is mainly based on anti-competiveness and abuse of dominant market position. As such, it looks at mergers and acquisitions and is not so much focused on, for example, the source of funding. Does it come from state-aided companies? And what are the levels of transparency? Member States, on the other hand, because of their national security competencies, do have the ability to screen for national security concerns. In fact, twelve Member States already have such mechanisms in place. So, the idea is to bring the differences between Member States a bit closer together, to encourage information sharing, but the European Commission's proposal is still quite loose. It is non-binding, and I think it should also be seen more strategically as taking a position in a debate much more than coming down with hard regulations.

In our internal market, it only makes sense to have similar criteria between Member States. What do you screen for, what is acceptable and what considerations do you have? It is obvious that critical infrastructure impacts the energy sector, transport and finance sectors, but increasingly, digitisation takes us to artificial intelligence, dual-use goods, cybersecurity goods, telecom and digital infrastructure. And these are just areas we can think off now. The list will only keep growing.

There are currently two categories of Member States: those that conduct FDI screening and those that do not. But, those that do screen also use different criteria, in terms of the percentages that are stake as well as the definition of sectors. It makes sense to think about this on the European level. Yet we have to do so in a way that is actually feasible. If we go overboard, we risk losing credibility. I believe the European Parliament is well aware of this, and will in the coming trialogues support increased coordination between the Member States. We also need to keep in mind that we are talking about non-binding measures. This could be a good compromise between those that are concerned about more top-down measures on the European level and those that believe the EU is not doing enough.

What is slumbering throughout this entire debate is a certain wave of protectionist desires. The discussion about investment screening in particular has brought this to the fore of the political debate. We should definitely not be naive about this. The reality is that there is an increasing mutual dependence between the EU and other countries including China. We cannot only listen to importers or exporters. The consequences of an actual deterioration in our relationships with other countries, any sort of standoff or even talking about a trade war will not be without consequence for us in Europe too.

I believe this perspective needs to be an integral element of these ongoing discussions which we need to address head on.

I would like to point to some lessons that we have learned in this regard which may inspire some more caution. Some time ago, the European Commission was investigating the dumping of solar panels on European markets. In that situation, it was Germany that actually obstructed the investigation out of concern for its own economic considerations; importing cheaper solar panels to facilitate an energy transition, but also simple market access for German cars that it feared losing if China retaliated. This dynamic will undoubtedly also play a role in the ongoing discussions. We need to understand and assess these in order to take them into account while moving forward.

I will conclude by going back to where I started. We need to put the question of FDI screening and other measures meant to protect critical infrastructures in a broader context. On the European level, we just adopted modernised trade defence instruments, another category of measures to deal with unfair trade practices. The European Parliament also just adopted a report on digital trade, which extends our rules-based trade to the digital sphere as well. Yet such measures cannot adequately address the challenges we face in today's intertwined global economy – especially in relation to China – if they are not placed within an overall EU-China Strategy. That strategy is currently non-existent, but should at least also include the private sector.

How do we want to engage with our partners and what responsibility do they have in relation to us? Think about the United States and how some of their proposed anti-dumping measures vis-à-vis China can also negatively impact us in Europe. How do we feel about China's policies and their side-effects in Africa? We need to address these questions from a broader perspective. This is why the entire question of FDI screening needs to be seen in a context. We should see all the factors for what they are and then make a decision that cannot be seen as a form of veiled protectionism. Beyond the mechanism and laws that are currently being designed, I believe willingness to actually act is what this debate is really about. It is about a calculation of self-interest, and it is about a calculation of a potential backlash. Therefore, it is essential that the question of political will is part of this discussion. If you seek to influence decision-makers, the question is how to foster will. I will leave it there, and I am happy to answer any questions you might have.

CHAPTER 7

Reading Between the Lines of the EU Regulation Establishing a Framework for Screening FDI into the Union

*Régis Bismuth**

§7.01 INTRODUCTION

On 13 September 2017, the European Commission published its proposal for a regulation establishing a framework for screening foreign direct investments (FDI) into the European Union (EU)[1] (hereinafter the 'Regulation Proposal'), more specifically on the grounds of security and public order.[2] This proposal eventually led to the adoption, in March 2019, of Regulation 2019/52 (hereinafter 'the Regulation' or 'Regulation 2019/52').[3]

When released, this proposal seemed quite surprising, particularly when one recalls the sceptical – and at times reluctant – position of the Commission with regards to domestic FDI screening mechanisms. This was, for instance, the case in 2006 when the Barroso Commission decided to scrutinise a new French decree establishing authorisation procedures for foreign investments in certain sectors of activities that

---

* The author is grateful to Mikaël Schinazi (PhD student at Sciences Po Law School) for his useful comments on a previous draft. The views expressed in this chapter are those of the author only and any errors or omissions are his sole responsibility. We thank Professor F. Baetens (University of Oslo) for having performed graciously the peer review.

1. European Commission, Proposal for a Regulation of the European Parliament and the Council Establishing a Framework for Screening of Foreign Direct Investments into the European Union, COM(2017)487, 2017/0224(COD), 13 Sept. 2017 https://ec.europa.eu/info/law/better-regulation/initiative/111803/attachment/090166e5b5075ff8_en, accessed 25 Apr. 2018.
2. *See* Arts 3 and 4 of the Regulation Proposal.
3. Regulation 2019/452 establishing a framework for the screening of foreign direct investments into the Union, OJEU L 79 I/1, 21 Mar. 2019.

affect public policy, public security or national defence.[4] The Commission initiated infringements proceedings to the extent that some of the provisions of the new decree could have been in contradiction with EU treaty rules on the free movement of capital and the right of establishment.[5] The Commission expressed similar concerns, which were subsequently alleviated, when the French Government adopted a new decree on 'economic patriotism' in 2014 extending the list of business sectors (energy, water, transport, telecommunications, infrastructure and public health) in which the Ministry of Economy had the right to screen foreign investments.[6]

These precedents highlighting the suspicions weighing on FDI screening mechanisms under EU law[7] could lead us to raise a somewhat ironic question: would the Barroso Commission have reacted negatively to the 2017 Juncker Commission's proposal establishing a framework for screening FDI into the EU on the grounds of security and public order?

It seems clear that Regulation 2019/452 is the result of an evolution of the Commission's stance with regards to non-EU FDI flows. As such, this chapter first explores this evolution (section 7.02), before analysing Regulation 2019/452 further and criticising it on a number of grounds. To begin, this regulation has limited added value for Member States' existing FDI screening mechanisms (section 7.03). It also imposes on Member States an implied obligation to establish FDI screening mechanisms (section 7.04). Additionally, this regulation could serve as a basis of a 'soft blocking power' – at little expense – for the Commission (section 7.05). Perhaps most important, it rests on Article 207 TFEU, which is a fragile and questionable legal basis for the type of framework envisaged by the Regulation (section 7.06). Lastly, it can be seen as a missed opportunity to the extent that it does not address the key issue of competitive neutrality in FDI transactions (section 7.07).

§7.02 DECIPHERING THE EUROPEAN COMMISSION'S NEW 'PROTECTIVE NARRATIVE'

It is indeed possible to notice some changes in the vocabulary the Commission has used when describing the control of non-EU FDI flows and, more generally, the defence of EU interests in economic globalisation, whilst remaining determined to challenge restrictions on capital flows in an intra-EU context.[8] The Commission sent an important signal in its May 2017 paper on 'Harnessing Globalization,' in which it noted that 'concerns have recently been voiced about foreign investors, notably state-owned

4. Decree n° 2005-1739 of 30 Dec. 2005, [2005] Journal Officiel de la République Française 20779.
5. *See*, European Commission, IP/06/438, 4 Apr. 2006; European Commission, IP/06/1353, 12 Oct. 2006.
6. Decree n° 2014-479 of 14 May 2014, [2014] Journal Officiel de la République Française 8062.
7. *See also* Till Müller-Ibold, 'Foreign Investment in Germany: Restrictions Based on Public Security Concerns and Their Compatibility with EU Law' (2010) 1 European Yearbook of International Economic Law 203.
8. For instance, the Commission initiated infringement proceedings against Bulgaria, Hungary, Latvia, Lithuania and Slovakia which adopted new laws regulating potentially restricting EU individuals and companies from buying farmland (IP/16/1827, 26 Mar. 2016).

enterprises, taking over European companies with key technologies for strategic reasons' while raising the issue of reciprocity by pointing out that 'EU investors often do not enjoy the same rights to invest in the country from which the investment originates'.[9] It is also not a coincidence that the Regulation Proposal was released on the same day as Juncker's State of the Union address, in which he underlined that 'Europe must always defend its strategic interests' and announced, 'we are not naïve free traders'.[10]

It is somehow difficult to determine whether the evolution of the positions of the Commission is genuinely sincere. It must be stressed that the proposal did not call into question the overarching principle of free movement of capital embedded in the TFEU. Besides, on an almost systematic basis, the statements made on behalf of the European Commission on the issue of FDI screening combine a normative dimension ('openness to foreign investment remains a key principle for the EU ... ') as well as an economic prescription ('openness to foreign investment remains ... a major source of growth.')[11] The Commission has been very careful within the framework of this initiative, positioning itself as a shield that can protect EU citizens and industries from the downsides of globalisation, as well as constantly reaffirming its commitment to the free movement of capital as part of its DNA.

Nevertheless, this 'cautious protective narrative' should not obscure the fact that the Commission does not seem ideologically and politically at ease with this initiative subject to ideological dilemmas as well as divergent political forces. The proposal was neither the result of a proactive strategy for globalisation nor the (even very) early stage of an industrial policy at the EU level.[12] It is not also the result of a genuine initiative of the Commission as it was primarily a request of France, Germany and Italy. In their joint letter sent to the European Commission in February 2017, the French, German and Italian governments expressed their concerns as to the growing number of acquisitions of European companies in strategic sectors carried out by non-EU investors as well as the lack of reciprocity with respect to the admission of FDI or government procurement in certain countries.[13] They updated their position in a document published in July

9. European Commission, Reflection Paper on Harnessing Globalization, 10 May 2017, p. 15, https://ec.europa.eu/commission/sites/beta-political/files/reflection-paper-globalisation_en.pdf, accessed 25 Apr. 2018.
10. President Jean-Claude Juncker's State of the Union Address 2017, Brussels, 13 Sept. 2017, http://europa.eu/rapid/press-release_SPEECH-17-3165_en.pdf, accessed 25 Apr. 2018.
11. European Commission (n 9) 15. *See also* European Commission, State of the Union 2017, Press Release, 14 Sept. 2017 (citing Vice-President Jyrki Katainen: 'the EU is and will remain one of the most open investment regimes in the world. Foreign direct investment is an important source of growth, jobs and innovation').
12. Besides, as pointed out by the European Parliament, non-EU investments targeting European companies are 'part of strategic industrial policies' of non-EU countries (European Parliament, Proposal for a Union Act on the Screening of Foreign Investment in Strategic Sectors, B8-0302/2017, 26 Apr. 2017).
13. *See* https://www.bmwi.de/Redaktion/DE/Downloads/S-T/schreiben-de-fr-it-an-malmstroem.pdf?__blob=publicationFile&v=5, accessed 25 Apr. 2018. *See also* Proposals for Ensuring an Improved Level Playing Field in Trade and Investment, February 2017, https://www.bmwi.de/Redaktion/DE/Downloads/E/eckpunktepapier-proposals-for-ensuring-an-improved-level-playing-field-in-trade-and-investment.pdf?__blob=publicationFile&v=4, accessed 25 Apr. 2018.

2017 in which they pointed out that some of these non-EU investments also affect the level playing field since they are 'directly or indirectly subsidised by government agencies'.[14] However, while the Commission's proposal included certain provisions concerning the screening of investment in strategic sectors, it does not deal with the issue of reciprocity and does not clearly address the anti-competitive effects of subsidised acquisitions.

The Commission also had to deal with the disagreement of certain EU Member States over the potential establishment of a screening mechanism at the EU level. It must be noted that only twelve of them have so far put in place FDI screening mechanisms at the national level,[15] differing in scope and design.[16] Nordic countries as well as Ireland, Spain, Portugal and Greece viewed the Regulation Proposal as a protectionist enterprise.[17] The UK government considered that it would 'place additional burden and uncertainty on prospective investors, which is at odds with the UK's stance as an open and liberal investment destination'.[18]

The Commission was therefore in a rather awkward position when drafting this proposal. First, it intended to erect an FDI screening mechanism at the EU level while similar mechanisms established at the domestic level have usually been subject to the scrutiny of the Commission. Second, the initiative was the result of a minority of EU Member States who are willing to tighten the control of non-EU FDI and have raised concerns as to the level playing field and reciprocity in international trade and investment. Third, it is clear that it was difficult to reach a consensus among EU Member States between those supporting the initiative, those hostile towards screening mechanisms supposedly sending protectionist signals, and those not ready to accept that the Commission would exercise certain prerogatives in the field of security and public order which have been the responsibility of EU Member States up to now.[19] Fourth, on top of that, the Commission perhaps saw this initiative as an opportunity to consolidate the new exclusive competence it has acquired in the field of FDI as part of

14. European Investment Policy: A Common Approach to Investment Control, 28 Jul. 2017, https://g8fip1kplyr33r3krz5b97d1-wpengine.netdna-ssl.com/wp-content/uploads/2017/08/17 0728_Investment-screening_non-paper.pdf, accessed 25 Apr. 2018.
15. This is the case of Austria, Denmark, Germany, Finland, France, Latvia, Lithuania, Italy, Poland, Portugal, Spain and the United Kingdom.
16. European Commission, Welcoming Foreign Direct Investment while Protecting Essential Interests, COM(2017)494, 13 Sept. 2017, p. 7, https://eur-lex.europa.eu/legal-content/EN/TXT/PDF /?uri = CELEX:52017DC0494&from = EN, accessed 25 Apr. 2018.
17. Fabrizio Di Benedetto, A European Committee on Foreign Investment?, Columbia FDI Perspectives, No. 214, 4 Dec. 2017.
18. UK Department for International Trade, Explanatory Memorandum, 5 Oct. 2017 [20], https://www.parliament.uk/documents/lords-committees/eu-external-affairs-subcommittee/foreign-direct-investment/EM-foreign-direct-investment.pdf, accessed 25 Apr. 2018.
19. Article 65(1)(b) of TFEU provides that the principle of free movement of capital is without prejudice to the right of Member States 'to take measures which are justified on grounds of public policy or public security'. Pursuant to Art. 4(2) of TEU, 'The Union ... shall respect their essential State functions, including ... maintaining law and order and safeguarding national security. In particular, national security remains the sole responsibility of each Member State.' *See also* Hermann-Josef Blanke, 'Article 4 [The Relations Between the EU and the Member States]' in Hermann-Josef Blanke and Stelio Mangiameli (eds), *The Treaty on European Union (TEU) – A Commentary* (Springer 2013) 228.

the Common Commercial Policy (CCP) since the Lisbon Treaty pursuant to Article 207 TFEU. Not surprisingly, the Commission chose this provision as the legal basis of its Regulation Proposal, and it was also the legal basis retained in the final text of the regulation – even though, as will be seen later, this choice is questionable.

§7.03 A LIMITED ADDED VALUE FOR MEMBER STATES' EXISTING FDI SCREENING MECHANISMS

An analysis of Regulation 2019/452 should start with one simple question: what is exactly the added value of this regulation compared to currently applicable rules under EU law? Answering this question requires distinguishing the position of Member States and the position of the Commission. As to the Member States, it appears that the Regulation 2019/452 neither enhances the possibility for them of exercising control over non-EU FDI nor compels them to do so.

Regulation 2019/452 specifies the legal framework of Member States' FDI screening mechanisms on the grounds of security or public order. It must be recalled that pursuant to Article 65 TFEU, the freedom of movement of capital set out in Article 63 TFEU is without prejudice to the right of Member States 'to take measures which are justified on grounds of public policy or public security' to the extent that they do not 'constitute a means of arbitrary discrimination or a disguised restriction on the free movement of capital'.[20] In a nutshell, the Regulation provides that such mechanisms shall be transparent and non-discriminatory between third countries, shall 'set out the circumstances triggering the screening, the grounds for screening and the applicable detailed procedural rules'[21] and 'apply timeframes under their screening mechanisms'.[22] Moreover, foreign investors and undertakings concerned 'shall have the possibility to seek recourse against screening decisions of the national authorities.[23]

Most of the requirements of the Regulation are nothing more than a detailed codification of the principles identified in the Court of Justice's case law on freedom of movement of capital. These include, *inter alia*, the necessity to indicate the specific circumstances in which prior authorisation is required,[24] observance of a principle of proportionality requiring 'that the measures adopted be appropriate to secure the attainment of the objective which they pursue and not go beyond what is necessary in order to attain it',[25] and access to legal redress for any person affected by a restrictive measure.[26] Only a few procedural obligations listed in the Regulation (notification of screening mechanisms under Article 3(7) and cooperation mechanism under Articles 6 and 7) go beyond the existing requirements under the TFEU. To this extent, the

20. Articles 65(1)(b) and 65(3) TFEU.
21. Regulation 2019/452, Art. 3(2).
22. Regulation 2019/452, Art. 3(3).
23. Regulation 2019/452, Art. 3(5).
24. ECJ, Case C-54/99 (*Association Église de Scientologie de Paris and Scientology International Reserves Trust v. The Prime Minister*) 14 Mar. 2000, ECLI:EU:C:2000:124 [21].
25. ECJ, Case C-112/05 (*Commission of the European Communities v. Federal Republic of Germany*) 23 Oct. 2007, ECLI:EU:C:2007:623 [72].
26. ECJ, Case C-54/99 (n 24) [17].

Regulation can also be depicted as an attempt to better discipline and control domestic screening procedures.

This raises the question as to whether Article 207 TFEU should have been used as the exclusive legal basis of the Regulation. It seems indeed that, as least with respect to the aforementioned provisions, Article 64(2) TFEU would have been a more appropriate legal basis since it clearly empowers the EU to adopt, through the ordinary legislative procedure, 'the measures on the movement of capital to or from third countries involving direct investment – including investment in real estate – establishment, the provision of financial services or the admission of securities to capital markets'. Rather, the Commission made the choice to ground the Regulation in the CCP on which it has exclusive competence but, according to Opinion 2/15, does not cover non-direct foreign investments.[27] The issue of the appropriateness of the legal basis will also be discussed below.

§7.04 AN IMPLIED OBLIGATION FOR MEMBER STATES TO ESTABLISH FDI SCREENING MECHANISMS

Regulation 2019/452 provides that Member States may 'maintain, amend or adopt mechanisms to screen foreign direct investments on the grounds of security or public order'.[28] It does not clearly indicate whether Member States may 'abolish' existing screening mechanisms, but current debates in the European Parliament show that the insertion of a 'ratchet mechanism' in the final text is conceivable.[29]

The Regulation does not explicitly require Member States to establish an FDI screening mechanism at the national level. Nevertheless, one might wonder whether it is implicitly required under some of its provisions. Under Article 3(7) of the Regulation, Member States have an obligation to notify their existing screening mechanisms to the Commission. But Member States that have not established such mechanisms shall also provide the Commission with an annual report covering foreign direct investments 'that took place in their territory, on the basis of information available to them ...'.[30] Member States willing to comply bona fide with this obligation will probably establish at least a mandatory reporting system for statistical purposes.[31]

27. CJEU, Opinion 2/15 (*EU-Singapore FTA*), 16 May 2017, ECLI:EU:C:2017:376 [225–238]. *See also* Nikos Lavranos, 'Mixed Exclusivity: The CJEU's Opinion on the EU-Singapore FTA' (2017) 2 European Investment Law and Arbitration Review 11.
28. Regulation 2019/452, Art. 3(1).
29. *See, for instance,* the proposal of the Committee on International Trade: 'Member States may maintain, amend, *tighten up* or adopt mechanisms to screen foreign direct investments ...' (European Parliament, Committee on International Trade, Draft Report, COM(2017)0487 – C8-0309/2017 – 2017/0224(COD), 7 Mar. 2018).
30. Regulation 2019/452, Art. 5(1).
31. It is noteworthy to mention that an amendment introduced under the auspices of the Committee on International Trade of the European Parliament – not retained in the final text – specified that the annual report must be provided, 'on the basis of information available to them, *and the efforts made to obtain that information*' (European Parliament, Committee on International Trade (n 29)).

Other provisions of the Regulation suggest that Member States will have to establish a more invasive FDI screening mechanism, not just for informational purposes. Under Article 6 of the Regulation, a Member State which considers that an FDI is likely to affect its security or public order may provide 'comments' to the Member State where the FDI is planned or completed.[32] Likewise, if it considers that an FDI is likely to affect security or public order in one or more Member States, the Commission may issue an 'opinion' addressed to the Member State in which the FDI is planned or has been completed.[33] In both cases, the host state of the investment 'shall give due consideration to the comments' of the other Member States and to the opinion of the Commission.'[34] Also, under Article 8 of the Regulation, where it considers that an FDI 'is likely to affect projects or programmes of Union interest on grounds of security and public order, the Commission may issue an opinion.'[35] The Member State where the investment is planned or has been completed 'shall take utmost account of the Commission's opinion and provide an explanation to the Commission if its opinion is not followed'.[36]

It seems that a Member State which has not instituted an FDI screening mechanism faces conflicting obligations. On the one hand, it may follow another Member State's 'comments' or the Commission's 'opinion' and condition or prohibit the transaction. However, adopting this approach without a clear legal basis in domestic law could constitute a violation of the obligation that FDI screening mechanisms shall be transparent and 'set out the circumstances triggering the screening, the grounds for screening and the applicable detailed procedural rules'[37]. On the other hand, if the Member State disregards such comments or opinions, it fails to give them 'due consideration'. In the case of a programme of Union interest, a Member State without an FDI screening mechanism is not likely to be in the position to 'take utmost account of the Commission's opinion'. In both cases, the Commission may initiate infringement proceedings against that Member State for failure to fulfil its obligations under the regulation. An effective way to avoid this risk would be to establish a full-fledged domestic FDI screening mechanism in order 'to assess, investigate, authorise, condition, prohibit or unwind foreign direct investments'.[38] Such mechanism would be triggered if the circumstances so require under Regulation 2019/452.

§7.05 A 'SOFT BLOCKING POWER' OF THE COMMISSION: AT LITTLE EXPENSE

From the EU's perspective, it seems at first sight that Regulation 2019/452 does not vest the European Commission with substantial responsibilities and prerogatives: Member

32. Regulation 2019/452, Art. 6(2).
33. Regulation 2019/452, Art. 6(3).
34. Regulation 2019/452, Art. 6(9).
35. Regulation 2019/452, Art. 8(1).
36. Regulation 2019/452, Art. 8(2)(c).
37. Regulation 2019/452, Art. 3(2).
38. Definition of 'screening' under Art. 2(3) of Regulation 2019/452.

States shall notify the Commission of their existing screening mechanisms,[39] and inform the Commission of any FDI undergoing screening.[40] The Commission may also request information from Member States[41] and, as pointed out above, issue 'opinions' to Member States where it considers that an FDI is likely to affect security or public order.[42] The Commission has the power to screen – in the restrictive sense of investigating, finding out information or assessing – but does not have the *de jure* power to block transactions on the grounds of security or public order in the same manner as set forth in the context of the Committee on Foreign Investment in the United States (CFIUS). There is no such thing as a *de jure* federal blocking power at the EU level.

Despite this apparently lax regulatory framework under which the European Commission intends to operate, it is possible to identify the various means by which it could exercise a *de facto* control over foreign investments within the EU.

In the practice of screening procedures, formal decisions rejecting an acquisition are fairly rare. For instance, since the creation of the CFIUS and more specifically since the Exon-Florio amendment – adopted in 1988 and granting the US President the power to block 'mergers, acquisitions or takeovers' – only five transactions have been rejected,[43] while many more have been abandoned at the initiative of the acquirer because of concerns raised by members of CFIUS during the review process.[44] Beyond pure formalism, the significance of administrative guidance and moral suasion in such circumstances should not be overlooked. This is perhaps where the future *de facto* power of the Commission under the Regulation is to be found. The Commission's opinion raising security or public order concerns would not bind Member States but would place on them an onus to explain why they are not following the Commission's opinion.[45] This 'soft blocking power' could be used as a strategic tool by the European Commission by modifying the schedule of acquisitions so as to generate a chilling effect for investors having ties with foreign governments and/or opportunities for potential European purchasers.

It also appears that the Commission's soft blocking power would come at little expense as there is an asymmetry of obligations between the loose framework under which the Commission would operate and the detailed obligations of Member States. For instance, there are transparency requirements for the latter but not the former. On the one hand, the Regulation does not specify that the Commission would have the duty to state reasons while issuing an opinion when it comes to project of Union interest. But, on the other hand, it requires the Member States 'to provide an

39. Regulation 2019/452, Art. 3(7).
40. Regulation 2019/452, Art. 6(1).
41. Regulation 2019/452, Arts 7(5) and 9.
42. Regulation 2019/452, Arts 6(3), 7(2) and 8(1).
43. James K. Jackson, The Committee on Foreign Investment in the United States (CFIUS), Congressional Research Service, RL33388, 13 Mar. 2018, p. 7, https://fas.org/sgp/crs/natsec/RL33388.pdf, accessed 25 Apr. 2018.
44. *Ibid*, p. 57.
45. Stephen Adams, Screen Tests: The EU's Proposed New Framework for Foreign Investment, 20 Nov. 2017.

explanation to the Commission in case its opinion is not followed'.[46] Moreover, given that the Commission's opinions would not be legally binding – at least from a formal standpoint – 'member States would ultimately be responsible for the decision to block a foreign investment'.[47]

This has two significant implications. First, from a sole EU law perspective, the soft law dimension of the Commission's intervention implies that its 'opinions' do not 'produce legal effects vis-à-vis third parties' within the meaning of Article 263 TFEU and could not be challenged before the CJEU within the framework of an action for annulment. Second, from an international law perspective, the blocking decision, even though stemming from a Commission's opinion, would be attributable to the Member State. If this decision constitutes a violation of an international investment agreement to which the EU is a party, the Member State concerned shall bear the financial responsibility arising from such a violation.[48] Eventually, the European Commission would be shielded from litigation in relation to its advisory function under the regulation.

§7.06 A FRAGILE AND QUESTIONABLE LEGAL BASIS

The Commission chose to use Article 207 TFEU as the exclusive legal basis of the regulation. It stated in its proposal: 'Foreign direct investment is included in the list of matters falling under the common commercial policy pursuant to Article 207(1) TFEU. In accordance with Article 3(1)(e) TFEU, the European Union has exclusive competence with respect to the common commercial policy. Accordingly, only the Union may legislate and adopt legally binding acts within that area.'[49] This is also mentioned in the preamble of the Regulation.[50]

As pointed out above, this choice is debatable when it comes to areas that touch upon Member States' screening mechanisms codifying EU rules and principles on freedom of movement of capital. More fundamentally, there is somehow a disharmony – not to say a kind of contradiction – between, on the one hand, EU's exclusive competence with respect to FDI as part of the CCP and, on the other hand, the substance of the Regulation dealing with screening FDI on the grounds of security or public order, which have been the responsibility of Member States thus far. The Preamble of the Regulation itself mentions that it is 'without prejudice to sole responsibility of Member States for safeguarding their national security, as provided for in Article 4(2) TEU. It is also without prejudice to the protection of their essential security interests in accordance with Article 346 TFEU'.[51]

46. Regulation 2019/452, Art. 8(2)(c).
47. Lourdes Catrain and Eleni Theodoropoulou, 'EU Overview' (2017) 5 The Foreign Investment Regulation Review 84.
48. Article 3(1)(b) of Regulation 912/2014 establishing a framework for managing financial responsibility linked to investor-to-state dispute settlement tribunals established by international agreements to which the European Union is party, OJEU L 257/121, 28 Mar. 2014.
49. European Commission (n 1) p. 8.
50. Regulation 2019/452, Preamble [6].
51. Regulation 2019/452, Preamble [7].

The recent CJEU's Opinion 2/15 noted that Article 207(1) TFEU 'refers generally' to FDI 'without drawing a distinction according to whether the acts concern the admission or the protection of such investments'.[52] However, the Court did not suggest that the exclusive competence over FDI under Article 207 TFEU affects the right of Member States to take measures which are justified on grounds of public policy or public security under Article 65(1)(b) TFEU.[53]

Moreover, the Court pointed out that a provision in the EU-Singapore FTA recognising the right to apply measures necessary to maintain public order or to public security 'lays down not a commitment but the possibility of applying a derogation,' under which 'a member State will be able, for overriding reasons relating to public order, public security [etc.] to treat Singapore investors less favourably than its own investors'.[54] In a nutshell, Article 207 TFEU does not grant the EU an exclusive competence over matters concerning Member States' public policy or public security concerns when in relation to FDI. It rather implies, in combination with Article 65 TFEU, the possibility of inserting a public order and public security carve-out for Member States in EU international investment agreements.

While Article 207 TFEU is a questionable legal basis, the framework does not seem, at least as it currently stands, to effectively encroach Member State's latitude to regulate public policy or public security concerns. However, in light of the above, a full-fledged FDI screening mechanism that would be operated at the Commission's level could be contrary to EU treaties.[55] This must be kept in mind if the Commission's intent was to adopt a 'foot-in-the-door' strategy by devising a soft cooperation mechanism that would serve as a basis to expand its authority in the future.[56]

§7.07 A MISSED OPPORTUNITY CONCERNING COMPETITIVE NEUTRALITY IN FDI TRANSACTIONS

In light of the foregoing discussion about the fragile legal basis of the Regulation, one may be led to wonder whether Regulation 2019/452 constitutes a missed opportunity to address issues of reciprocity and of the level playing field in FDI, in particular the absence of specific rules dealing with non-EU investments benefiting from subsidised financing or other types of government support.

52. CJEU, Opinion 2/15 (n 27) [87].
53. *See also*, for a different perspective based on previous case law, Ramon Vidal Puig, 'The Scope of the New Exclusive Competence of the European Union with Regard to "Foreign Direct Investment"' (2013) 40 Legal Issues of Economic Integration 133, 157–160.
54. CJEU, Opinion 2/15 (n 27) [101].
55. The Commission also noted that the option 'to propose an FDI screening mechanism entirely operated at EU level [...] could be very difficult to operate [...] due to the fact that national security remains the sole responsibility of Member States' (Commission Staff Working Document Accompanying the Regulation Proposal, COM(2017)487, 2017/0224(COD), https://eur-lex.europa.eu/legal-content/EN/TXT/PDF/?uri=CELEX:52017SC0297&from=LT, accessed 25 Apr. 2018).
56. The UK noted that the proposed regulation 'sets an unhelpful precedent both in relation to security matters and in respect of other areas of Member State competence. Should even a small overstep be accepted in this case, it is possible that this could be taken as a precedent to expand further in future' (UK Department for International Trade (n 18) [22]).

With regards to the scope of the EU and Member States' competence with respect to FDI involving non-EU investors, a distinction may be drawn between two types of 'protective measures'. First, as previously mentioned, protective measures adopted for public policy or public security concerns fall within the scope of Member States' prerogatives.[57] Second, under Article 207(1) TFEU, the EU CCP already explicitly includes, in the field of international trade, 'measures to protect trade such as those to be taken in the event of dumping or subsidies'.[58] By way of analogy, the exclusive competence of the EU on this basis shall also include the safeguard of competitive neutrality in the area of FDI. Henceforth, the EU has exclusive competence to establish a screening mechanism aimed at targeting and sanctioning anti-competitive practices in the context of non-EU inward investment, for instance acquisitions made by subsidised foreign firms, through the support of government agencies, state-owned enterprises or sovereign wealth funds.[59]

The Regulation does not deal comprehensively with the issue of subsidised FDI and seems to treat it more as a political issue than an economic one. The Regulation indeed provides that 'in determining whether a foreign direct investment is likely to affect security or public order, Member States and the Commission may also take into account, in particular … whether the foreign investor is directly or indirectly controlled by the government, including state bodies or armed forces, of a third country, including through ownership structure or significant funding'.[60] The presence of foreign sovereign investment and/or foreign sovereign funding can therefore provide a relevant indication to characterise an underlying foreign policy objective – and potentially a risk relating to public policy or public security for the host State. However, the Regulation does not discipline subsidised financing as an unfair competitive advantage from an economic perspective. While drafting the Regulation Proposal, the Commission ignored the joint request of France, Germany and Italy to address the issue of government subsidies in FDI when such countries stressed that 'due consideration should be given to the extent to which the actual acquisition is funded or co-financed by government-controlled or government-influenced agencies, and the extent to which the investor's bid for the target company clearly exceeds the market price'.[61] Such an initiative would have filled a vacuum, to the extent that it is not possible to challenge such economic distortions within the framework of the WTO Agreement on Subsidies and Countervailing Measures (applicable only to trade in goods) and of State aid rules under the TFEU (applicable only to EU Member States).

Interestingly, the US already envisaged to integrate competitive neutrality concerns in its FDI screening mechanism after China National Offshore Oil Corporation

57. *See also* Emanuel Castellarin, *La participation de l'Union européenne aux institutions économiques internationales* (Pedone 2017) 102.
58. *Ibid.*, 324–327.
59. Gary Hufbauer, Thomas Moll and Luca Rubini, Investment Subsidies for Cross-Border M&A: Trends and Policy Implications, United States Council Foundation Occasional Paper No. 2, April 2008, https://www.uscib.org/docs/usc_foundation_investment_subsidies.pdf, accessed 25 Apr. 2018.
60. Regulation 2019/452, Art. 4(2)(a).
61. European Investment Policy: A Common Approach to Investment Control (n 14).

(CNOOC)'s attempt to purchase Unocal in 2005. CNOOC received privileged funding from state-owned entities and its bid was significantly higher than Chevron's offer (the bid was eventually dropped because of vehement political attacks from the US Congress).[62] This led to a debate as to whether the jurisdiction of CFIUS should be extended. The Treasury was indeed 'considering, non-national security issues related to potential distortions from a larger role of foreign governments in markets'.[63] More recently, the US Congress has discussed possibilities of amending the CFIUS framework to better integrate the issue of subsidised financing.[64] One of the options would be to place 'some form of restriction or penalty on foreign direct investors who receive financing at below-market rates or receive some other form of subsidization directly or indirectly by their home government'.[65]

Undoubtedly, the EU has an exclusive competence to devise such an economic defence mechanism under Article 207 TFEU. This could also serve as a basis for addressing concerns with regards to reciprocity, notably the lack of reciprocal access to the Chinese market for EU companies.[66] It is somehow surprising that the EU chose not to go down that road with a crystal-clear legal basis and to ignore the concerns expressed by certain members of the European Parliament on these issues.[67]

---

62. Ben White, Chinese Drop Bid to Buy US Oil Firm, Washington Post, 3 Aug. 2005.
63. David H. McCormick Testimony Before the House Committee on Financial Services, 3 May 2008, https://www.treasury.gov/press-center/press-releases/Pages/hp861.aspx, accessed 25 Apr. 2018 (adding that 'Through inefficient allocation of capital, perceived unfair competition with private firms, or the pursuit of broader strategic rather than strictly economic return-oriented investments, sovereign wealth funds could potentially distort markets').
64. For instance, the Senate minority leader recently declared that 'Democrats believe that the CFIUS model should extend not just to national security but to economic security. When China attempts to steal our best technology by buying American companies – whether it is robotics, AI, or chips on Qualcomm – we ought to block it. China doesn't play fair' ([2018] 164(44) Congressional Record – Senate, 13 Mar. 2018, S1648).
65. James K. Jackson (n 43) 43–44.
66. Thilo Hanemann and Mikko Huotari, EU-China FDI: Working Towards Reciprocity in Investment Relations, Mercator Institute for China Studies (MERICS), 17 Apr. 2018, https://www.merics.org/en/papers-on-china/reciprocity, accessed 25 Apr. 2018.
67. *See*, for instance, European Parliament, Committee on International Trade, COM(2017)0487 – C8-0309/2017 – 2017/0224(COD), Draft Report by Franck Proust, 12 Apr. 2018, Amendment No. 284 (mentioning *inter alia* the following criteria for screening: 'the presence of significant funding, which may take the form of subsidies, or a political presence in its decision-making centres', 'the investment can reinforce or lead to a monopolistic structure or the control of a value chain', 'access to the sector in the foreign investor's country of origin is open, restricted or banned and there is no reciprocity or a level playing field'); European Parliament, Committee on International Trade, COM(2017)0487 – C8-0309/2017 – 2017/0224(COD), Draft Opinion by Reinhard Bütikofer, 2 Mar. 2018, Amendment No. 208 (mentioning *inter alia* the following criteria for screening: 'The degree of reciprocity in openness to foreign direct investments', 'whether the foreign investor: [...] Receives substantial state aid').

CHAPTER 8

Summary of the Discussion of the Final Panel on the EU's FDI Screening Proposal

Nikos Lavranos

The last panel of this colloquium discussed the EU's FDI screening proposal by way of an interactive debate, rather than on the basis of full-fledged presentations. This summary reflects the main points of the discussion.

The panel consisted of the following panellists.

Prof. Marco Bronckers (Leiden University), Mr Golsong (Goodyear), Ms McNelis (MLex), Mr Hueckmann (FTI consulting), Ms Farouq (US Embassy) and Mr Reshetnyak (Russian Embassy). Accordingly, the panellists discussed the EU's FDI screening proposal from various perspectives (academic, business, media and policy-making).

From the business perspective, Mr Golsong emphasized that the global trading system works best when everybody plays by the rules. There is a need to retain open investment regimes, as this is critical for the future economic and social development of countries. Accordingly, he emphasized the need for a common approach across the EU because differing standards must be avoided; otherwise, forum shopping will take place, which will likely have a negative impact. In that sense, having uniform standards regarding FDI within the EU is preferable compared to the current situation where half of the Member States have some sort of FDI screening mechanisms in place whereas the other half of the Member States does not.

However, Mr Golsong shared the broadly held view among the other panellists, namely, that the proposed Regulation on FDI screening is too broad. In particular, the proposed Regulation needs a clear definition on public order and security, which in turn would create the necessary legal certainty for foreign investors. Indeed, if investments from abroad have an impact on public order and security within the EU, these cases must be clearly and definitely delineated, since uncertainty is likely to create disturbances and tensions. Moreover, he emphasized the importance of focusing more on the protection of IP rights and protection of transfer of know-how, which are of relevance for the protection of EU interests.

Another aspect raising concerns is the difficulty of distinguishing between state-owned/state-controlled FDI and private FDI. In particular, the question arises: what are the precise criteria?

Moving towards the practical implementation of EU FDI screening, Mr Golsong also emphasized that the process of monitoring the FDI screening process is critical, in particular as regards the protection of sensitive commercial information.

Finally, Mr Golsong also highlighted the importance of the WTO and G20 to strive for open markets and secure reciprocity – also for EU investments abroad.

In addition, from a business perspective, Jan Hueckmann presented his views on the proposed EU FDI screening mechanism by sharing FTI's experience with the US FDI screening mechanism CFIUS. In particular, it is worth looking at the CFIUS because it can give us an idea of how the new EU investment screening framework will work in practice.

In this regard, it is noteworthy that CFIUS is set up to ensure confidentiality of the investment being screened on national security grounds.

The recent case of Financial Ants and MoneyGram is instructive. In theory, the process should take maximum two and half to three months. However, the Financial Ants and MoneyGram case took twelve months with multiple delays. The reason was that rivals were seeking to politicize the case by involving law-makers, social media and academics to create political pressure on CFIUS to block the investment. Obviously, this runs counter to the certainty and speed in reaching the decision, which is what businesses prefer and indeed need.

If we then look at the EU screening proposal itself, it is clear that the ambition is rather limited. There is no obligation to set up a screening procedure for Member States and the emphasis seems to be on coordination and information sharing.

However, the EU proposal adds further complexity by adding new stakeholders/participants to the procedure in two instances. First, the European Commission can issue a non-binding opinion on foreign investments that are of 'Union interest'. Second, Member States can ask for information and issue objections if they feel that they are impacted by a particular foreign investment. This means that potentially 29 further – after Brexit 28 – new players can give input and request for more information, creating delays and more controversies. While neither the European Commission nor other Member States have a formal veto power, politically this might be different.

Surprisingly, businesses so far have not woken up to this threat on how they can conduct or receive investments in Europe. Indeed, the interest in the proposal so far has been rather subdued from industry. Essentially, businesses that have formed their opinion on the proposal fall into two camps. The first, more numerous camp, does not like the proposed EU screening framework because it will create further complexity and delays to investments. Some also object to further restraints on how to conduct their business' investments on principle. Others still worry about a possible retaliation from China. The second, smaller camp, sees benefits in the proposal because it will limit unfair competition from state-led economies.

From a journalist's perspective, Natalie McNelis has been following the EU's FDI screening proposal very closely. Indeed, this proposal could be seen as potentially a foot in the door for the EU to take a more supranational role in vetting foreign investments within the EU.

In this context, it is fascinating to see the differences of opinion: the European Commission, who sees its text as a mere framework, the European Parliament, who speaks of it as a long-overdue tool to protect the EU market, and various EU Member States, some who support the initiative and others who vehemently oppose it, seeing it as a power grab by the European Commission and powerful EU Member States.

Prima facie, the draft that the European Commission has put on the table is relatively vague and open ended. Also, it does not impose any hard and fast obligations on the Member States. At the same time, it does not open the door to protectionism by EU Member States either.

But, if one looks at the way the European Parliament speaks of the text, there seems to be a lot more room for protectionism in it. In particular, the MEP Rapporteur Mr Proust speaks of the need to counter unfair competition from foreign investors. He says the EU should check whether foreign trading partners offer reciprocal access to their markets before opening the EU market to them. These points are, however, not included in the draft text.

In contrast, certain small Member States in the Council have reacted quite vociferously to the proposal, saying it will handicap their ability to attract badly needed foreign investments, that it will impose onerous bureaucratic obligations on them, and that it will be a means for the European Commission and other Member States to pressure them in setting their own foreign investment policy.

In many ways, the proposal seems to be mainly useful for EU Member States which are contemplating taking measures to block foreign investments. These Member States will feel reassured that their actions are unlikely to be opposed by the EU or other Member States.

Overall, it is fair to say that the final text will look very different from the current draft proposal.

From an academic perspective, Prof. Bronckers focused mainly on the fact that there have been a lot of concerns in the EU about a lack of reciprocity in the investment relations with China: European investors do not enjoy the same market access in China as the other way around.

However, the European Commission's proposal does not address these concerns, but is solely limited to national security considerations. According to him, the European Commission should address these reciprocity concerns head on. In fact, it is not good enough to hide behind technical arguments that any restrictions on Chinese investments could raise concerns about potential inconsistency with WTO law. The real issue is the reciprocity and not necessarily national security. For this reason, the European Commission should consider focusing in its proposal also on the reciprocity issue.

In sum, it can be concluded that the European Commission's FDI screening proposal is lacking precision and fails to address the real concern of reciprocity with China, i.e., enable better access of European investments into the EU. In this context, the focus on national security is rather artificial and misses the point. Moreover, the experience with the US CFIUS illustrates the risks of politicization and delays, which in the context of the EU and large number of stakeholders might be even greater. Nonetheless, there seems to be political support for an EU FDI screening mechanism in many Member States, in particular large ones, and within the European Parliament. In other words, sooner rather than later, such a mechanism will be endorsed and implemented. In light of that, it is surprising and rather ill-advised that businesses seem not be interested in this topic and thus not actively engage in the debate. After all, it is businesses that need to deal with it. The good news is, there is still time to try and influence the final text of this proposal.

Note: Meanwhile, on 19 March 2019 Regulation (EU) 2019/452 of the European Parliament and of the Council establishing a framework for the screening of foreign direct investments into the Union has been adopted and entered into force, largely unchanged compared to the proposal discussed above.[1]

1. OJ L 79I, 21.3.2019, p. 1–14.

Part IV The WTO Context and the US Experience

CHAPTER 9

The EU Proposal for FDI Control: The WTO on the Sidelines?*

*Justine Fassion & Bregt Natens***

§9.01 INTRODUCTION

The law of the World Trade Organization ('WTO') disciplines how governments regulate *trade*. As modern-day trade is no longer just about moving boxes, trade increasingly became inseparable from foreign direct investment ('FDI').[1] For example, due to lower transport costs and instant communication tools, companies have been able to maximize efficiencies by globalizing their production chains. This, in many circumstances, requires FDI in the country hosting part of the production chain. As a result of such changes to modern-day trade, WTO rules are increasingly relevant to how governments regulate *FDI*.

It is well-established that there is an overlap between trade *rules* and investment *rules*, and several WTO agreements are relevant to FDI. This relevance may be tangential: the Agreement on Subsidies and Countervailing Measures regulates how governments can counteract subsidization of investors, and the Agreement on Trade-Related Aspects of Intellectual Property Rights protects intellectual property rights of foreign investors. That said, the WTO agreements do not purport to provide an integrated set of rules on investment, or cover all aspects of investment. In fact, already

* The views expressed in this chapter are exclusively those of the authors and do not necessarily reflect those of Sidley Austin LLP and its partners. This chapter has been prepared for academic purposes only and does not constitute legal advice. This information is not intended to create, and receipt of it does not constitute, a lawyer-client relationship. Readers should not act upon this without seeking advice from professional advisers. We thank Professor K Van der Borght (Free University of Brussels) for having graciously performed the peer review.

** Asja Serdarevic and Julia Tiskowiec provided research assistance. Any errors or omissions are the authors' own.

1. *See* section 9.03[A] for the working definition of FDI used in this chapter.

in 1996, the WTO set up a working group to further analyse the complex relationship between trade and investment, and trade rules and investment rules.[2]

Other authors have already addressed overlaps, convergence, and parallels between trade rules and investment rules.[3] We seek to contribute to this body of literature by assessing the potential relevance of WTO rules specifically for (inward)[4] *FDI control*.[5] To that end, we first set out the WTO rules disciplining FDI control, before, by way of case study, we apply these rules to the European Union ('EU') proposal for FDI control. We conclude that it is likely that (application of) the EU proposal for FDI control creates WTO-inconsistencies, and that these inconsistencies are not necessarily justifiable under the applicable exceptions.

§9.02 WTO RULES DISCIPLINING FDI CONTROL

Two WTO agreements are particularly relevant from the perspective of disciplining FDI control: (i) the Agreement on Trade-Related Investment Measures ('TRIMs Agreement'), which covers trade in goods and furthers the rules set out in the General Agreement on Tariffs and Trade ('GATT') 1994;[6] and (ii) the General Agreement on Trade in Services ('GATS'). Before setting out the substantive obligations relevant to FDI control in these agreements, it is useful to recall that the GATT 1994 and GATS also contain disciplines on 'good governance', such as procedural fairness, transparency, and reasonable administration.[7]

2. *See* WT/MIN(96)/DEC, 'Singapore Ministerial Declaration', 18 Dec. 1996, para. 20. The work of the working group was carved out of the Doha Round. *See* WT/L/579, 'General Council Decision' 1 Aug. 2004.
3. *See, e.g.*, Nicholas DiMascio and Joost Pauwelyn, 'Non-Discrimination in Trade and Investment Treaties: Worlds Apart or Two Sides of the Same Coin?', *American Journal of International Law* 102:1, 2008; Sungjoon Cho Jürgen and Kurtz, 'Converging Divergences: A Common Law of International Trade and Investment', Chicago-Kent College of Law Research Paper No. 2015-02.
4. On restrictions to outward FDI, *see* Rudolf Adlung, 'Opportunity at a Cost: Confronting Restrictions on FDI Outflows', E15 Initiative Opinion, 2017, available at https://www.ictsd.org/opinion/opportunity-at-a-cost-confronting-restrictions-on-fdi-outflows.
5. *See*, on this topic, also Zhu (Judy) Wang, 'CFIUS under Review: National Security Review in the US and the WTO', *Journal of World Trade* 50:2, 2016. Wang assesses US domestic judicial review of an FDI control measure, and briefly draws a comparison to the security exceptions under WTO law, which we discuss below in section 9.02[D].
6. *See* Panel Report, *India – Solar Cells*, paras 7.74–7.75 and 7.78.
7. *See* Andrew Mitchell, Elizabeth Sheargold and Tania Voon, 'Good Governance in International Economic Law: A Comparative Analysis of Trade and Investment', *Journal of World Investment & Trade* 17:1, 2016; Rudolf Adlung, 'International Rules Governing Foreign Direct Investment in Services: Investment Treaties versus the GATS', *Journal of World Investment and Trade* 17, 2016, pp. 58–61.

[A] Disciplines on Good Governance

WTO rules on good governance are 'conceptually similar to the notion of fair and equitable treatment' typically found in investment rules.[8] From the perspective of FDI control, the requirement of reasonable administration is particularly relevant.

Article X:3(a) of the GATT 1994 and the parallel obligation in Article VI:1 of the GATS[9] require a government to administer all measures of general application (i.e., measures that apply to an unidentified number of economic operators)[10] in a reasonable, objective, and impartial manner – but they are *not* a tool for WTO adjudicators to test the consistency of domestic rulings with domestic regulations.[11] It has been argued that, instead, they should be seen as manifestations of the principles of consistency and predictability.[12]

Thus, when *regulating* FDI control, governments should ensure that the rules permit reasonable, objective, and impartial administration.[13] And when administering the rules on FDI control, governments should ensure they do so in a reasonable, objective, and impartial manner. In other words, these provisions also concern *how* FDI control is administered in practice (much like domestic law provisions on good governance[14]).

[B] Disciplines on Trade in Goods: The TRIMs Agreement

Where FDI concerns investment in companies that sell goods, WTO rules on trade in goods – and in particular the TRIMs Agreement – affect how a government can regulate FDI control.

WTO rules on goods not only protect trade in goods directly but also *indirectly*. As the WTO Appellate Body explained, 'measures that did not directly regulate goods, or the importation of goods, have nonetheless been found to contravene GATT obligations'.[15] The rights of investors were explicitly mentioned as an example of such an indirect measure.[16]

8. *See* Rudolf Adlung, 'Multilateral Investment Disciplines: Don't Forget the GATS', *Columbia FDI Perspectives*, 2014, p. 2.
9. Article VI:1 of the GATS applies only to sectors in which specific commitments have been scheduled. *See* below section 9.02[B].
10. *See* Appellate Body Report, *US – Certain Anti-Dumping Methodologies (China)*, para. 5.130.
11. *See* Panel Report, *US – Stainless Steel*, para. 6.50.
12. Panagiotis Delimatsis, 'Due Process and "Good" Regulation Embedded in the GATS – Disciplining Regulatory Behaviour in Services Through Article VI of the GATS', *Journal of International Economic Law* 10:1, 2007, p. 28.
13. Cf. Appellate Body Report, *EC – Selected Customs Matters*, paras 200–201, where the Appellate Body found that the substance of a measure can be examined under Art. X:3(a) of the GATT 1994 if this substance is alleged to lead to an unreasonable, subjective, or partial administration.
14. *See* Judy Wang, 'Ralls Corp. v. CFIUS: A New Look at Foreign Direct Investments to the US', *Columbia Journal of Transnational Law* 54, 2016, p. 30.
15. *See* Appellate Body Report, *China – Publications and Audiovisual Products*, para. 227.
16. *See* Appellate Body Report, *China – Publications and Audiovisual Products*, para. 227.

The TRIMs Agreement applies to 'investment measures related to trade in goods', or TRIMs.[17] The term Trade-Related Investment Measure ('TRIM') has been interpreted broadly as comprising any measure that has investment objectives and features or refers to investment programmes.[18] The TRIMs Agreement prohibits WTO Members from applying a TRIM that discriminates between domestic goods and like imported goods (Article 2.1 of the TRIMs Agreement and Article III of the GATT 1994); and (ii) constitutes a quantitative restriction on imports (Article 2.1 of the TRIMs Agreement and Article XI of the GATT 1994).[19] The TRIMs Agreement provides an illustrative list of measures that constitute such violations, which contain, for instance, measures imposing local content requirements,[20] and restrictions of access to foreign exchange.[21]

[C] Disciplines on Trade in Services: The GATS

Where FDI concerns investment in companies that provide services, the GATS affects how a government can regulate FDI control.

The GATS has a broad scope of application: in principle, it applies to any measure by a WTO Member that affects the supply of any service.[22] The wide notion of 'services' includes processes with close relationships to goods, such as contract manufacturing. Trade in services is defined by reference to four modes of supplying a service:[23]

(1) Mode 1 or cross-border supply: The service supplier of country A crosses the border to country B to supply a service to the consumer in country B.
(2) Mode 2 or consumption abroad: The consumer in country A crosses the border to country B to consume the service supplied by the service supplier of country A.
(3) Mode 3 or commercial presence: The service is supplied in country A to a consumer in country A through a commercial presence in country A of a service supplier of country B for the purpose of supplying a service.
(4) Mode 4 or temporary presence of natural persons: A natural person of country A temporarily moves to country B to supply services.

---

17. *See* Art. 1 of the TRIMs Agreement.
18. *See*, for an overview of the case law, Panel Report, *India – Solar Cells*, paras 7.59–7.64.
19. These obligations apply without prejudice to other rights and obligations under the GATT 1994. *See* Art. 2.1 of the TRIMs Agreement. For example, governments maintain the right to discriminate in government purchases, subject to the conditions set out in Art. III:8(a) of the GATT 1994. *See* Appellate Body Report, *Canada – Renewable Energy/Feed-In Tariffs*, paras 5.20–5.28.
20. *See* paragraph 1(a) to the Annex to the TRIMs Agreement.
21. *See* paragraph 2(b) to the Annex to the TRIMs Agreement.
22. There are limited exceptions. For example, by virtue of Art. I:3(b)–(c), the GATS does not apply to services supplied in the exercise of governmental authority.
23. *See* Art. I:2 of the GATS.

Mode 3 is of central importance to FDI.[24] Every company that sets up a commercial presence, i.e., any type of business or professional establishment,[25] in another country for the purpose of supplying a service engages in international trade in services. Mode 3 covers greenfield establishments as well as acquisitions, and applies both pre- and post-establishment.[26] This confirms that GATS disciplines apply to 'entities that seek to establish' a commercial presence,[27] or 'across all stages of a commercial project'.[28] The one limitation is that the GATS only applies in case of majority ownership or control but,[29] *would* apply to a measure that prevents an entity from obtaining majority ownership or control.[30] Once there is ownership or control, it is difficult to imagine a Mode 3 service transaction that is not underpinned by FDI.[31] The consequence is that governments regulating FDI control should abide by their obligations under the GATS.

Several GATS disciplines may play a role in the regulation of FDI control, but we focus on the key disciplines concerning non-discrimination and market access.[32] The GATS prohibits discrimination between like services and service suppliers of two exporting countries (Article II). The obligation to accord Most-Favoured Nation ('MFN') treatment is limited only by each WTO Member's list of exemptions.[33] The EU did not schedule relevant exemptions for FDI control.[34] Further, the GATS contains a market access obligation (Article XVI) and an anti-discrimination provision, called national treatment, between domestic and foreign like services and service suppliers (in Article XVII). The market access and national treatment obligations apply *only* to

24. Mode 4 is of relevance insofar as it 'encompasses the investment-related movement of natural persons', and Modes 1 and 2 'have the potential to influence investment behaviour'. *See* Sidonie Descheemaeker, 'Ubiquitous Uncertainty: The Overlap between Trade in Services and Foreign Investment in the GATS and EU RTAs', *Legal Issues of Economic Integration* 43:3, 2016, pp. 272–273 and figures 2 and 3 (emphasis omitted).
25. Article XXVIII(d) of the GATS defines commercial presence as 'any type of business or professional establishment, including through (i) the constitution, acquisition or maintenance of a juridical person, or (ii) the creation or maintenance of a branch or a representative office, within the territory of a member for the purpose of supplying a service'.
26. *See* S/C/W/314, Council for Trade in Services, 'Mode 3 – Commercial Presence: Background Note by the Secretariat', 7 Apr. 2010, para. 9.
27. *See* Panel Report, *China – Publications and Audiovisual Products*, para. 7.974.
28. *See* Rudolf Adlung, 'Multilateral Investment Disciplines: Don't Forget the GATS', *Columbia FDI Perspectives*, 2014, p. 1.
29. *See* Art. XXVIII(n)(i) and (ii) of the GATS.
30. *See* S/C/W/314, Council for Trade in Services, 'Mode 3 – Commercial Presence: Background Note by the Secretariat', 7 Apr. 2010, para. 13.
31. *See*, for the same view, Gaetan Verhoosel, 'The Use of Investor-State Arbitration under Bilateral investment Treaties to Seek Relief for Breaches of WTO Law', *Journal of International Economic Law* 6:2, 2003, pp. 494 and 505; Sidonie Descheemaeker, 'Ubiquitous Uncertainty: The Overlap between Trade in Services and Foreign Investment in the GATS and EU RTAs', *Legal Issues of Economic Integration* 43:3, 2016, p. 271.
32. *See, e.g.*, on GATS disciplines on capital transfers and their interplay with the market access and national treatment obligations, Gabriel Gari, 'GATS Disciplines on Capital Transfers and Short-term Capital Inflows: Time for a Change?', *Journal of International Economic Law* 17, 2014, p. 399.
33. *See* Art. II:2 of the GATS.
34. *See* GATS/EL/31, European Communities and their Member States, 'Final List of Art. II (MFN) Exemptions', 15 Apr. 1994.

the services sectors that the importing Member agreed to by scheduling specific commitments.[35]

The GATS non-discrimination obligations are, in essence, no different from their well-known counterparts in Articles I and III of the GATT 1994. But the GATS market access obligation has an autonomous meaning. In a nutshell, it lists six[36] types of measure which a WTO Member shall not maintain or adopt in sectors where specific commitments are scheduled, unless the schedule contains a relevant limitation. The first four types of measure prohibit quantitative limitations (on the number of service suppliers, transactions or assets, operations or service output, or employment).[37] The fifth type of measure prohibits limitations on the form of establishment and covers, for instance, the requirement for foreign service suppliers to use contractual joint ventures to supply services in the host country.[38] The sixth type of measure, which is obviously related to FDI,[39] prohibits limitations on the participation of foreign capital.[40]

[D] Exceptions Justifying Violations of WTO Rules

Both WTO rules on trade in goods and on trade in services contain exceptions on the basis of which regulators can justify violations of WTO obligations. Most relevant are the general exceptions set out in Article XX of the GATT 1994 (for goods) and Article XIV of the GATS (for services), and the security exceptions found in Articles XXI of the GATT 1994 and XIV *bis* of the GATS. The GATT 1994 exceptions are also available to justify a violation of the TRIMs Agreement.[41]

There are three steps to assessing whether a measure is justified under the general exceptions.

First, the measure must concern one of a closed list of policy grounds that governments may invoke as the reason for violating WTO rules. The list contains, *inter alia*, (i) the protection of public morals or, under the GATS only, to maintain public

35. Articles XVI and XVII of the GATS apply only to measures affecting trade in services: (i) in sectors for which commitments have been undertaken in the WTO Member's Schedule of specific commitments; and (ii) insofar as that Member did not schedule a limitations to the specific commitment. *See* S/C/W/314, Council for Trade in Services, 'Mode 3 - Commercial Presence: Background Note by the Secretariat', 7 Apr. 2010, table 5 for an overview of commitments in selected subsectors and para. 56 for an overview of the types of scheduled limitations. The EU's consolidated list of specific commitments is enshrined in S/C/W/273, European Communities and its Member States, 'Certification: Draft Consolidated GATS Schedule', 9 Oct. 2006.
36. The list is exhaustive. *See, e.g.*, Panel Report, *US – Gambling*, para. 6.264.
37. *See* Appellate Body Report, *US – Gambling*, para. 246.
38. *See* Panel Report, *China – Publications and Audiovisual Products*, para. 7.1356.
39. Eighteen WTO Members' Schedule contain limitations on the participation of foreign capital. *See* S/C/W/314, Council for Trade in Services, 'Mode 3 - Commercial Presence: Background Note by the Secretariat', 7 Apr. 2010, para. 57.
40. *See*, on various interpretations of the scope of this provision, Bart De Meester and Dominic Coppens, 'Mode 3 of the GATS: A Model for Disciplining Measures Affecting Investment Flows?' in Zdenek Drabek and Petros C. Mavroidis (eds), *Regulation of Foreign Investment: Challenges to International Harmonization* (World Scientific 2013), p. 105.
41. *See* Art. 3 of the TRIMs Agreement.

order;[42] (ii) the protection of human, animal, or plant life or health;[43] or (iii) the securing of compliance with domestic laws or regulations that themselves are not inconsistent with WTO rules.[44]

Second, if a measure falls within the ambit of one of the listed policy grounds, the government must establish that the measure has the requisite nexus with the policy ground. For the three example policy grounds, the requisite nexus is that the measure is *necessary*.[45] In a nutshell, a measure is necessary if: (i) it contributes to attaining their policy objective;[46] and (ii) there is no reasonably available alternative measure that would make the same contribution but is less trade restrictive.[47] The WTO adjudicator will also consider the restrictive impact of the measure on trade[48] and the relative importance of the interests or values furthered by the challenged measure.[49] The latter means that a regulator is granted more leeway if the interest or value concerned is 'vital' – the classic example being the protection of human life.[50]

Third, once a measure is deemed necessary to obtain a policy ground set out in the general exceptions, it must still pass the requirements of the so-called chapeau.[51] The purpose of the chapeau is to prevent abuse of the general exceptions by focusing on how the measure is being applied.[52] A measure will fail to satisfy the conditions of the chapeau if it is applied in a manner that: (i) constitutes an arbitrary or unjustifiable discrimination between countries where like conditions prevail; or (ii) is a disguised restriction on trade. These standards are 'broad in scope and reach',[53] and their application is highly factual.

In turn, the security exceptions provide a potentially less stringent framework for justifying certain violations of WTO rules. They provide, in relevant part, that nothing in the relevant WTO rules shall be construed to: (i) require disclosure of information where *a WTO Member considers* such disclosure contrary to its essential security interests;[54] or (ii) prevent a WTO Member from taking any action *it considers necessary* for the protection of its essential security interests.[55] The second ground for exception does require, again in relevant part, that the 'action' is: (a) related to supplying a military establishment; or (b) taken in time of war or other emergency in international

42. *See* Art. XX(a) of the GATT 1994 and Art. XIV(a) of the GATS.
43. *See* Art. XX(b) of the GATT 1994 and Art. XIV(b) of the GATS.
44. *See* Art. XX(d) of the GATT 1994 and Art. XIV(c) of the GATS.
45. *See* Art. XX(a), (b) and (d) of the GATT 1994 and Art. XIV(a)-(c) of the GATS.
46. *See, e.g.*, Appellate Body Report, *US – Gambling*, para. 306.
47. *See, e.g.*, Appellate Body Report, *US – Gambling*, para. 307.
48. *See, e.g.*, Appellate Body Report, *US – Gambling*, para. 306.
49. *See, e.g.*, Appellate Body Report, *US – Gambling*, para. 306.
50. *See, e.g.*, Appellate Body Report, *EC – Asbestos*, para. 172.
51. *See* Art. XX of the GATT 1994 and Art. XIV of the GATS.
52. *See, e.g.*, Appellate Body Report, *US – Gasoline*, p. 22.
53. *See* Appellate Body Report, *US – Shrimp*, para. 120.
54. *See* Art. XXI(a) of the GATT 1994 and Art. XIV *bis* (a) of the GATS.
55. *See* Art. XXI(b) of the GATT 1994 and Art. XIV *bis* (b) of the GATS.

relations.[56] At the time of writing, there is no jurisprudence on the security exceptions, although the issue appears to be live in pending disputes.[57]

§9.03 HOW WTO RULES DISCIPLINE FDI CONTROL IN THE EU LEGAL FRAMEWORK

In principle, the economy of the EU is open to FDI, pursuant to the fundamental principle of free movement of capital between the EU and third countries.[58] However, free movement of capital is not necessarily *unconditional*. Member States might want to ensure that such openness is reciprocal and that an adequate protection of the essential interests of the EU or its Member States is guaranteed.[59] The EU treaties provide for several legal bases to control FDI.

That said, the disinterest of the EU to propose legislation on this point until now left the Member States with discretion to impose their own FDI control regime. As a result, there is a certain level of FDI control in the EU, but this is operated mainly by the Member States. The need for better coordination at the EU level, heightened by the increasing number of foreign takeovers of EU strategic companies,[60] led the European Commission ('Commission') to propose the adoption of common rules for FDI control at the EU level in September 2017.[61]

[A] The EU Legal Framework for FDI Control

Unlike in the United States, where the Committee on Foreign Investment in the United States ('CFIUS') reviews certain FDI with national security implications, the current EU legal framework does not currently provide for a systematic and harmonized FDI control mechanism.[62] That said, the EU treaties empower Member States to impose restrictions on FDI, within certain limits that are set in the case law of the Court of Justice of the EU ('Court'). Of the twenty-eight Member States, almost half currently

56. *See* Art. XXI(b)(ii) and (iii) of the GATT 1994 and Art. XIV *bis* (b)(i) and (iii) of the GATS.
57. *See* European Union's third-party written submission in *Russia – Measures Concerning Traffic in Transit*; United States' responses to questions from the Panel in *Russia – Measures Concerning Traffic in Transit*; Johannes Fahner, 'Qatar under Siege: Chances for an Article XXI Case?', *EJIL Talk*, 9 Jan. 2018, available at https://www.ejiltalk.org/qatar-under-siege-chances-for-an-article-xxi-case/.
58. *See* Art. 63(1) of the Treaty on the Functioning of the European Union ('TFEU').
59. *See* European Commission, *Communication from the Commission to the European Parliament, the European Council, the Council, the European Economic and Social Committee and the Committee of the Regions Welcoming Foreign Direct Investments while Protecting Essential Interests*, COM(2017) 494 final, 13 Sept. 2017, p. 2.
60. *See* 'Brussels Seeks Tighter Vetting of Foreign Takeovers', *Financial Times*, 13 Aug. 2017.
61. European Commission, *Proposal for a regulation of the European Parliament and of the Council establishing a framework for screening of foreign direct investments into the European Union*, COM(2017) 494 final, 13 Sept. 2017 ('Communication of 13 September 2017').
62. *See* Recital 5 to draft regulation 'establishing a framework for screening of foreign direct investments into the European Union' in the Communication of 13 Sept. 2017.

have FDI control legislation in place.[63] The review process, the sectors concerned, the modalities of the judicial review, and the responsible authorities for carrying out FDI control vary considerably between the Member States.[64]

The main objective pursued by FDI control is the protection of public security, which is understood in the EU legal framework as encompassing strategic sectors of the EU economy in various domains: energy, infrastructure, telecommunication, defence, etc. The legal basis for Member States to operate FDI control for national security purposes is found in the provisions on the free movement of capital. Article 63(1) TFEU guarantees that 'all restrictions on the movement of capital between Member States and between Member States and third countries [are] prohibited'.[65] This general principle of free movement of capital is limited by a number of exceptions that permit Member States to control FDI. Among those exceptions, one is a general exception in the EU treaties, which specifically protects the defence/security sector as it relates to the 'protection of the essential interest of [Member States'] security which are connected with the production of or trade in arms, munitions and war material'.[66]

Another important exception is a derogation specific to the free movement of capital.[67] Pursuant to this exception, Member States retain the right to impose restrictions 'on grounds of public policy or public security'.[68] The public security exception has consistently been interpreted narrowly in the case law of the Court. According to the Court, restrictions on FDI imposed by Member States (e.g., an authorization regime) can be justified on grounds of public security to the extent that: (i) there is 'a genuine and sufficiently serious threat to a fundamental interest of society'; (ii) the restrictions do not serve purely economic ends; (iii) the investor affected by the restriction has access to legal redress; and (iv) the restriction is proportionate to the public security/policy objective and the objective cannot be achieved by less restrictive measures.[69]

[B] The European Commission Proposal for FDI Control

After a series of foreign takeovers of EU-based companies in strategic sectors, certain Member States (primarily France, Germany, and Italy) criticized the lack of a harmonized screening mechanism at EU level and called for a better protection of critical EU

63. *See* European Parliament, 'Foreign Direct Investment Screening. A Debate in Light of China-EU FDI flows', *European Parliamentary Research Service Briefing*, May 2017, p. 7.
64. *See* F. Werhlé and J. Pohl, 'Investment Policies Related to National Security: A Survey of Country Practices', *OECD Working Papers on International Investment*, 2016/02, OECD Publishing, pp. 14–15 for a comparison between some Member States (i.e., Austria, Finland, France, Germany, Italy, Lithuania, United Kingdom).
65. *See* Art. 63(1) TFEU.
66. *See* Art. 346(1)(b) TFEU.
67. *See* Art. 65(1)(b) TFEU.
68. *See* Art. 65(1)(b) TFEU.
69. *See, e.g.*, judgments of 14 March 2000, *Association Eglise de Scientologie de Paris v. The Prime Minister*, C-54/99, paras 17–18; of 4 Jun. 2002, *Commission v. France*, C-483/99, para. 48 (and case law cited therein).

businesses.[70] In this context, the Commission put forward a proposal, in the form of a draft regulation, 'establishing a framework for screening of foreign direct investments into the European Union' ('Draft Regulation') on 13 September 2017.[71]

We have explained above that FDI control is left to the discretion of Member States, with nearly half of them operating their own screening, based on national legislation, under which the scope and procedures vary.[72] The Draft Regulation is meant to address the concerns of certain Member States by creating a common framework for Member States and the Commission to screen FDI from third countries that may threaten security or public order.[73] Importantly, the Draft Regulation does not oblige Member States that currently do not have an FDI screening mechanism in place to establish such a mechanism. Yet, the Draft Regulation also does not create an EU-wide FDI control mechanism to vet and block foreign takeovers in strategic sectors of the EU economy based on the model of CFIUS.

The Draft Regulation will establish substantive and procedural rules for FDI screening in EU Member States.

In terms of substantive rules, the Draft Regulation will limit the grounds for reviewing FDI from third countries to 'security or public order'.[74] Although the Draft Regulation contains a non-exhaustive list of factors that may be taken into account when determining whether FDI affects 'security or public order' (e.g., critical infrastructure, critical technologies, security of supply of critical input, the fact that the foreign investor is controlled by the government of a third country, including through significant funding), the term 'security or public order' is not defined.[75] Importantly, when determining whether a particular FDI is likely to affect security or public order, the Member States and the Commission may take into account whether the foreign investor is controlled by the government of a third country, including through significant funding.[76]

In terms of procedural rules, the Draft Regulation will impose an obligation of cooperation and exchange of information between individual Member States and the Commission. The screening mechanisms of the Member States will need to meet certain basic procedural requirements, such as the requirement to provide for clear timeframes to issue decisions and the possibility to seek judicial redress of decisions.[77]

70. *See, e.g.*, the common letter sent by the Finance Ministers of France, Germany and Italy to the EU Trade Commissioner Malmström in February 2017, available at https://www.bmwi.de/Redaktion/DE/Downloads/S-T/schreiben-de-fr-it-an-malmstroem.pdf?__blob = publicationFile &v = 5.
71. Communication of 13 September 2017.
72. *See also* Recital 4 to Draft Regulation.
73. The definition of FDI laid down in the Draft Regulation mirrors the definition provided by AG Sharpston in Opinion 2/15 (*see* Art. 2(1) of Draft Regulation).
74. *See* Art. 3(1) and (2) of Draft Regulation.
75. *See* Art. 4 of Draft Regulation.
76. *See* Art. 4 of Draft Regulation.
77. *See* Art. 6 of Draft Regulation. Some of those basic procedural requirements are derived from the case law of the Court.

[C] The Relevance of WTO Rules for EU FDI Control

As explained above, a number of WTO rules are relevant to the field of FDI control. Any piece of EU legislation on FDI control would have to comply with WTO rules.

We note at the outset that the Draft Regulation of the Commission refers expressly to the EU and Member States' commitments undertaken in the WTO sphere in that respect.[78] More specifically, the Draft Regulation recognizes that:

> [t]he implementation of this Regulation by the Union and the Member States should comply with the relevant requirements for the imposition of restrictive measures based on grounds of security or public order stipulated in EU law, in the Agreement on the European Economic Area (EEA Agreement), in the WTO Agreement (including in particular Article XIV(a) and Article XIV bis of the GATS) and in other trade and investment agreements or arrangements to which the Union or Member States are parties.[79]

This makes clear that it is also the EU's understanding that FDI control likely raises issues with substantive WTO obligations. These issues may concern the Draft Regulation in itself ('as such') or specific instances of application of FDI control on the basis of the Draft Regulation ('as applied'). The legal standard for a finding of an 'as such' violation is that the measure at issue 'restricts, in a material way, the discretion' of the authority to apply the measure in a WTO-consistent manner.[80] Although any assessment of WTO-consistency of a measure is by nature fact-dependent, we see three points in the Draft Regulation that merit further discussion.

The *first* point concerns the question whether the Draft Regulation may give rise to an 'as such' claim under the GATS MFN obligation (or its equivalent for goods in the GATT 1994) because it discriminates between third countries. The EU attempts to preclude this issue in Article 6(1) of the Draft Regulation by providing that 'Member States' screening mechanisms shall ... not discriminate between third countries.' This may make an 'as such' MFN claim more difficult to make. On an 'as applied' basis, MFN claims may be easier to make (for instance, in a case where two investors, from two countries, wish to make the same investment and only one investment is screened).

The *second* point concerns the scope of obligations under the GATS. As explained above, the GATS contains important flexibilities (such as the Schedule of specific commitments) that permitted each WTO Member to modulate the extent of its obligations. This issue is much less poignant for trade in goods, but the factual circumstances in which there may be a violation of goods rules based on the Draft Regulation also seem more narrow.

The *third* point is that it is not obvious that the Draft Regulation contains 'as such' violations of the good governance obligations contained in the GATT 1994 and the GATS. Any such issues are more likely to be found in Member States' domestic rules on

78. *See* Recital 3 to Draft Regulation.
79. *See* Recital 22 to Draft Regulation.
80. Appellate Body Report, *EU – Biodiesel*, para. 6.229.

FDI control (one can think, in certain circumstances, of e.g., requirements to comprehensively translate voluminous documents). On an 'as applied' basis, the good governance obligations may be less relevant, because their scope is limited to measures of general application.

Once – and if – the Draft Regulation, whether 'as such' or 'as applied' is found to violate WTO rules, the question becomes whether the violation can be justified. The Draft Regulation suggests that two exceptions would likely be invoked: the measure is necessary to maintain public order, or the measure falls under the security exceptions.

First, the EU could attempt to justify the measure under the 'public order' exception in Article XIV(a) of the GATS. As noted above, Article XIV(a) concerns 'public morals' and 'public order'. In contrast, Article XX of the GATT 1994 only concerns 'public morals'. It is notable that the Draft Regulation does *not* refer to public morals. It thus seems as if the EU has foreseen a 'public order' exception only for violations of the GATS. If a measure falls within the scope of Article XIV(a) of the GATS, it must also be shown to be 'necessary'.

Second, the Draft Regulation makes it clear that a challenge of a decision on a specific FDI will also be defended under the security exceptions in Articles XXI of the GATT 1994 or XIV *bis* of the GATS. As noted above, there is, to date, no jurisprudence on the security exceptions, but some cases in which the security exception may be invoked are currently being litigated. The positions expressed by WTO Members on the security exception vary from those leaving the entire margin of discretion to the Member invoking such exception, to those acknowledging that WTO adjudicators need to carry out some sort of substantive analysis of the exception.[81]

The EU itself has in the past supported the idea that members could decide for themselves what is 'necessary to protect [their] essential security interests',[82] but more recently also said that '[w]hile GATT provided for security exemptions, the scope of such exemptions was circumscribed by specific situations and conditions'.[83] It is, according to the EU,[84] for the responding WTO Member invoking the security exception to show that these situations are present and these conditions are met.[85] This requires showing four elements.

81. *See, e.g.*, G/C/M/129, WTO Council for Trade in Goods, 'Minutes of the Meeting of 30 June 2017', ss 5 and 16.
82. *See, e.g.*, Roger P. Alford, 'The Self Judging WTO Security Exception', *Scholarly Works*, Paper 330, 2011, p. 714, referring to the position of the European Economic Community in the context of the trade embargo imposed on Nicaragua by the United States in 1985. More recently, the EU suggested that the invoking WTO Member has a 'certain margin of discretion', but not 'unfettered discretion'. *See* European Union's third-party written submission in *Russia – Measures Concerning Traffic in Transit*, paras 28 and 35.
83. *See, e.g.*, G/C/M/129, WTO Council for Trade in Goods, 'Minutes of the Meeting of 30 June 2017', para. 16.7.
84. Other WTO Members have different views. For instance, the United States and Russia seem to suggest that invocation of the security exception is non-justiciable, i.e., cannot be reviewed by a panel or the Appellate Body. *See* United States' responses to questions from the Panel in *Russia – Measures Concerning Traffic in Transit*.
85. *See* European Union's third-party written submission in *Russia – Measures Concerning Traffic in Transit*, para. 24.

First, there is a situation in which the security exception provides justification. This is so, in the EU's view, only for the three situations listed in the provisions, which contain 'objective' and 'verifiable' elements or factual situations: a relationship with fissionable materials and traffic in arms, or the existence of an armed conflict or any other sufficiently grave emergency in international relations.[86]

Second, that situation must threaten the responding Member's 'essential security interests'.[87] Such an interest 'must relate genuinely to "security" and be "essential"', not just protectionist or a minor security interest.[88]

Third, the measure must be 'designed "for" the protection of the relevant essential security interests against that threat'.[89] This requires that the measure 'is "capable" of protecting the relevant essential security interests', based on its 'content, structure and expected operation'.[90]

Fourth, the responding Member considers the measure 'necessary'.[91] The adjudicator should 'review ... whether [the] invoking Member can plausibly consider that the measure is necessary', based on an assessment of: (i) the relative importance of the objective pursued by the measure; (ii) the contribution of the measure to that objective; and (iii) the trade restrictiveness of the measure.[92]

Finally, as an overarching consideration, the EU considers that WTO adjudicators should ensure that the security exception is 'applied in light of the principle of good faith' in light of 'the customary international law principle of *pacta sunt servanda*'.[93]

By the EU's own standard, thus, the security exception may not contain an easy way out to justify violations of WTO rules caused by FDI control. Experience also shows that justifying a measure under the general exceptions is not a straightforward task.

§9.04 CONCLUSION

In this contribution, we examined the relevance of WTO rules for the EU proposal to establish a framework for FDI control – the Draft Regulation. The most relevant WTO rules for FDI control are obligations found in the TRIMs Agreement (for goods) and the

86. *See* European Union's third-party written submission in *Russia – Measures Concerning Traffic in Transit*, paras 40–45.
87. *See* European Union's third-party written submission in *Russia – Measures Concerning Traffic in Transit*, para. 38.
88. *See* European Union's third-party written submission in *Russia – Measures Concerning Traffic in Transit*, para. 50.
89. *See* European Union's third-party written submission in *Russia – Measures Concerning Traffic in Transit*, para. 38.
90. *See* European Union's third-party written submission in *Russia – Measures Concerning Traffic in Transit*, para. 53.
91. *See* European Union's third-party written submission in *Russia – Measures Concerning Traffic in Transit*, para. 56.
92. *See* European Union's third-party written submission in *Russia – Measures Concerning Traffic in Transit*, paras 58 and 62.
93. *See* European Union's third-party written submission in *Russia – Measures Concerning Traffic in Transit*, para. 36.

GATS (for services), as well as the key exceptions that could justify violations of WTO rules.

The Draft Regulation seeks to set up substantive and procedural rules for all Member States to screen FDI on public security grounds. Although the Draft Regulation contains some obligations in terms of screening process or scope, Member States will continue to enjoy a certain margin of discretion in the way they operate their screening mechanisms.

The Draft Regulation may raise issues with certain substantive WTO obligations. These issues may concern the Draft Regulation in itself ('as such') or specific instances of application of FDI control by Member States on the basis of the Draft Regulation ('as applied'). This should not come as a surprise, as the Draft Regulation itself foreshadows the need to justify violations of WTO rules.

However, it is not at all straightforward that the general exceptions and the security exception (by the EU's own standard) will be an easy-to-reach safe haven for the Draft Regulation or any instance of application.

CHAPTER 10
CFIUS Overview

James Mendenhall & Riana Terney[*]

This chapter provides a summary of the current laws and procedures governing the Committee on Foreign Investment in the United States ('CFIUS'), as well as the new CFIUS reform legislation, known as the Foreign Investment Risk Review Modernization Act of 2018 (FIRRMA), which at the time of this writing has not been fully implemented. Section 10.01 concerns the scope of CFIUS legal authority, participating agencies, and jurisdiction. Section 10.02 explains the different types CFIUS filings. Section 10.03 summarizes the required contents of a CFIUS notice or declaration. Section 10.04 explains the timeframes for CFIUS reviews and investigations. Section 10.05 lists the criteria CFIUS considers in evaluating a transaction. Section 10.06 highlights possible outcomes of a CFIUS review or investigation. Section 10.07 discusses the (very limited) extent of judicial review of CFIUS determinations.

As at the time of this writing, the US Treasury Department has not yet issued implementing regulations for FIRRMA. Therefore, unless stated otherwise, the descriptions below are based on the regulations in force prior to the implementation of FIRRMA.

§10.01 SCOPE

[A] CFIUS Legal Authority

CFIUS is an interagency committee chaired by the Secretary of the Treasury, which has authority to assess the national security implications of transactions that could result in

* We thank Professor D Prevost (University of Maastricht) for having graciously performed the peer review.

control of a US business by a foreign person.[1] When there is credible evidence that the foreign person might take action that threatens to impair US national security, and when no other provision of law (other than the International Emergency Economic Powers Act) provides suitable authority to protect national security, the President is authorized to suspend or prohibit the transaction. CFIUS may require mitigation (such as a modification of the transaction or a limitation on the governance rights of the investor) as a condition for clearing a transaction.

[B] Participating Agencies

The Secretary of the Treasury chairs CFIUS. Other CFIUS members are the respective heads of eight major government agencies.[2] Five offices within the Executive Office of the President participate in CFIUS as observers.[3] The Director of National Intelligence (DNI) and the Secretary of Labor are non-voting, ex officio members of CFIUS. CFIUS decisions are generally taken by consensus. DNI's primary role is to provide CFIUS with an analysis of any threat to the national security of the US posed by any covered transaction, taking into account the views of all affected or appropriate agencies of the intelligence community with respect to the transaction.

[C] Scope of CFIUS Jurisdiction

[1] Scope of CFIUS Jurisdiction Prior to the Adoption of FIRRMA

CFIUS has jurisdiction over transactions in all sectors, regardless of size. However, prior to the adoption of FIRRMA, CFIUS only had jurisdiction over transactions 'by or with a foreign person, which could result in control of a U.S. business by a foreign person' (31 C.F.R. § 800.601). CFIUS continues to have jurisdiction over such transactions post-FIRRMA, but as will be explained in the section 10.02, FIRRMA expands the scope of CFIUS jurisdiction to certain non-control transaction.

A 'foreign person' means '[a]ny foreign national, foreign government, or foreign entity; or ... [a]ny entity over which control is exercised or exercisable by a foreign national, foreign government, or foreign entity' (31 C.F.R. § 800.216).

1. CFIUS' basic authority arises under s. 721 of the Defense Production Act, codified at 50 U.S.C. § 4565 (also referred to as the Exon-Florio Amendment). CFIUS regulations are codified at 31 C.F.R. Part 800. The Congress amended the statute in 2007 with the Foreign Investment and National Security Act (FINSA). Congress amended the statute again in 2018 with the passage of FIRRMA. As at the time of this writing, Treasury has not issued regulations fully implementing FIRRMA, but it has adopted regulations to implement a 'pilot programme' under FIRRMA. *See* 31 C.F.R. Part 801.
2. The heads of the following departments and offices are members of CFIUS: Department of the Treasury, Department of Justice, Department of Homeland Security, Department of Commerce, Department of Defense, Department of State, Department of Energy, Office of the US Trade Representative, and the Office of Science and Technology Policy.
3. These offices are the Office of Management and Budget, Council of Economic Advisors, National Security Council, National Economic Council, and Homeland Security Council.

'US business' means 'any entity, irrespective of the nationality of the persons that control it, engaged in interstate commerce in the United States, but only to the extent of its activities in interstate commerce' (31 C.F.R. § 800.226). A US business would include the assets of a company that can function as a business.

'Control' means 'the power, direct or indirect, whether or not exercised, through the ownership of a majority or a dominant minority of the total outstanding voting interest in an entity ... or other means, to determine, direct, or decide important matters affecting an entity' (31 C.F.R. § 800.204(a)). Control is interpreted broadly. CFIUS regulations list the following ten examples of such matters:

(1) The sale, lease, mortgage, pledge, or other transfer of any of the tangible or intangible principal assets of the entity, whether or not in the ordinary course of business.
(2) The reorganization, merger, or dissolution of the entity.
(3) The closing, relocation, or substantial alteration of the production, operational or research and development facilities of the entity.
(4) Major expenditures or investments, issuances of equity or debt, or dividend payments by the entity, or approval of the operating budget of the entity.
(5) The selection of new business lines or ventures that the entity will pursue.
(6) The entry into, termination, or non-fulfilment by the entity of significant contracts.
(7) The policies or procedures of the entity governing the treatment of non-public technical, financial, or other proprietary information of the entity.
(8) The appointment or dismissal of officers or senior managers.
(9) The appointment or dismissal of employees with access to sensitive technology or classified US Government information.
(10) The amendment of the Articles of Incorporation, constituent agreement, or other organizational documents of the entity with respect to the matters described in paragraphs (a)(l)–(9) of this section.

31 C.F.R. § 800.204(a). The regulations also include a list of minority shareholder protections (such as the ability to prevent share dilution) that generally would not be deemed to confer control.

Under current regulations, CFIUS does not have jurisdiction over greenfield investments or acquisitions of 10% or less of the voting equity of the target business that are solely for the purpose of a passive investment. An acquisition is solely for the purpose of a passive investment 'if the person holding or acquiring such interests does not plan or intend to exercise control, does not possess or develop any purpose other than passive investment, and does not take any action inconsistent with holding or acquiring such interests solely for the purpose of passive investment' (31 C.F.R. § 800.223). The safe harbour for passive investments of 10% or less of the voting equity of a US business is difficult to apply in practice, as it is not always clear what sort of rights or economic arrangements would render an investment non-passive.

CFIUS will implement FIRRMA through new regulations. As at the time of this writing, CFIUS has not yet issued even draft implementing regulations. It is possible that CFIUS will revise the regulatory definition of control, including, e.g., the scope of minority shareholder protections that are deemed not to confer to control, the definition of greenfield investments and the safe harbour.

[2] Scope of CFIUS Jurisdiction after the Adoption and Implementation of the FIRRMA

Expanded Bases of Jurisdiction

As noted, under FIRRMA, CFIUS will continue to have jurisdiction to review transactions that result in control of a US business by a foreign person. In addition, FIRRMA expands the scope of CFIUS jurisdiction to certain categories of investments that do not involve the acquisition of control over a US business.
The expanded categories of CFIUS jurisdiction include:

- Real Estate: The purchase, lease, or concession of real estate located in the United States that is part of a port, is in close proximity to a sensitive military/government installation, provides the ability to collect intelligence at such installation, or poses a risk of foreign surveillance.
- 'Other Investments' in sensitive US businesses: 'Other investment' in a US critical infrastructure or critical technology business or a US business that maintains sensitive personal information of US citizens that can be exploited in a manner that threatens national security.
- Evasion: Transactions designed to evade or circumvent CFIUS jurisdiction. (It should be noted, however, that even under the pre-FIRRMA rules, CFIUS could assert jurisdiction over '[a]ny transaction or other device entered into or employed for the purpose of avoiding section 721 ... ' (31 C.F.R. § 800.104)).

FIRRMA contemplates that certain categories of investors will be exempt from the application of the real estate and 'other investment' bases of jurisdiction. CFIUS will identify such exempt investors based on, e.g., 'how a foreign person is connected to a foreign country or foreign government, and whether the connection may affect the national security of the United States' (50 U.S.C. § 4565(a)(4)(E)).

'Other Investment'

Of these the new categories of covered transactions, the 'other investment' category is likely to be the most significant, and it is also one of the more complicated bases of jurisdiction to apply. The 'other investment' category covers a direct or indirect investment by a foreign person in a US business that:

(1) owns, operates, manufactures, supplies, or services critical infrastructure;
(2) produces, designs, tests, manufactures, fabricates, or develops one or more critical technologies; or

(3) maintains or collects sensitive personal data of US citizens that may be exploited in a manner that threatens national security;

and the investment affords the foreign person any one or more of the following rights:

(1) access to any material non-public technical information in possession of the US business;
(2) membership or observer rights on the board of directors or equivalent body or the right to nominate such an individual (special rules apply to LP investments in funds); or
(3) any involvement, other than through voting shares, in substantive decision-making of the business regarding:
   - the use, development, acquisition, safekeeping, or release of sensitive personal data of US citizens maintained or collected by the sensitive US businesses;
   - the use, development, acquisition, or release of critical technologies; or
   - the management, operation, manufacture, or supply of critical infrastructure.

FIRRMA defines critical technology to include essentially *any* technology on an export control list, primarily the US Munitions List (USML) (sensitive military items) or the Commerce Control List (CCL) (commercial, dual-use and less sensitive military items); certain nuclear and nuclear-related facilities, equipment and materials; select agents and toxins; and a new category of 'emerging and foundational technologies' that will be subject to export controls. New export control reform legislation, the 'Export Control Reform Act of 2018' (ECRA), sets out interagency process to identify 'emerging and foundational technologies'. The Department of Commerce has begun the process for identifying emerging and foundational technologies, but, at the time of this writing, has not yet issued draft regulations.

New regulations should provide additional guidance on the scope of critical infrastructure and sensitive personal information.

[D] FIRRMA Pilot Programme

On 11 October 2018, the US Treasury Department published interim regulations that established a pilot programme to address specific risks to US critical technologies.[4] At the time of this writing, the pilot programme remains in effect.

The pilot programme expands the scope of transactions subject to review by CFIUS to include certain non-controlling investments made by foreign persons in US businesses involved in critical technologies related to any one of the twenty-seven

4. Determinations and Temporary Provisions Pertaining to a Pilot Program to Review Certain Transactions Involving Foreign Persons and Critical Technologies, 31 C.F.R. Part 801, 83 Fed. Reg. 51322 (11 Oct. 2018).

specific industries. It also requires parties to file a mandatory declaration for all transactions that fall within the scope of the pilot programme.

In order to fall within the scope of the pilot programme, all of the following criteria must be met:

(1) The transaction closed on or after 10 November 2018. However, the pilot programme does not apply to transactions for which, prior to 11 October 2018: (i) there is an executed binding written agreement; (ii) a party has made a public offer to shareholders to buy shares; or (iii) a party has solicited proxies in connection with a board election.
(2) The US business produces, designs, tests, manufactures, fabricates, or develops 'critical technology' that is either utilized in one or more 'pilot programme industries' or designed specifically for use in one or more pilot programme industries. 'Critical technology' includes certain agents and toxins, as well as certain technologies that are subject to US export controls.
(3) The transaction results in control over the US business or affords the foreign investor any of the following rights: (a) access to material non-public technical information; (b) board or board observer rights; or (c) any involvement in substantive decision-making – other than voting shares – regarding the use, development, acquisition, or release of critical technology.

The pilot programme includes exceptions for investment funds contemplated under FIRRMA. The safe harbour described above for passive investments of 10% or less of the voting equity of a US business does not apply in the context of the pilot programme.

For transactions covered by the pilot programme, mandatory declarations must be submitted to CFIUS by 10 November 2018, or promptly thereafter if the transaction completion date is between 10 November 2018 and 25 December 2018, or forty-five days before the transaction completion date, if the completion date is after 25 December 2018.

§10.02 NOTICES AND DECLARATIONS

In most cases, CFIUS filings are voluntary; however, in the absence of such voluntary notice, CFIUS may initiate review of a transaction by an 'agency notice'.

Although CFIUS notices are voluntary, parties may decide to file because: (a) the transaction is in a sector about which they know CFIUS is concerned; (b) they want to mitigate political fallout; and/or (c) they seek legal certainty – once CFIUS approves a deal, CFIUS cannot come back later to revisit the issue.

Within three years after a transaction has closed, any CFIUS agency may request CFIUS review of a transaction for which no voluntary notice was filed by filing an agency notice to the Committee. After three years, only the Deputy Secretary of the Treasury Department may request such review. CFIUS has the authority to order divestment or take other action, as discussed in section 10.06.

In addition, FIRRMA contemplates an abbreviated filing process that would allow parties to submit a 'declaration' in lieu of a notice, and obtain a decision in a shorter timeframe. Most declarations will be voluntary, but some will be mandatory.

FIRRMA provides for mandatory declarations (or notices) for covered transactions that result in the acquisition of a 'substantial interest' in a US. business involved in critical infrastructure, critical technology, or sensitive data by a foreign person in which a foreign government has, directly or indirectly, a 'substantial interest'. CFIUS will define 'substantial interest' in implementing regulations, and, in doing so, shall consider the means by which a foreign government could influence the actions of a foreign person. Investments that do not involve the kinds of rights that would result in an 'other investment' or an interest that is < 10% voting interest is not a substantial interest. FIRRMA also allows CFIUS to require (as it did in the pilot programme) mandatory declarations (or, if the investor's so chooses, a notice in lieu of a declaration) for investments that involve a US business that produces, designs, tests, manufactures, fabricates, or develops one or more critical technologies.

At the time of this writing, CFIUS has not yet implemented the declaration process for investments that are not within the scope of the pilot programme.

§10.03 CONTENTS OF NOTICE OR DECLARATION

A formal notice to CFIUS must include detailed information on the transaction, the transaction parties, and the US business that is the subject of the transaction. The necessary information includes, among other things: transaction documents (e.g., the joint venture agreement, share purchase agreement, or asset purchase agreement), 'personal identifier information' ('PII') for directors and executives of the foreign person (e.g., passport and visa information), and organizational charts for the foreign person and the US business post-transaction. Collecting some of this information, in particular the PII, can be burdensome and time-consuming. CFIUS may request additional information during the course of a review or investigation.

FIRRMA authorizes CFIUS to charge a filing fee for every notice. The fee may be no higher than the lower of 1% of the value of the transaction or USD 300,000, adjusted annually for inflation.

A declaration should be no longer than five pages. The declaration would identify the foreign person and US business, explain the interest and rights being acquired, describe the critical technology developed by the US business, list the US business' government contracts, etc. CFIUS has provided a template for a declaration on its website.[5]

5. *See* https://home.treasury.gov/system/files/206/Declaration-Submission-Form-for-Critical-Technology-Pilot-Program_0.pdf.

§10.04 TIMING

[A] Processing of Declarations

FIRRMA contemplates that CFIUS will make a decision on a declaration within thirty days. At the end of that time, CFIUS may: (a) clear the transaction; (b) request a formal notice; (c) determine that it cannot complete the review on the basis of the declaration (in which case, the parties must independently decide whether to submit a notice); or (d) initiate a unilateral review.

[B] Processing of Notices

Table 10.01 below is a simplified timeline of the preparation and processing of a CFIUS notice. The timeframes, other than those defined in the statute, are estimates. At any point during the process, CFIUS may request that the parties withdraw the notice in order to restart the timeline and provide CFIUS more time to review the transaction. As indicated in the timeline, the process begins by preparing and providing CFIUS with draft notice. Currently, there is no statutory timeline for CFIUS to provide comments on the draft notice. When implemented, FIRRMA will require that CFIUS provide comments within ten days, if the parties stipulate that the transaction is a covered transaction:

Event	*Time*
Prepare and submit draft notice	1–2 months (approx.)
Respond to questions from CFIUS, at the end of which time a formal notice is submitted	1 week–3 months (approx.)
CFIUS ensures notice is complete and initiates a formal review	1–6 weeks (approx.)
Formal review	45 days
Formal investigation (if necessary)	45 days
Review by the President (if necessary)	15 days

CFIUS may approve the transaction during the forty-five-day review. However, if CFIUS believes it needs more time, it may initiate an investigation, which must be completed within the next forty-five days. CFIUS will initiate an investigation if any national security concerns have not been mitigated. In addition, there is a rebuttable presumption that CFIUS will conduct an investigation if the acquirer is foreign government-controlled, or if the transaction concerns 'critical infrastructure' and there are unmitigated national security concerns. The presumption can be rebutted if the CFIUS Chair and any assigned 'lead agency' determine that the transaction does not threaten the national security (31 C.F.R. § 800.502(c)).

If CFIUS has not cleared a transaction at the end of the investigation period, CFIUS must refer the transaction to the President for decision with its recommendations. In such cases, the President must announce a decision within fifteen days of CFIUS completing the investigation. If CFIUS informally advises the parties that it will not approve a transaction, and satisfactory mitigation measures cannot be agreed, the parties customarily withdraw their application before the matter is submitted to the President.

Parties to a transaction may ask to withdraw their notice at any time during a review or investigation. Such a request must be approved by CFIUS, and CFIUS's approval may be contingent upon the parties' agreement to update CFIUS on the status of the transaction or refile in the event they proceed with the transaction (presumably in a modified form). CFIUS sometimes requests a withdrawal to allow more time for the negotiation of a mitigation agreement or for changes in the transaction to address CFIUS concerns.

Once (1) CFIUS determines that a notified transaction is not 'covered,' or (2) CFIUS or the President determines that a transaction does not present national security risks (or that risks have been mitigated), CFIUS cannot reopen a review and investigation of the transaction. However, if a transaction subsequently materially changes in a way that implicates national security, or if a party fails to comply with a mitigation agreement, CFIUS may intervene, potentially seeking modification or rescission of the transaction.

§10.05 CRITERIA

In reviewing a covered transaction, CFIUS evaluates all relevant national security considerations and the particular facts and circumstances of a transaction in order to determine whether the transaction will pose a national security risk. Among the factors that CFIUS takes into account are the following, listed in section 721(f) of the Defense Production Act of 1950:

(1) domestic production needed for projected national defence requirements;
(2) the capability and capacity of domestic industries to meet national defence requirements, including the availability of human resources, products, technology, materials, and other supplies and services;
(3) the control of domestic industries and commercial activities by foreign citizens as it affects the capability and capacity of the United States to meet the requirements of national security;
(4) the potential effects of the proposed or pending transaction on sales of military goods, equipment, or technology to certain countries;
(5) the potential effects of the proposed or pending transaction on US international technological leadership in areas affecting US national security;
(6) the potential national security-related effects on US critical infrastructure, including major energy assets;
(7) the potential national security-related effects on US' critical technologies;

(8) whether the covered transaction is a foreign-government-controlled transaction;
(9) as appropriate,
   (a) the adherence of the subject country to non-proliferation control regimes;
   (b) the relationship of the subject country with the US, specifically its record on cooperating in counter-terrorism efforts;
   (c) the potential for transshipment or diversion of technologies with military applications;
(10) the long-term projection of US' requirements for sources of energy and other critical resources and material; and
(11) such other factors as the President or the Committee may determine to be appropriate, generally or in connection with a specific review or investigation.

In its annual report to Congress, CFIUS also lists factors it has considered in recent national security reviews. In its most recent report, for CY 2015, CFIUS listed the following factors that have given rise to concerns:[6]

(1) Foreign control of US businesses that:
   - Provide products and services to an agency or agencies of the US government, or state and local authorities that have functions that are relevant to national security.
   - Provide products or services that could expose national security vulnerabilities, including potential cyber security concerns, or create vulnerability to sabotage or espionage. This includes consideration of whether the covered transaction will increase the risk of exploitation of the particular US business' position in the supply chain.
   - Have operations, or produce or supply products or services, the security of which may have implications for US national security, such as businesses that involve infrastructure that may constitute critical infrastructure; businesses that involve various aspects of energy production, including extraction, generation, transmission, and distribution; businesses that affect the national transportation system; and businesses that could significantly and directly affect the US financial system.
   - Have access to classified information or sensitive government or government contract information, including information about employees.
   - Are in the defence, security, and national security-related law enforcement sectors.
   - Are involved in activities related to weapons and munitions manufacturing, aerospace, satellite, and radar systems.

6. *See* Unclassified CFIUS Annual Report (report period CY 2015) 23–24.

- Produce certain types of advanced technologies that may be useful in defending or in seeking to impair US national security, which may include businesses engaged in the design and production of equipment or components that have both commercial and military applications. Such transactions have included, for example, businesses engaged in the design, production, or provision of goods and services involving network and data security. They have also included businesses that produce semiconductor manufacturing equipment, design integrated circuits, and fabricate integrated circuits, in light of the fact that semiconductors are an enabling technology for a range of national security critical devices, systems, and functions. They have also included businesses that are in the biotechnology sector, given the potential military applications of such technology and the sensitivity of the information such companies may collect.
- Engage in the research and development, production, or sale of technology, goods, software, or services that are subject to US export controls.
- Are in a field with significant national security implications in which there are few alternative suppliers or in which a loss in US technological competitiveness would be detrimental to national security.
- Have operations or facilities that are in proximity to military or other sensitive US government facilities.
- Hold substantial pools of potentially sensitive data about US persons and businesses that have national security importance. Such businesses could be in any number of sectors, including, for example, the insurance sectors, health services, and technology services.

(2) Acquisition of control by foreign persons that:
- Are controlled by a foreign government.
- Are from a country with a record of non-proliferation and other national security-related matters that raise concerns.
- Have historical records of taking or intentions to take actions that could impair US national security.
- Have a history of doing business in sanctioned countries.

§10.06 MITIGATION AND OTHER POTENTIAL OUTCOMES

As the CFIUS filing process is a voluntary process, there are no sanctions for failure to file. However, as noted above, CFIUS can initiate review of a covered transaction *sua sponte*, and the consequences of review can be significant, particularly where a transaction has already been completed. Once CFIUS is seized of jurisdiction, CFIUS has the authority to block a transaction (if not yet completed), order divestment (if completed), or order mitigation measures. Mitigation measures CFIUS has previously negotiated and adopted have included:[7]

- Ensuring that only authorized persons have access to certain technology; that only authorized persons have access to US government, company, or customer information, and that the foreign acquirer not have direct or remote access to systems that hold such information.
- Establishing a Corporate Security Committee and other mechanisms to ensure compliance with all required actions, including the appointment of a US government-approved security officer or member of the board of directors and requirements for security policies, annual reports, and independent audits.
- Establishing guidelines and terms for handling existing or future US government contracts, US government customer information, and other sensitive information.
- Ensuring that only US citizens handle certain products and services, and ensuring that certain activities and products are located only in the US.
- Notifying security officers or relevant US government parties in advance of foreign national visits to the US business for approval.
- Security protocols to ensure the integrity of goods or software sold to the US government.
- Notifying customers regarding the change of ownership.
- Assurances of continuity of supply for defined periods, and notification and consultation prior to taking certain business decisions, with certain rights in the event that the company decides to exit a business line. Established meetings to discuss business plans that might affect US government supply or national security considerations.
- Exclusion of certain sensitive assets from the transaction.
- Providing the US government with the right to review certain business decisions and object if they raise national security concerns.

§10.07 JUDICIAL REVIEW

The substance of a CFIUS determination is not subject to judicial review.[8] However, the Circuit Court of the District of Columbia ('D.C. Circuit') held in the landmark case, *Ralls Corp v. Committee on Foreign Investment in the United States*, No. 13-5315 (D.C. Cir. 15 July 2014), that CFIUS determinations are nevertheless subject to review on constitutional procedural grounds to safeguard due process.

In the *Ralls* case, Ralls Corporation ('Ralls'), a US entity owned by two Chinese nationals, had entered into a series of transactions to acquire property leases for wind

7. *See* Unclassified CFIUS Annual Report (report period CY 2015) 21–22.
8. *See* s. 721(e) of the Defense Production Act of 1950, as amended ('Actions and Findings Nonreviewable.---The actions of the President under paragraph (1) of subsection (d) and the findings of the President under paragraph (4) of subsection (d) shall not be subject to judicial review').

farm sites located under and in close proximity to restricted airspace used by the US Navy for training purposes. Ralls did not file a voluntary CFIUS notice prior to completing these transactions. After closing, CFIUS informed Ralls that it would initiate a review if Ralls did not file a CFIUS notice, after which point Ralls filed a notice. In the course of the thirty-day review and forty-five-day investigation period, CFIUS determined that Ralls' acquisition was a national security risk and ordered interim mitigation measures. The matter was then referred to the President, who concluded that the transaction threatened the national security of the US and ordered Ralls to divest, in addition to imposing other restrictions relating to the access and use of the sites in question.

Ralls challenged CFIUS' decision and the President's order on constitutional due process grounds, among others. Ralls argued that CFIUS had not informed Ralls of the evidence it relied upon in determining that the transaction posed a national security threat, nor, Ralls argued, had CFIUS given Ralls an opportunity to rebut the evidence in question.

The District Court for the District of Columbia dismissed Ralls' claims, but the D.C. Circuit reversed, finding that Ralls had a vested, constitutionally protected property right. The D.C. Circuit concluded that Ralls had a right to review the unclassified evidence that informed the government's decision and to have an opportunity to rebut that evidence, before the government took any action. In other words, the court found that, in order to pass constitutional muster: (1) before taking official action, the government must provide the parties with unclassified evidence on which the President relies; and (2) the parties must have the opportunity to rebut this evidence. Notably, this decision does not affect the substance of CFIUS determinations (as CFIUS determinations are not subject to substantive review), only the process by which the determination is made.

Two consequences of the *Ralls* decision are worth noting. First, as a practical matter, if CFIUS decides that it cannot clear an investment, it will provide a detailed letter listing the factors playing into its decision. Second, CFIUS will generally inform parties that they can refile and request CFIUS review again. This means that parties are more likely to file repeatedly for the same transaction.

§10.08 CONCLUSION

The law and practice pertaining to CFIUS proceedings is changing rapidly. The scope of CFIUS jurisdiction is expanding, and the scrutiny CFIUS will give to sensitive transactions is likely to increase. As at the time of this writing, it is too early to know whether the recent CFIUS reforms will curtail investment or require longer timeframes for closing transactions. Investors from all countries will need to keep a close eye of future developments.

Part V The EU Regulation as Adopted

CHAPTER 11

The Adoption of the Regulation Establishing a Framework for Screening of Foreign Direct Investments into the European Union

*Anders Neergaard**

§11.01 INTRODUCTION

On 20 November 2018, the European Parliament and the Council of the European Union reached political agreement on the Commission Proposal for a Regulation establishing a framework for screening of foreign direct investment into the European Union (EU).[1] After some further technical and legal-linguistic fine-tuning, the agreement was endorsed by COREPER on 5 December 2018 and by the Committee on International Trade on 10 December 2018. The European Parliament subsequently adopted its resolution on 14 February 2019, and the Council adopted the Regulation formally on 5 March 2019.[2]

The legal basis for the Regulation is Article 207(1) TFEU, the legal basis for the Common Commercial Policy (CCP). Since the entry into force of the Treaty of Lisbon, this provision also covers uniform principles on foreign direct investment. In terms of procedure, Article 207(2) TFEU provides that the European Parliament and the Council shall adopt regulations in accordance with the ordinary legislative procedure.

---

* Any opinions expressed in this chapter are strictly personal and do not necessarily reflect a position of the Legal Service. I thank Dr M. Chamon (lecturer at the University of Maastricht) for having graciously performed the peer review.

1. European Commission, Proposal for a regulation establishing a framework for screening of foreign direct investment into the European Union (COM(2017) 0487, 2017/0224 (COD)) (hereinafter: Commission Proposal).
2. To be published in the Official Journal on 21 Mar. 2019.

As the title indicates, the present chapter aims at providing a first overview of the provisions of the Regulation as well as some succinct comments on the legal issues raised in the process of its adoption. Contentious aspects were notably the scope and the screening factors that Member States authorities were supposed to take into account when examining foreign investments in their territory.

[A] Background and Context

The Regulation will establish an optional framework for screening by the Member States of foreign direct investment (FDI) into their territories on the grounds of security and public order. Although it is in the form of a regulation, the act does not introduce any EU-wide compulsory legal framework. Member States remain free to decide whether to establish or maintain such a system or not. This optional nature should be seen against the background of the sensitivity of issues concerning security and public order in the Member States, as well as the divergences in the positions of Member States on the need for this type of mechanism.

Actually, the situation sought to be addressed by the Regulation poses a dilemma. On the one hand, foreign investment is a major source of growth.[3] On the other hand, there have been some 'concerns about foreign investors, notably state-owned enterprises, taking over European companies with key technologies for strategic reasons' and 'EU investors often do not enjoy the same rights to invest in the country from which the investment originates'.[4] The Proposal should thus respond to a need to protect the legitimate interests of the EU and its Member States against investments detrimental to them.[5] Nevertheless, reaching this objective may prove challenging. While many of the Member States have systems for screening of foreign investments, others do not.[6] It may well be that different Member States see the issue from quite different perspectives.[7] It should also be noted that investments may also be 'screened' for other reasons than the ones of security and public order, in particular in the context of merger control and of prudential assessments in the financial sector.

Investment screening may also raise questions in relation to trade and WTO law, to the freedom of capital movements and the freedom of establishment as well as to a number of Union policies. In its Proposal, the Commission outlines these issues and finds that the proposal is consistent with the policies concerned. While it is not possible to provide a complete analysis of the relationship to such other fields of law, some brief comments are provided in section 11.06 below.

---

3. According to the Commission Proposal, explanatory memorandum, p. 2.
4. Commission Proposal, explanatory memorandum, p. 2; European Commission, Reflection Paper 'Harnessing Globalisation', COM(2017) 240, 10 May 2017.
5. Commission Proposal, explanatory memorandum, p. 2.
6. According to the Communication from the Commission to the European Parliament, the European Council, the Council, the European Economic and Social Committee and the Committee of regions '*Welcoming Foreign Direct Investment while Protecting Essential Interests*' (COM(2017) 494), p. 7, Austria, Denmark, Germany, Finland, France, Latvia, Lithuania, Italy, Poland, Portugal, Spain and the United Kingdom have in place mechanisms for screening FDIs.
7. *See* Elvire Fabry and Jacopo Maria D'Andria, *The Challenges of Chinese Investment Control in Europe*, Notre Europe, Jacques Delors Institute.

[B] The Regulation

Addressing first the question why there should be a framework for the screening of FDI into the EU, the Regulation refers in the Preamble to the positive effect of FDI on growth and states that the Union and the Member States have an open investment environment. Following an amendment of the European Parliament, the Regulation recalls in Recital 2 that in accordance with Article 3(5) TEU, the EU shall, in its relations with the wider world, uphold and promote its values and interests and contribute to the protection of its citizens. The Preamble then points out that the commitments taken in the context of the WTO allow restrictive measures in the area of FDI on the grounds of security or public order.[8] Moreover, several Member States have put in place measures according to which they may restrict capital movements on such grounds.[9] The Regulation continues by recalling that there is no comprehensive EU framework for the screening of FDI, while the major trading partners of EU have developed such frameworks (Recitals 1-5). Furthermore, the framework should provide the Commission and the Member States with the means to address risks to security and public order (Recital 8).

§11.02 OBJECTIVES, SCOPE AND OPTIONAL NATURE

[A] Objectives and Scope

Against this background, the Regulation establishes a framework for screening FDI into the EU by the Member States and for a cooperation mechanism between them and the Commission with regard to the FDI likely to affect security or public order (Article 1). Furthermore, the Regulation is without prejudice to the Member States' sole responsibility for the maintenance of national security as provided for in Article 4(2) TEU and the right to protect their essential security interests under Article 346 TFEU. It is also explicitly specified that the Regulation does not limit the right of each Member State to decide whether to screen a particular foreign investment or not.

Clearly, it was important for the Council to explicitly state that the Regulation does not apply to portfolio investment. While Recital 9 states that a broad range of investments should be covered, following an amendment in Council, it now also affirms that portfolio investment is not covered. Strictly speaking this is already clear from the fact that the Regulation covers only FDI (as mentioned in the title and in the provisions of the Regulation), as portfolio investment does not fall under that category. This limitation is in turn the logical consequence of the fact that the legal basis, Article 207 TFEU, only covers FDIs.[10] It should also be noted that the Regulation concerns FDI into the Union and not investment flows between the Member States.

8. Under which circumstances WTO may become relevant is discussed in section 11.06, 'Legal Basis and Compatibility with Other Fields of Law', [C] Trade Law.
9. Such measures would still have to comply with Art. 65(1) TFEU.
10. *See below* under section 11.06, 'Legal Basis and Compatibility with Other Fields of Law'.

On the issue of the scope, one may notice that the Parliament had suggested a number of amendments to the definitions, notably regarding the definition of FDI. The Parliament proposed that investments into its exclusive economic zone declared pursuant to the United Nations Conventions on the Law of the Sea (UNCLOS) and the continental shelf also be explicitly covered, and wanted to specify that the control of an investor over an investment could be either direct or indirect. These amendments were however not accepted in the end.[11] At the same time, the Council suggested certain modifications of the scope and of the definitions that were ultimately taken on board, though it does not seem that this led to any radical changes overall.[12]

In respect of the objective and scope of the Regulation, it should finally be underlined that it contains no provisions about the consequences of screening of an FDI. It is thus left entirely to the Member States to define what kind of measures they will adopt if they find that there is an issue affecting security or public order.

[B] Optional Nature

There was no disagreement between the Institutions that the instrument should be optional for the Member States. These will thus be able to decide whether to have a screening procedure or not. Nevertheless, the Council insisted on making it absolutely clear that there is no obligation for Member States to have a screening mechanism and that national security is the responsibility of the Member States because of the sensibility of these issues in the Member States (amendments to Article 1 and to Recitals 3, 4, 7, 8 and 17).

Article 3 thus makes clear that Member States may maintain, amend or adopt mechanisms to screen FDIs in their territory on grounds of security or public order but no provision obliges them to do so. However, if the Member States do maintain or establish such a mechanism, this mechanism must comply with the provisions of the Regulation. The rules and procedures shall notably be transparent and not discriminatory between third countries. Member States shall set out circumstances triggering screening, grounds for screening and the detailed procedural rules. Timeframes must be defined, and the mechanism shall allow the taking into account of other Member States' comments and of the Commission's opinion. Confidential information must be protected and foreign investors concerned must have the possibility to seek recourse against screening decisions.

Member States that have a screening mechanism shall also ensure that there is a mechanism for identifying and preventing circumvention of the mechanism and screening decisions (Article 3(6)). The prevention of circumvention was of particular importance to the Parliament, emphasised mainly in the light of the use of shell

11. The scope thus covers 'foreign direct investments into the Union', and the specific situation of the exclusive economic zone where third countries may have certain rights is not touched.
12. *See* Art. 1 'Subject matter and scope', in particular the reference to a cooperation mechanism and paras 2 and 3, and Art. 2 'Definitions', in which the terms 'assess, investigate, authorise, condition, prohibit or unwind' and the definition of 'foreign direct investment undergoing screening' were added on the initiative of Council.

companies to avoid legal or tax obligations. This provision must nevertheless be read in the light of Article 1(3), which states explicitly that nothing in the Regulation shall limit the right of each Member State to decide whether or not to screen a particular foreign investment. In other words, it is not only the decision whether to have a mechanism or not that is left entirely to the Member States, but also the decision to make use of it in any specific case.

Most of the conditions laid down in the Regulation are formulated in very general terms and leave a wide margin of discretion to the Member States. In other words, the options available may not be limited simply to the question of whether to have a mechanism or not but also to how such a mechanism should be designed more precisely. It may indeed be consistent with the optional nature of the framework to avoid too much detail.

It follows from these multilayer options that even if the aim was to address the fact that the Union does not have a framework for investment screening, the Regulation does not strictly speaking ensure that FDIs are actually screened. One may therefore wonder what the purpose of introducing the framework actually was. In this regard, Recital 7 underlines the need to provide legal certainty. Following amendments in the Council and Parliament, it is now clear that this legal certainty is for the Member State screening mechanisms. After amendments in Council, the limitations of the Union power are once again recalled by stating that the common framework is without prejudice to the sole responsibility of the Member States for safeguarding national security as provided for in Article 4(2) TEU and to the protection of essential security interests in accordance with Article 346 TFEU (Article 1(2)).

§11.03 SCREENING FACTORS

Article 4 lists a number of factors that the Member States and the Commission may, *inter alia*, consider when deciding whether an FDI is likely to affect security or public order. It follows from the Preamble that the list of factors that may be taken into consideration when determining whether an FDI is likely to affect security or public order is intended to guide Member States and the Commission as well as to provide transparency to investors.

The three Institutions all agreed that the list of the factors to be taken into consideration when deciding whether to screen an investment should be non-exhaustive (Recital 11). Notwithstanding this, their definition was a particularly sensitive subject during the negotiations between the Institutions. The Parliament wanted a longer and more detailed list, the Council a slightly shorter and less detailed one, and the Commission had proposed a list with even less detail. The Parliament had also sharpened the language by suggesting two sets of conditions. For one set of factors, Parliament proposed that the Member States 'may' take them into account, while for another, Parliament suggested replacing 'may' in the operative sentence in Article 4 with 'shall'. In that sense, those factors would have been compulsory.

Of the factors finally retained, one may note the effects on critical infrastructure, critical technologies, supply of critical inputs, access to sensitive information and the freedom and pluralism of the media (Article 4(1)). Furthermore, the Member States and the Commission may under Article 4(2) also take into account whether the foreign investor is controlled by the government of a third country, whether the investor has already been involved in activities affecting security or public order, whether there is a serious risk that the investor engages in illegal or criminal activities.

Following an amendment in the Parliament, Recital 11 states that Member States should be able to assess risks to security or public order arising from significant changes in the ownership structure or key characteristics of a foreign investor. The Parliament had also proposed that this should be a factor mentioned in Article 4, but this was not accepted.

Following from more far-reaching amendments in the Parliament, Recitals 13 and 14 add further elements to the screening. Recital 13 states that the Member States and the Commission should be able to take into account the context and circumstances of the FDI, in particular, whether it is controlled or funded by a third country pursuing state-led outward projects or programmes. Member States might according to Recital 14 consider information from economic operators, civil society organisations and social partners. The Parliament had also wanted to include a number of risks of a different nature, such as risks to intellectual property rights, to human rights and core ILO standards as well as aspects of reciprocity (Article 3(2a) and Recital 12a), but this was not accepted.

Taking into account the non-exhaustive nature of the list of screening factors, it may be of particular interest to notice also the statements in the Preamble. Strictly speaking, the factors mentioned in the provisions may be taken into account but Member States are not obliged to do so. The same goes for screening factors mentioned only in the recitals. Moreover, factors not mentioned could also be taken into account. The absence of a certain factor or circumstance in the provisions simply means that these aspects are not regulated. Member States are thus not prevented by the absence of such provisions from actually providing these possibilities. Nevertheless, the mention of a factor may have the effect of inciting that it is taken into account. Even if the Preamble should provide a statement of reasons for the provisions or stating their context, rather than complementing them, the difference in effect between a non-exhaustive list of factors in an article that may be taken into account and a recital mentioning the factor, is not obvious. Whether a factor is mentioned or not does not seem to be determining for the question whether the screening and the measures it lead to are justified in relation to the security exceptions provided for in Article XXI GATT and in Article XIV (a) GATS (*see* under section 11.06).

It may be noted that the amendments of the Parliament seem to be a part of a wider ambition of the Parliament to bring civil society and social partners into the political debate, as well as to promote human rights, sustainable development and adherence to ILO conventions.[13] The screening factors are further commented on below in section 11.06 on the compatibility with international and Union laws.

---

13. *See, for instance*, Regulation (EU) 2017/2321 amending Regulation (EU) 2016/1036 on protection against dumped imports from countries not members of the European Union and Regulation

§11.04 MECHANISM FOR COOPERATION

[A] Cooperation Between Member States

The Regulation provides, in Articles 6 and 7, for a mechanism for cooperation between Member States. Article 6 lays down the procedure where an investment is undergoing screening and Article 7 where this is not the case. This distinction, proposed by Council, seeks to provide a greater nuance compared to the Commission Proposal, so procedures are differentiated not on the basis of whether the Member State in question formally has a screening mechanism, but on the basis of whether a screening procedure is actually initiated.

Under Article 6(1), the Member States are required to notify the Commission and the other Member States of any FDI in their territory undergoing screening as soon as possible. The notification may include a list of Member States whose security or public interest is deemed likely to be affected. The information to be notified is specified in Article 9(2).

A Member State that considers that its security and public order are affected can, by using this mechanism, provide comments to the Member State where the investment is undergoing screening (Article 6(2)). This is also the case where a Member State considers that an investment planned or completed in another Member State that is not undergoing screening could have such an effect (Article 7(1)). The Commission may provide an opinion on the investment (Article 6(3) and Article 7(2). The Regulation stipulates that comments and opinions shall be duly justified (Article 6(5), Article 7(4)). They are addressed to the Member State where the screening takes place or, as appropriate, the Member State where the investment is planned or has been completed (Article 6(7) and Article 7(6)). In view of providing these comments and opinions, the Commission and the other Member States may also request additional information under Article 6(6) when the investment is undergoing screening but also under Article 7(5) when it is not undergoing screening. Possibilities for requesting and providing information between the Member States, and between them and the Commission, as well as a possibility to request opinions and comments where a Member State considers that its security interests are concerned have also been envisaged (Article 6(4) and Article 7(3)). A Member State receiving comments from another Member State or an opinion from the Commission should give them due consideration. Both cases, where an investment is undergoing screening and where this is not the case, Article 6(6)–(8) and Article 7(6)–(8), provide a set of tight deadlines for comments and opinions. The possibility to comment and give an opinion on investments not undergoing screening is limited to fifteen months after the completion of the investment (Article 7(8)).

The cooperation mechanism only applies to investments completed after the entry into force of the Regulation (Article 7(9), Recital 18).

(EU) 2016/1037 on protection against subsidised imports from countries not members of the European Union (OJ L338 of 19 Dec. 2017, p. 1).

The Regulation specifies that the Commission opinions in the cooperation mechanism are adopted in accordance with Article 288 TFEU. Thereby, it becomes clear (if there was any doubt about this) that they are non-binding (Recital 16). As the purpose of the cooperation mechanism is to protect security or public order, the measures taken in this framework are limited to this purpose, which is why the Preamble once again underlines that the final decision on the screening of the investment remains the sole responsibility of the Member State where the investment is planned or completed (Recital 17). The reason for the deadlines set would seem be the wish to provide legal certainty to investors (*see* Recital 21) but may also serve the purpose of efficiency.

[B] Commission Opinion on Investment Affecting Projects and Programmes of the Union

Under the Regulation, the Commission is given the possibility of providing an opinion on investments affecting projects and programmes of the Union. In this context, the Member States should 'take utmost account' of this opinion (Article 8, Recital 19). The procedures set out in Articles 6 and 7 apply *mutatis mutandis*. Nevertheless, a Member State may also indicate whether it considers that an FDI is likely to affect projects and programmes of Union interest. Therefore, the comments and opinions are sent to the other Member States (and not only the Member State screening it or where the investment is to take place). Furthermore, the Member State where the investment is planned or has been completed shall take utmost account of the Commission's opinion according to Article 8(2). The Parliament had suggested adding an obligation to take utmost account of the comments and opinions that an investment affected the security or public order of another Member State, if supported by one-third of the Member States. However, this was not taken up in the Regulation.

The scope of Article 8 are those programmes of Union interest which involve a substantial amount or a significant share of EU funding or which are covered by Union legislation regarding critical infrastructure, critical technologies or critical inputs, but only the ones that are specified in the annex (Article 8(3)). The annex accordingly lists eight projects or programmes of Union Interest.[14] The list in the annex is to be updated by the Commission through the delegated act procedure (Article 8(4), Recital 20).

An important difference between the Commission Proposal and the adopted act, on the one hand, and the position of the European Parliament, on the other, was that in the latter's view, the list of programmes would have been non-exhaustive, meaning that the Commission could have provided opinions on investments affecting a wider range of programmes.

14. The Annex lists the Regulation (EU) N° 1285/2013 on the European GNSS programmes (Galileo & EGNOS); Regulation (EU) N° 377/2014 on Copernicus; Regulation (EU) N° 1291/2013 Horizon 2020; Regulation (EU) N° 1315/2013 on Trans-European Networks for Transport (TEN-T); Regulation (EU) N° 347/2013 on Trans-European Networks for Energy (TEN-E); Regulation (EU) N° 283/2014 on Trans-European Networks for Telecommunications; Regulation (EU) 2018/1092 on the European Defence Industrial Development programme; and Council Decision of 6 Mar. 2018 establishing the list of projects to be developed under PESCO.

[C] Information Requirements

Article 9 specifies the information that is to be included in the notification under Article 6(1) or requested by the Commission and the other Member States pursuant to Article 6(6) or Article 7(5). This obligation covers, according to Article 9(2), the ownership structure of the investor and of the undertaking which the investment concerns, the approximate value of the investment, the products, services and business operations of the investor and the undertaking which the investment concerns, the Member States in which the investor and the undertaking which the investment concerns conduct relevant business operations, the funding of the investment and its source and the date of the investment. Nevertheless, Member States must provide additional information if available.

Article 9(4) is of a different nature. It provides that the Member State where the investment is planned or has been completed may request the foreign investor or the undertaking concerned by the investment to provide the information required under Article 9(2). The investor is obliged to provide the information without delay. If a Member State is unable to obtain the information, it shall according to Article 9(5) notify the Commission and the other Member States concerned. It shall duly justify the reasons for not providing the information and explain the best efforts undertaken to obtain it including a request pursuant to Article 9(4).

It should be noticed that Article 9(4) is formulated as if it was a power conferred on the Member State concerned. However, it would appear that this power is not created by this provision but is part of the Member States' competence to maintain security and public order. It could also be discussed what relation this provision has with national rules that might restrict or set conditions for such a procedural step. The obligation to provide the information is also different to most of the provisions of the regulation in that it imposes an obligation directly on the investor. These specificities do not seem problematic and Article 9(4) and (5) provide clarity as to the how the Member States can cope with issues related to the legal and practical difficulties that may be involved in getting the relevant information.

[D] Contact Points

A provision of great practical importance would seem to be Article 11, under which each Member State and the Commission shall appoint a contact point for the implementation of the Regulation. The Commission shall provide a secure and encrypted system to support direct cooperation and exchange of information between the contact points (Article 11, Recitals 26 and 27). This obligation applies to all Member States.

[E] Confidentiality

Under Article 10, information received under the application of the Regulation shall be used only for the purpose for which it was requested. Member States and the Commission shall ensure the protection of confidential information acquired in application of the Regulation and that it is not downgraded or declassified without the consent of the originator.

Taking up the language proposed by Council, Recital 30 specifies that Member States and the Commission should protect confidential information in compliance in particular with Commission decision (EU, Euratom) 2015/443 on security in the Commission, Commission decision (EU, Euratom) 2015/444 on the security rules for protecting EU classified information and the Agreement between the Member States of the EU, meeting within the Council, regarding the protection of classified information exchanged in the interests of the EU. The Commission decisions referred to were adopted on the basis of Article 249 TFEU, which allows the Commission to adopt its rules of procedure.

It may be noticed that the limitation of the use of the information to the purpose for which it was received would seem to exclude that the competent authorities pass it on to fiscal authorities or even police authorities in case it might indicate fiscal fraud or other types of criminal activity. It could be discussed, however, whether there are not some limitations to this restriction, for instance, where security and public order are concerned. While there may be an interest in underlining the need to ensure the respect for confidentiality and refer to relevant acts as a context of the legislative act, it should be noticed that the Commission decisions referred to in Recital 30 concern only the internal organisation of the Commission and belong to the responsibility and competence of the Commission. It is also for this institution to decide on any modification of them.

[F] International Cooperation

On the initiative of the Parliament, a provision on cooperation with third countries was introduced in Article 13. Strictly speaking, this cooperation concerns the authorities of third countries and the Commission and the Member States 'may' cooperate with such authorities. Parliament had suggested 'shall cooperate', but this was not accepted. Recital 29, based on an amendment in the Parliament, encourages cooperation with authorities of like-minded third countries and adds that the Commission should be able to monitor such cooperation.

§11.05 POLITICAL CONTROL

[A] Annual Reporting by the Member States

By 31 March every year, the Member States shall, according to Article 5(1), provide the Commission with an annual report, covering the preceding year, including aggregated information on FDI that took place in their territory and aggregated information on the requests received from other Member States pursuant to Articles 6(6) and 7(5). The report is to be based on information available to the Member State. Member States maintaining a screening mechanism shall in addition provide aggregated information on the application of their screening mechanisms.

The obligation to provide information applies to all Member States, including those that do not have a screening mechanism, although the Member States that have such a mechanism have an additional information obligation. It may seem obvious that a Member State will have to base its report on the information available to it. Presumably, the inclusion of this limitation should be seen against the background that the level of information available in Member States may vary, in particular depending on whether the Member State has a screening mechanism or not and the position that Member States should not be required to seek further information to comply with their reporting obligation.

[B] Annual Reporting by the Commission and Parliament Scrutiny

Under Article 5(3), the Commission shall provide an annual report on the implementation of the Regulation to the European Parliament and the Council, which shall be made public. In the Preamble, it is reminded that the Commission should draw up this report with due respect for the confidential nature of certain information included in the reports from the Member States. Nevertheless, the Commission's report shall be made public (Recital 32). The Parliament has, on the other hand, been given the possibility to invite the Commission to ad hoc meetings to its responsible committee to explain systemic issues related to the implementation of the Regulation (Article 5(4), Recital 33). Finally, in connection with the text of the Regulation, the Commission also agreed to make a statement that it would share with the Parliament the standardised forms that it will prepare for the Member States to follow in order to comply with the annual reporting obligations.

The special role for the Parliament in this context constitutes an interesting step forward in the political control by the European Parliament, even if similar mechanisms exist in the economic policy coordination field (introduced through the so-called six-pack and two-pack legislation).[15] It should nevertheless be underlined that the Parliament's invitation shall concern 'systemic issues' only, which is in line with the

15. Provisions on an economic dialogue have been introduced in:

- Art. 2-ab of Regulation No. 1466/97 on the strengthening of the surveillance of budgetary positions and the surveillance and coordination of economic policies (as modified by Regulation No. 1175/2011) (OJ L 306, 23 Nov. 2011, pp. 12–24);
- Art. 2a of Regulation (EC) No. 1467/97 on speeding up and clarifying the implementation of the excessive deficit procedure (as amended by Regulation No 1177/2011 of 8 Nov. 2011) (OJ L 306, 23 Nov. 2011, pp. 33–40);
- Art. 3 of Regulation (EU) No. 1173/2011 on the effective enforcement of budgetary surveillance in the euro area, (OJ L 306, 23 Nov. 2011, pp. 1–7);
- Art. 6 of Regulation (EU) No. 1174/2011 on enforcement measures to correct excessive macroeconomic imbalances in the Euro area (OJ L 306, 23 Nov. 2011, pp. 8–11);
- Art. 14 of Regulation (EU) No. 1176/2011 on the prevention and correction of macroeconomic imbalances (OJ 306, 23 Nov. 2011, pp. 25–32);
- Art. 15 of Regulation (EU) No. 473/2013 on common provisions for monitoring and assessing draft budgetary plans and ensuring the correction of excessive deficit of the Member States in the Euro area (OJ L 140, 27 May 2013, p. 1);
- Art. 18 of Regulation (EU) No. 472/2013 allows Parliament to invite the Council and the Commission into a dialogue on the application of the regulation.

institutional supervisory role of the European Parliament. The ad hoc meetings are therefore not meant to be a mechanism for interfering in individual cases. Indeed, the question of how far the mechanism could go in practice was the subject matter of significant debate during the negotiations.

The obligation for the Commission to maintain confidentiality in its annual reporting to the European Parliament may be an indication of the sensitivity of the subject matter of the Regulation. As Member States are only obliged to provide aggregated information, one could expect that the need for confidentiality would be less stringent. Confidentiality might certainly also apply in the context of the ad hoc meetings in the responsible committee in Parliament. Nevertheless, it should be noted that the Parliament has established its own mechanisms for maintaining confidentiality in special interinstitutional agreements with the Commission and Council.[16] Therefore, it cannot be excluded that the Parliament could have access to confidential information under the proposed mechanism, although such information must be limited to systemic issues.

[C] Delegated Acts

In Article 8(4), power is delegated to the Commission to amend the list of projects and programmes of Union interest. This list is essential for determining the applicability of the Commission screening mechanism. Article 16 lays down the applicable procedure and provides for an indeterminate duration of the delegation, for the possibility for the Parliament and Council to revoke the mandate as well as for objecting to the delegated acts and thereby preventing it from entering into force (*see also* Recital 20).

It should be recalled that a power delegated under Article 290 TFEU must not allow any modifications of the essential elements of a legislative act. The power conferred in Article 8(4) on the Commission allows a modification which affects the scope of the Regulation, as it alters the list of projects and programmes to which the screening by the Commission under Article 8 applies. However, this can hardly be seen as an effect on any essential element of the Regulation, because the choice of which type of projects and programmes should be covered is already defined in Article 8(3). This power does not allow the adoption of political choices within the meaning of the case law of the Court.[17] It may also be noted that the drafting follows the standard formula agreed in the 'Common Understanding' of the Interinstitutional Agreement

16. Framework agreement on the relations between the European Parliament and the European Commission (OJ L304 of 20 Nov. 2010, p. 47), Interinstitutional agreement Between EP and Council concerning the forwarding to and handling by EP of classified information held by Council and matters other than those in the area of CFSP (OJ C 95, of 1 Apr. 2014, p. 1) and Interinstitutional agreement of 20 Nov. 2002 between the European Parliament and the Council concerning access by the European Parliament to sensitive information of the Council in the field of security and defence policy (OJ C 298, of 30 Nov. 2002, p. 1). *See also* the Rules of Procedure of the European Parliament, notably Rule 210a.
17. *See, for instance,* Case C-363/14, Parliament *v.* Council, ECLI:EU:C:2015:579, notably paragraphs 46ff; Case C-427/12, Commission *v.* Parliament and Council, ECLI:EU:C:2014:170, notably paras 43–51; Case C-355/10, Parliament *v.* Council, ECLI:EU:C:2012:516, paras 64–66.

between the European Parliament, the Council and the Commission on Better Law-Making.[18]

[D] Expert Group

A Commission expert group on the screening of FDIs into the EU composed of representatives of the Member States shall support the development and implementation of comprehensive and effective policies (Article 12, Recital 28). The Commission shall consider seeking advice of the group on systemic issues relating to the implementation of the Regulation.

The establishment of the expert group was subject to extensive discussions during the negotiations, because the Parliament insisted on a 'coordination group' that would discuss open issues of investment protection. As a solution, it was agreed to refer to an existing expert group established by a Commission decision, and it follows from Recital 28 that it is this group that will also be involved in view of the adoption of delegated acts under Article 16(4). While the group may be consulted on the implementation of the regulation, there are no specific implementing powers conferred on the Commission which are subject to the procedures laid down in Regulation 182/2011 under Article 291 TFEU.

[E] Review Clause

Under Article 15, the Commission shall three years after the beginning of the application of the Regulation and thereafter every five years evaluate its functioning and present a report to the European Parliament and the Council. Member States shall be involved and if necessary provide the Commission with information. The report may be accompanied with legislative proposals (*see also* Recital 26).

§11.06 LEGAL BASIS AND COMPATIBILITY WITH OTHER FIELDS OF LAW

[A] Legal Basis

The Regulation is based on Article 207(1) TFEU.

In *Opinion 2/15* of 16 May 2017, the Court of Justice found that the use of the words 'FDI' in Article 207(1) TFEU is an unequivocal expression of the intention of the Member States not to include 'other foreign investment' (non-direct or portfolio investment) in the CCP (paragraph 83). Moreover, the Opinion also makes clear that the admission of investments falls within the scope of Article 207(1) TFEU (paragraphs 85 and 86). As the Proposal is limited in terms of subject matter to the admission of FDI,

18. Interinstitutional Agreement between the European Parliament, the Council of the European Union and the European Commission of 13 Apr. 2016 on Better Law-Making (OJ L 123 of 12 May 2016).

Article 207(1) TFEU is in principle the correct legal basis. It is certainly true that the Member State competence for security and public order was a very important element in the design of the Regulation, notably its optional nature. However, the fact that Member States may be competent to decide on such issues does not contradict the fact that provisions relating to the control of investments may be directly related to trade and thus fall under the legal basis of Article 207 TFEU. In any case, as the aim and content of the Regulation have been designed, there is no reason for doubting that Article 207 TFEU is the correct legal basis.[19]

[B] Compatibility with Other Fields of Law

As a general remark, it must be underlined that the requirements under the Regulation are of a general nature and leave a margin of discretion to the Member States in their implementation. This may be a consequence both of the divergence of approaches between the Member States and the sensitivity of the issue of security and public order, as illustrated both in Article 346 TFEU and in the multiple references to this provision in the Regulation. The absence of provisions regarding the decisions to be taken if an issue of security or public order were identified should also be understood in this light. This general nature, the margin of discretion left to the Member States and the absence of provisions on the consequences of the screening also seem to make it less likely that the provisions of the Regulation could be considered as requiring anything that would enter into conflict with other provisions of international or Union laws.

[C] Trade Law

As regards trade law, Recital 3 of the Regulation refers to the commitments taken in the World Trade Organisation, in the Organisation for Economic Cooperation and Development and in trade and investment agreements. According to the Recital, these commitments do not prevent the EU and the Member States from adopting restrictive measures to FDI on the grounds of security or public order, subject to certain requirements. It is specified in the recital that the Regulation concerns inward FDI and not outward investment.[20] At the other end of the Preamble, Recital 35 states that the implementation of the Regulation by the Union and the Member States:

> should comply with the relevant requirements for the imposition of restrictive measures on grounds of security and public order in the WTO Agreements (including in particular Article XIV (a) and Article XIV bis of the GATS). It should also comply with EU law and be consistent with the commitments made under other trade and investment agreements and arrangements to which the Union or Member States are adherents or parties.

---

19. It could perhaps be discussed whether Art. 64(2) TFEU could have provided the legal basis for this Regulation. Art. 64(2) also applies to direct investment but it applies '*without* prejudice to the other chapters of the Treaties'. *See also* comment under footnote 11.
20. It does thus not concern potential export restrictions which could be prohibited under Art. XI GATT.

Article XIV(a) GATS provides that:

> subject to the requirement that such measures are not applied in a manner which would constitute arbitrary or unjustifiable discrimination between countries where like conditions prevail, or a disguised restriction on trade in services, nothing in the agreement shall be construed to prevent the adoption or enforcement by any Member of measures: (a) necessary to protect public morals or to maintain public order ... .

According to a footnote: 'The public order exception may be invoked only where a genuine and sufficiently serious threat is posed to one of the fundamental interests of society.' Article XIV*bis* makes clear that GATS does not require Members to provide information that they consider contrary to their essential security interests. Furthermore, it provides that GATS does not prevent certain actions relating to the supply of services for military purposes, fissionable or fusionable materials or measures taken in time of war or other emergencies in international relations.

As the recitals indicate, it is in particular in the context of the implementation of the Regulation that the issue of WTO compatibility could come up. It is worth noting that the provisions quoted in Recital 35 refer to exceptions. As it follows from the footnote in Article XIV GATS, the exception for public order appears to be rather restrictive. Nevertheless, before an exception becomes relevant, it is necessary to find that the Regulation or its implementation could be incompatible with one of the commitments under GATS. It may be noted in this connection that the exceptions in Article XIV are similar, albeit not identical, to the exceptions in Article 346 TFEU.

As a hypothesis, it could be considered that the screening of FDI and the measures that would be taken on the basis of that screening would concern an investment to be made in the context of the establishment in the Member State and thus concern trade in services within the meaning of Article I GATS. This could give rise to questions of compatibility with Article II GATS on the Most-Favoured-Nation Treatment, Article XVI on Market Access and Article XVII on national treatment. It would seem that in particular the application of the screening factors identified in Article 4 of the Regulation could be of interest in this respect. Nevertheless, given the general nature of the provisions of Article 4, it still seems highly unlikely that those provisions could enter into conflict with any of the provisions of the GATS. The absence of a provision on what consequences there should be after screening is completed does not exclude the possibility of a restrictive effect in conflict with WTO rules, but the risk for such an effect seems considerably reduced. On the other hand, it is always possible that national measures could go further.

In the hypothetical case that such a national measure restricts the possibility to invest, the question is first whether there is a commitment under the relevant schedule for the service in question. In that case, one would have to assess whether the relevant potential effects would be compatible with the relevant provision of GATS. If this is not the case, the question comes up whether it could fall under any of the exceptions. It is not entirely clear to what extent the provisions of GATS quoted above allow the taking into account of the government control and the ownership structure. The GATS provisions may therefore merit a particular attention from the national authorities when they apply Article 4(2) in this context. On the other hand, it does not seem that those provisions of GATS would put into question the taking into account of criminal activities and previous activities affecting security.

[D] Consistency with Other Fields of Union Law

As regards the freedom of capital movements under Article 63 TFEU, Recital 4 states that the 'Regulation is without prejudice to the right of Member States to derogate to the free movement of capital as laid down in Article 65(1)(b) TFEU'. In the explanatory memorandum, the Commission Proposal recalled that FDI is a capital movement within the meaning of Article 63 TFEU, that restrictions of such movements are prohibited and that an investment screening mechanism may constitute such a restriction. However, the restrictions may be justified when necessary and proportionate for the achievement of objectives defined in the Treaty, including public security and public policy grounds under Article 65 TFEU or for overriding reasons in the general interest as defined by the Court of Justice. Furthermore, the Commission Proposal refers to case law according to which such public interests may be relied on only if there is a genuine and sufficiently serious threat to a fundamental interest of society. According to the Proposal, the Regulation is consistent with these requirements as it confirms that Member States may screen the investments and sets out basic procedural requirements for this.[21]

In respect of the freedom of establishment, the Commission Proposal simply notes that Article 49 TFEU does not apply to the establishment of third-country nationals in the EU. Recital 36 states that the application of the screening mechanism should be consistent with the application of the Merger Regulation,[22] notably in respect of the interpretation of the notion of legitimate interest within the meaning of the third paragraph of its Article 21(4). Recital 37 moreover states that the Regulation should not affect EU rules for prudential assessment of acquisitions of qualifying holdings in the financial sector.

As already noted, the requirements under the Regulation are of a general nature and leave a margin of discretion. It is therefore unlikely that they could be considered as requiring anything that would enter into conflict with the provisions on the free movement of capital or the freedom of establishment. The same may be said of Recitals 36 and 37 on the relation with the merger regulation and with EU rules on prudential assessment in the financial sector respectively. However, in all three cases, it is nevertheless useful to remind of the obligation to respect that legislation in view of the application of the screening mechanisms.

---

21. Commission Proposal, explanatory memorandum, p. 4, which refers to Case C-463/00, Commission *v.* Spain, ECLI:EU:C:2003:272, para. 34; Case C-212/09 Commission *v.* Portugal, para. 83 and Case C-244/11, Commission *v.* Greece, para. 67.
22. Regulation 1389/2004.

[E] Data Protection

Under Article 14, any processing of personal data pursuant to the Regulation shall be carried out in accordance with Regulation (EU) 2016/679 and Regulation (EC) N°45/2001 and only in so far as is necessary for the screening of FDI and for ensuring the effectiveness of the cooperation provided for in the Regulation. The personal data collected shall be kept only for the time necessary for achieving the purposes for which they were collected. Article 14 on data protection as well as Recital 31 justifying it in fact came into the text relatively late in the procedure, as they were not included in the Commission Proposal. As the obligations of data protection referred to apply generally, it may be discussed whether these references add anything to the legal situation of the Regulation. Nevertheless, issues relating to data protection could very well arise in the application of the Regulation in specific cases. As the provisions of the Regulation are of a general nature and leave a wide margin of discretion to the Member States, it is unlikely that the provisions of the Regulation could enter into conflict with the rules of data protection.

§11.07 CONCLUSIONS AND COMMENTS

It follows from the above that the Regulation does not establish any European investment screening mechanism and does not lay down any obligation to screen FDIs or to establish a mechanism for investment screening. Member States retain their discretion both in respect of whether to screen an FDI and in respect of which screening factors to apply. Indeed, the Parliament wanted to go further but the divergent positions and the sensitivities of the Member States must also be taken into account when assessing the outcome of the legislative procedure. In the light of this, it is important not to underestimate the interest in establishing this framework for investment screening. It would seem likely that the mechanism for cooperation, with its obligations to notify, the possibilities to comment and adopt opinions on FDIs in the Member States, will strengthen the capacity of the Member States and of the Union to coordinate and address risks to security and public order as stated in Recitals 7 and 8. Likewise, the political control established provides a democratic legitimacy to the framework. Over time, both the mechanism for cooperation and the political control established would seem suitable for gathering an increased knowledge of FDIs and their potential effects on security and public order.

CHAPTER 12

The EU Regulation on Screening Foreign Direct Investment: Another Piece of the Puzzle

Jacques H.J. Bourgeois & Eliza Malathouni[*]

§12.01 INTRODUCTION

In its Communication of July 2010, setting out the objectives of the Union's future international investment policy, the European Commission stated that it was best poised to 'ensure that EU investors abroad enjoy a level playing field, which assures uniform and optimal conditions for investment through the progressive abolition of restrictions on investment'.[1] The originally perceived objective of the EU Regulation on Screening Foreign Direct Investment (hereinafter 'the Regulation') – as stated by the European Commission – was 'to provide legal certainty to both EU and foreign investors',[2] an objective which also figures in the Preamble of the actual Regulation, but in a slightly different and qualified form.[3] The Regulation recognizes that: '[i]t is important to provide legal certainty for Member States' screening mechanisms ... and to ensure Union-wide coordination and cooperation on the screening of foreign direct investments' while clarifying that:

* Any errors or omissions are the authors' own. The views expressed in this chapter are exclusively those of the authors. This chapter has been prepared for academic purposes only and does not constitute any legal advice.

1. European Commission, *Towards a Comprehensive European International Investment Policy*, Communication from the Commission to the Council, the European Parliament, the European Economic and Social Committee and the Committee of the Regions, COM (2010) 343 final (7 Jul. 2010), 4.
2. *Ibid.*, 1.
3. Regulation (EU) 2019/452 of the European Parliament and of the Council of 19 Mar. 2019 Establishing a Framework for the Screening of Foreign Direct Investments into the Union, OJ L 791, 21 Mar. 2019, 1.

> [t]he framework for the screening of foreign direct investments and for cooperation should provide Member States and the European Commission with the means to address risks ... in a comprehensive manner, and to adapt to changing circumstances while maintaining the necessary flexibility for Member States to screen foreign direct investments ... .[4]

The Regulation should not be read however outside its actual context. A reading devoid of the actual circumstances that led to its enactment would prompt us to seriously question whether the Regulation is apt to actually pursue this objective of legal certainty, clarity and stability, given it does not establish an EU-wide investment screening process for inward foreign direct investment (hereinafter 'FDI') but relies on national screening mechanisms established in Member States (hereinafter 'MS'). The Regulation merely envisages a dual mechanism, which fosters cooperation and the exchange of views between MS, and the European Commission in terms of screening FDI, while reserving some kind of screening for the European Commission when it comes to projects of European interest. The type of screening contained within the Regulation, however, differs significantly from any kind of regulation encountered in the territories of the main EU trading and investment partners. Hence, one should read the Regulation within its proper context. The Regulation comes largely as a response to the lack of reciprocity faced by EU investors abroad and mainly in China. While the EU strives to maintain an open EU investment policy, it is not prepared to do so at all costs. It therefore wishes to level the playing field, and it does so by looking inward into its own territory.

At the same time that discussions on the Regulation were taking place in Europe, heated debate was also conducted across the Atlantic, as concerns the investment screening procedure undertaken by the Committee on Foreign Investment in the US (hereinafter 'CFIUS'). Discussions ultimately led to the enactment of the Foreign Investment Risk Review Modernization Act (hereinafter 'FIRRMA') aiming to modernize and strengthen the existing investment screening review on grounds of national security conducted under the auspices of CFIUS. The modernization and strengthening were prompted by concerns over Chinese investments within the US.[5]

The current chapter takes these developments into consideration and provides a critical assessment of the Regulation. Section 12.02 provides background information in relation to FDI in Europe and FDI in China, with a view to fostering a better understanding of the context that prompted the enactment of the Regulation. Section 12.03 briefly analyses the Regulation by focusing on key characteristics and commenting in particular on its take on FDI, the limited grounds of review the factors to be considered and the definition of foreign investors as undertakings of a third country. Given that both in the EU and in the US, regulations were enacted as a result of concerns raised by Chinese inward FDI, the Regulation will be compared to the FIRMMA. Section 12.04 briefly presents and comments on the main mechanism. This section also recalls briefly the obligations established through the Regulation, that is, the cooperation mechanism, as well as the obligations for MS arising from EU Law and

4. *Ibid.*, Preamble Recitals 7 and 8.
5. Paul Rose, *FIRRMA and National Security* (Ohio State Public Law Working Paper No. 452, 10 Aug. 2018), https://ssrn.com/abstract=3235564 or http://dx.doi.org/10.2139/ssrn.3235564.

from the Regulation. Section 12.05 provides yet another context, that of the Organization for Economic Cooperation and Development (hereinafter 'OECD') and critically assesses the content of the EU Regulation against long-standing OECD investment principles. Section 12.06 attempts to place the Regulation itself within the broader EU context, arguing that it constitutes yet one more piece of the puzzle. Section 12.07 provides a conclusion.

§12.02 BACKGROUND

The Regulation is to be seen against the background of developments of FDI worldwide and of FDI in the EU and of FDI by EU companies.[6]

The global FDI outward stock grew between 1990 and 2017 from USD 2 to USD 30 trillion.[7] As Richard Baldwin showed[8] at the same time the growth in global trade is partly explained by the breakup of large multinational entities in to fragmented supply and value chains. No large company has enough resources to become specialized producer in all parts and components that it needs in order to produce a good or a service. Controlling the supply chain partly explains this quite remarkable increase in FDI.[9]

These developments have significant implications for governments considering policy measures on FDI and trade policy measures. Restrictive trade measures of country A could affect FDI by country A companies in country B: such FDI could be compromised to the extent that it is part of the supply chain to country A. Measures restricting FDI in country B could affect trade to country A: such trade could be compromised to the extent that FDI by country A companies is part of the supply chain to country A. The trade conflict between China and the US illustrates this. The considerable increase of US tariffs on Chinese goods is expressly designed by the US Administration to repatriate FDI in China by US companies.[10]

This goes hand in hand with an increase in the share of restrictive and regulatory investment policy measures worldwide. Some countries take a more critical stance towards foreign takeovers, in particular when they relate to national security or the sale of strategic domestic assets and technology firms.[11]

During the 2003–2015 period, foreign investors carried out projects in the EU amounting to a total value of more than EUR 2.6 billion.[12] At the end of 2017,

6. See supra *n. 3*.
7. United Nations Conference on Trade and Development (UNCTAD), *World Investment Report 2018: Investment and New Industrial Policies* (United Nations, 2018), 188, table 2.
8. *Passim* in: Richard Baldwin, *The Great Convergence: Information Technology and the New Globalization* (Harvard University Press 2016).
9. Enrique Martínez- Galán and Maria Paula Fontoura, *Global Value Chairs and Inward Foreign Direct Investment in the 2000s*, 42 World Economy 185, –186 (2019).
10. Jeff Stein, Taylor Telford, Gerry Shih and Rachel Siegel, *Trump Retaliates in Trade War by Escalating Tariffs in Chinese Imports and Demanding Companies to Cut Ties with China*, The Washington Post (24 Aug. 2019, 1:10 AM GMT + 2), https://www.washingtonpost.com/business/2019/08/23/china-hits-us-with-tariffs-billion-worth-goods-reinstates-auto-levies-state-media-report/?noredirect = on.
11. UNCTAD, *supra* n. 7, 17 referring to the situation in 2017.
12. Copenhagen Economics, *The World in Europe. Global FDI Flows Towards Europe: Extra-European FDI Flows Towards Europe* (Mar. 2018) 9, https://www.espon.eu/fdi.

investment stock in the EU held by the rest of the world amounted to EUR 6.295 billion.[13] The strong presence of traditional investors from advanced economies (USA, Canada, EFTA countries, Japan, Korea, Singapore and Taiwan) is accompanied by the emergence, in the last few years, of newcomers from emerging markets (China, Hong Kong and Macao) and Offshore Financial Centres.[14]

There is also significant EU outward FDI. At the end of 2017, net FDI stock held in the rest of the world by investors resident in the EU amounted to EUR 7.412 billion.[15]

FDI has obvious benefits for the EU. It supports directly economic activity in the EU, integrating in the EU supply chains and supporting jobs through backward and forward linkages with local firms. In addition, foreign undertakings often bring important technology, know-how and management skills that can benefit local undertakings through productivity spillovers.[16]

FDI has potential downsides, as well. Quite generally, a significant presence of investors of a given country increases the exposure of the EU economy to political and economic changes in that country. In the EU – as well as in the US – there is growing concern about foreign investors taking over EU companies with key technologies for strategic reasons.[17] That concern relates mainly, but not exclusively, to FDI by State-owned enterprises, which are seen as strangers in the midst of privately owned enterprises; through them foreign States can use assets held by EU companies to the detriment not only of the EU's technological edge but also to its security and public order.[18]

[A] Chinese Investments in the EU

Chinese FDI in the EU peaked at EUR 37 billion in 2016 and dropped over 50% to EUR 17.3 billion in 2018.[19] At the end of 2017, FDI stocks held by Chinese investors in the EU represented 3.4% of all FDI stock in the EU.[20]

With a few exceptions (Geely's investment in Volvo, Legend's acquisition of Banque Internationale à Luxembourg, Geely's acquisition of Saxo Bank, Kerui Tiancheng's acquisition of Biotest), large acquisitions in previous years (such as

13. Eurostat – News release 200/2018.
14. Commission Staff Working Document, *Foreign Direct Investment in the EU: Following up on the Commission Communication 'Welcoming Foreign Direct Investment while Protecting Essential Interests' of 13 March 2019*, SWD (2019) 108 final (13 Mar. 2019), 67.
15. Eurostat – News release 200/2018.
16. Copenhagen Economics, *supra* n. 12, 3.
17. European Commission, *Reflection Paper on Harnessing Globalisation*, COM (2017) 240 final, (10 May 2017), 15; European Commission, *A Balanced and Progressive Trade Policy to Harness Globalisation*, Communication from the Commission to the European Parliament, the Council, the European Economic and Social Committee and the Committee of the Regions, COM (2017) 492 final (13 Sept. 2017), 5.
18. *Ibid.*, 5.
19. Thilo Hanemann, Mikko Huatari and Agatha Kratz, *Chinese FDI in Europe: 2018 Trends and Impact of New Screening Policies* (Rhodium Group and Mercator Institute for China Studies, Mar. 2019), 9, https://www.merics.org/sites/default/files/2019-03/190306_MERICS-Rhodium%20Group_COFDI-Update_2019.pdf.
20. Eurostat – News release 200/2018.

Logicor, Pirelli and Supercell) gave way to a more equal and balanced spread of capital across sectors.[21]

The sharp decrease in the level of Chinese FDI in the EU is largely due to measures of the Chinese government affecting outward FDI and to increased scrutiny by EU MS, blocking or preventing several Chinese acquisitions giving access to critical technologies, sensitive information or influence over critical infrastructure.[22]

[B] EU Investments in China

At the end of 2017, FDI stocks held by EU investors in China amounted to EUR 328 billion, representing 4.3 % of FDI stock held in China.[23]

China has moved from an approval system (based on three lists of prohibited, restricted and encouraged sectors) to a new regulatory framework that will give foreign investors access to all sectors except the ones defined in a negative list.[24] Several sectors have recently been removed from that negative list. There remain a great many administrative practices, *inter alia*, restraining EU investors post-establishment.[25]

[C] Preliminary Steps

Against this background, various proposals were floated within the EU. The road leading to the Regulation illustrates the difficult search for some sort of compromise between conflicting policy requirements (FDI in the EU versus EU FDI abroad) and opposing views of MS and stakeholders (whether or not to regulate FDI in the EU and for what purpose).

In 2011, two members of the European Commission, Messrs Barnier and Tajani called for a debate on whether FDI in the EU needed to be investigated and proposed to set up a centralized committee to vet foreign acquisitions on strategic grounds. They met with opposition from Mr De Gucht, the member in charge of the EU trade policy, and criticism from a number of MS.[26] The matter was subsequently shelved.[27]

---

21. Hanemann, Huatari and Kratz, *supra* n. 19, 12–13.
22. *See* the country reports in: John Seaman, Mikko Huatari and Miguel Otero-Iglesias (eds), *Chinese Investment in Europe: a Country-Level Approach* (ETCN Report Dec. 2017), https://www.ifri.org/sites/default/files/atoms/files/etnc_reports_2017_final_20dec2017.pdf.
23. Eurostat – News release 200/2018.
24. Thilo Hanemann and Mikko Huotari, *EU-China FDI: Working towards Reciprocity in Investment Relations* (Rhodium Group and Mercator Institute for China Studies N°3 Update, May 2018), 14, https://www.merics.org/sites/default/files/2018-08/180723_MERICS-COFDI-Update_final.pdf.
25. *See* various surveys by the European Chamber of Commerce in China to be found on http//www.europeanchamber.com.cn/en/publications-archive; *see* in particular its Investment Working Group's Key Recommendations.
26. Juliane von Reppert-Bismarck, *Analysis: Rising Foreign Investment Fuels EU Vetting Debate*, Reuters (8 Mar. 2011, 1:46 PM), https://www.reuters.com/article/us-eu-industry-investment/analysis-rising-foreign-investment-fuels-eu-vetting-debate-idUSTRE72726P20110308.
27. Jakob Hanke, *EU's Big 3 Seek Greater Role for Brussels to Stop Chinese Takeovers*, Policito.eu (19 Aug. 2017, 12:10 PM CET, updated 21 Aug. 2017, 6:03 PM CET), https://www.politico.eu/article/eus-big-3-seek-greater-role-for-brussels-to-stop-chinese-takeovers/.

In February 2017, the German, French and Italian governments sent to the European Commission a joint letter and a key issues paper referring to state-led, strategic direct investments of non-EU investors in European key enabling technology companies, as well as issues around reciprocity of investment conditions. In July 2017, they provided an update of their position on a common approach to FDI control.

In June 2017, the European Council welcomed the European Commission initiative 'to analyse investments from third parties in strategic sectors, while fully respecting Member States' competences'.[28]

This opened the way for the European Commission, which submitted in September 2017 to the Council of the EU and the European Parliament a proposal for a regulation establishing a framework for screening.[29] In October 2017, the UK government voiced concern about this proposal.

The reaction of stakeholders was mixed.[30] National parliaments on the one hand asked for enhanced Commission competences and a convergence of national FDI screening mechanisms. Yet others voiced concerns over both the scope of the projects and programmes of Union interest, as well as the vagueness of the terms security and public order, which were to serve as grounds for investment screening. The industry also asked for clearer definitions and for the elimination of the patchwork of national screening mechanisms. They stressed however the importance of addressing the principle of reciprocity, adding additional factors for review and the protection of sensitive business information.[31]

The Regulation was adopted in March 2019, less than two years from the Commission's legislative proposal.[32]

§12.03 A BRIEF ANALYSIS

Up until the enactment and coming into force of the Regulation, FDI at a pre-entry level had either been scrutinized at MS level, primarily on public interests grounds – including national security – or on the basis of competition law and specifically the EU Merger Regulation, for those investments that qualified also as concentrations under the provisions of the latter. At a post-entry level, once an investment had been accepted in the territory of a MS, the Treaty on the Functioning of the European Union (hereinafter 'TFEU') provisions on freedom of establishment and free movement of capital become applicable. The Regulation comes to add yet another piece in the puzzle of the Common Commercial Policy (hereinafter 'CCP') and FDI in the Union by establishing a dual 'screening' mechanism. On the one hand, the Regulation promotes

28. European Council, *European Council Meeting 22 and 23 June 2017 – Conclusions*, EUCO 8/17 (22–23 Jun. 2017), paras 16–17.
29. European Parliamentary Research Service, Briefing: *EU Legislation in Progress: EU Framework for FDI Screening*, PE 614.667 (Apr. 2019), 6ff.
30. *Ibid.*, 6.
31. *Ibid.*, 6–9.
32. For an overview of the legislative process and the speed through which it passed through the relevant processes in the Council and the European Parliament, *see* Neergaard, Ch. 11, in this book.

the cooperation and exchange of information among MS, and between MS and the Commission, so as to raise awareness on cases of inward FDI likely to affect the security or public order of one or more MS. On the other hand, the Regulation provides that the Commission may screen FDI likely to affect projects or programmes of Union interest.

The detailed presentation of the provisions of the Regulation has been included elsewhere in this book and will not constitute the focal point of the present contribution. Rather, the present contribution purports to critically review the Regulation by addressing three main issues, relating to the Regulation's limited scope; first, the definition of investments, which is restricted to FDI and excludes portfolio investments (hereinafter 'PI'); second, as concerns the two exclusive grounds for screening mechanism, what do these two terms cover and how do they differ from similar terms employed in other FDI screening mechanisms, and, third, the implications of allowing MS to decide whether they will maintain or not a national screening mechanism. In addition, the present chapter briefly discusses the cooperation mechanism established by the Regulation and assesses the actual contribution of the cooperation mechanism, also with reference to international obligations of MS undertaken through the OECD and its long-standing investment principles.

[A] Some Characteristic Features

[1] Limited Scope

A mere reading of the title of the Regulation would prompt someone to reasonably expect that the Regulation actually establishes a system for screening inward FDI at EU level. Apart from the title, this initial expectation is further reinforced by the choice of legal basis, which is Article 207 of the TFEU, i.e., FDI as part of the CCP. Pursuant to Article 3(1)(e) of the TFEU, the CCP falls under the Union's exclusive competence, and the Court of Justice of the European Union (hereinafter 'CJEU') has further clarified in Opinion 2/15 that Article 207(1) TFEU covers both the admission and the protection of FDI. Accordingly, a screening mechanism of inward FDI at EU level would seemingly fall under the admission of FDI and hence, under the competence of the Union to legislate on this matter to the exclusion of the MS. However, a close reading of the actual content of the Regulation reveals a different reality.

The Regulation does not establish a typical FDI screening mechanism, similar to those contained at national level by FDI recipient countries around the world. National screening mechanisms usually entail the examination of inward (proposed) investments on the basis of specific grounds, with the view of allowing the investment to take place unequivocally, conditioning it, or blocking it. In certain cases, investments can also be unwound. National screening mechanisms constitute an expression of state sovereignty, and are a corollary of a recipient state's right to regulate who it admits in its own territory and under what conditions.

The Regulation does not deal with the exercise by an EU institution of its power to screen inward FDI. While recognizing that screening power on grounds of public order and security resides with the MS, the Regulation envisages a system of closer cooperation among the MS, and between MS and the European Commission, where either the MS or the European Commission deem that the (proposed) FDI likely affects security or public order. In addition, the provisions of the Regulation also empower the European Commission to issue an opinion where FDI likely affects the security or public order in relation to programmes and projects of Union interest.

The 'screening' mechanism adopted by the Regulation performs a complementary function to MS' national screening mechanisms. It is designed to assist the MS and the European Commission in collectively assessing potential cross-border threats.[33] The Regulation goes as far as to recognize that MS may either maintain, amend or adopt FDI screening mechanisms on the grounds of security or public order. It does not oblige the MS to adopt screening mechanisms on these grounds.

[2] Defining FDI

The Regulation applies solely to FDI – as opposed to the broader term of non-direct investments. It covers both mergers and acquisitions, as well as greenfield investments.

Following settled case law of the CJEU, FDI within the meaning of the Regulation is defined as 'investment of any kind by a foreign investor aiming to establish or to maintain lasting and direct links between the foreign investor and the entrepreneur to whom or the undertaking to which the capital is made available in order to carry on an economic activity in a Member State, including investments which enable effective participation in the management or control of a company carrying out an economic activity'.[34] The last part of the definition covers also acquisitions of shareholdings in companies limited by shares, provided the shareholdings enable the holder to effectively participate in the management or in the control of the company.[35] What the Regulation does not cover is non-direct investments.

The CJEU has explicitly excluded non-direct foreign investments, i.e., PI, from the purview of FDI, under Article 207 of the TFEU and the CCP;[36] this exclusion is logically taken over in the text and scope of application of the Regulation, since Article 207 of the TFEU serves as its legal basis.[37] Hence, the 'acquisition of company

33. Memo: Frequently Asked Questions on Regulation (EU) 2019/452 Establishing a Framework for the Screening of Foreign Direct Investments into the Union, http://trade.ec.europa.eu/doclib/docs/2019/june/tradoc_157945.pdf.
34. *See* Art. 2(1) of the Regulation, *supra* n. 3. *See also* Case C-446/04, *Test Claimant in the FII Litigation v. Commissioners of Inland Revenue*, ECLI:EU:C:2006:774, para. 181.
35. Joined cases C-105/12 to C-107/12, *Staat der Nederlanden v. Essent N.V., Essent Nederland B.V., Eneco Holding N.V. and Delta N.V.*, ECLI:EU:C:2013:677, para. 40 and case law cited.
36. Opinion 2/15 (*EU- Singapore Free Trade Agreement)*, ECLI:EU:C:2017:376, paras 225–245.
37. Paragraph 9 of the Preamble to the Regulation, *supra* n. 3, states in the relevant part:

> A broad range of investments which establish or maintain lasting and direct links between investors from third countries including State entities, and undertakings carrying out an economic activity in a Member State should be covered by this Regulation. It should, however, not cover portfolio investment.

securities with the intention of making a financial investment'[38] but without influencing the management or control of the undertaking amounts to a PI and is excluded from the Regulation's scope of application. This does not mean that PI are left unregulated under EU law. Portfolio investments fall under the free movement of capital provisions and as such, they constitute a shared competence between MS and the Union. The choice of Article 207 of the TFEU as the legal basis for the Regulation, consequently, resulted in the automatic exclusion of PI from the Regulation's scope of application. It is worth noting that the European Union remains an important hub of PI, with a total of EUR 12075.4 billion of outstanding liabilities, but also a major net borrower of PI amounting to EUR 3448.1 billion.[39]

[3] Screening Limited to Grounds of Security and Public Order

Similar to national screening mechanisms, the Regulation contains grounds on which FDI should be screened, as well as a list of factors to be weighed in when scrutinizing (proposed or completed) FDI. Despite the fact that the EU wanted to avoid setting up a screening mechanism similar to that of CFIUS, there are some striking similarities between the EU Regulation and the FIRMMA. The comparison is not across the board but is limited to grounds of review and factors to consider when conducting FDI screening. Accordingly, this section will first comment on the content of the terms security and public order as grounds for review within the EU Regulation, and; second, it will present briefly the factors and sectors pertaining to FDI screening within the EU Regulation from a comparative viewpoint.

Concerning the grounds for review, the Regulation recognizes security and public order as the only grounds on which MS may screen FDI.[40] National screening mechanisms usually refer to national security as a ground of review, although the term is often not defined.[41] In a similar fashion, the Regulation does not define the content of security and public order as the two grounds of review.

The Regulation employs the more general term 'security' as a ground for screening over the more commonly used 'national security' or 'essential security interests'.[42] Such a choice seems to be dictated by the choice of Article 207 TFEU as the Regulation's legal basis, as well as Article 1(2) of the Regulation which clearly states that the scope of application of the Regulation is without prejudice to Article 4(2) of the

38. Opinion 2/15, *supra* n. 36, para. 227.
39. *See Eurostat, Statistics Explained: International Investment Position Statistics* (25 Oct. 2019), https://ec.europa.eu/eurostat/statistics-explained/pdfscache/44015.pdf.
40. Article 1(1) of the Regulation, *supra* n. 3.
41. Under FIRMMA, national security includes any issues relating to homeland security; *see* 50 USC § 4565 (a)(1); the Investment Canada Act does not define or provide guidance on what is meant by investments possibly injurious to national security. In Australia 'national interest' is assessed on a case-by- case basis and is discussed in Australia's Foreign Investment Policy of 2019 (1 Jan. 2019), https://cdn.tspace.gov.au/uploads/sites/82/2018/12/1-January-2019-Policy_.pdf.
42. Frédéric Wehrlé and Joachim Pohl, *Investment Policies Relating to National Security: A Survey of Country Practices* (OECD Working Papers on International Investment 2016/02, 2016), https://www.oecd-ilibrary.org/finance-and-investment/investment-policies-related-to-national-security_5jlwrrf038nx-en.

Treaty on the European Union (hereinafter 'TEU') and Article 346 of the TFEU. Article 4(2) of the TEU states that national security remains the sole responsibility of MS. It is thus left to MS to define their own national security. Any 'essential security interests' are also the prerogative of MS to define, according to Article 346 of the TFEU.[43] As the Regulation permits MS to maintain their own national screening mechanisms, there is nothing in the text of the Regulation precluding them from screening FDI on grounds of national security or essential security interests, as defined however, under their own national regulations. In some screening mechanisms of the EU MS, the ground of protecting essential interests of national security is restricted to the defence sector and relates for example to the production or trade in arms, munitions, etc., but in most cases extends to the protection of other public interests.[44]

The only clarification provided, concerning the content of the term security, is that it does not cover issues of economic security, echoing in this regard also CFIUS' approach to 'national security'.[45] The clarification however is not provided in either the Preamble or the actual text of the Regulation, but rather on the DG trade website and the section of a memo on frequently asked questions.[46] Whether there is room for MS to include economic grounds under the security rubric is doubtful. By limiting the FDI screening to grounds of security and public order, the Regulation echoes TFEU provisions on the right of MS to derogate from the free movement of capital, also between MS and foreign countries.[47] Article 65 TFEU refers to the applicability of restrictions on the right of establishment laid down in Article 52 TFEU to foreign nationals on grounds of public policy, public security or public health. Under the Court's case law, these 'derogations must not be misapplied so as, in fact, to serve purely economic ends'.[48] The question arises whether MS could lawfully under EU law include on their own economic grounds in their screening mechanisms. The wording of Article 3(2) of the Regulation is ambiguous in this regard. It states that MS 'shall set out the circumstances triggering the screening, the grounds for screening … '. This could mean that economic grounds cannot be subsumed under security and public order grounds for investment screening. As FDI forms part of the matters coming within the scope of the EU's exclusive powers on the CCP, the EU would need to authorize specifically MS to screen FDI on economic grounds. The Regulation does clearly not do so.

43. Article 1(2) and para. 7 of the Preamble of the Regulation, *supra* n. 3, reiterate that national security and the protection of essential security interests remain the sole prerogative of MS.
44. European Commission, *Commission Staff Working Document Accompanying the Document Proposal for a Regulation of the European Parliament and of the Council Establishing a Framework for Screening of Foreign Direct Investments in to the European Union*, COM (2017) 487 final, SWD (2017) 297 final (13 Sep. 2017), 8.
45. Department of the Treasury, *Regulations Pertaining to Mergers, Acquisitions and Takeovers by Foreign Persons*, 31 C.F.R. Part 800, 73 F.R. (21 Nov. 2008), 70705; José W. Fernandez, *Lessons from the Trenches*, 33 IFLR, 44 (July/August 2014).
46. *Memo, supra* n. 33.
47. *See* Recital 4 of the Preamble of the Regulation, *supra* n. 3.
48. Case C-54/99, *Association Église de Scientologie de Paris*, Scientology International Reserves Trust v. the Prime Minister, ECLI:EU:C:2000:124, para. 17, referred to by M. Cremona, Ch. 2, in this book.

This raises another question in relation to Article 207 TFEU as a legal basis. Deciding on whether and how a given FDI in a given sector carries with it the risk of endangering public order and security is left to each MS.

EU law in general and the Regulation, as will be shown, impose nevertheless certain obligations on MS with regard to screening mechanisms that they maintain or introduce, such as adherence to strict time limits or with the obligation to provide foreign investors with an avenue of redress. These obligations are linked to the principles of accountability, transparency and proportionality.[49]

That the EU legislates on matters that under the TFEU are reserved to MS is at first blush paradoxical. Yet, there is a certain logic to it as is made clear in particular by the case law. In *Johnston v. Chief Constable of the Ulster Constabulary* in rejecting an argument put forward by the UK, the Court held that it is not possible to infer from derogations applicable in situations that may involve public safety that there is inherent in the (then EEC) Treaty a general proviso covering all measures taken for reasons of public safety, which AG Darmon called 'a no-go zone'.[50]

In Opinion 2/15, in the EU-Singapore Agreement, MS argued with respect to a clause in that agreement on public order, public security and other public interests that the EU cannot enter into commitments instead of MS in matters such as public order and public security and other public interests, which fall under exclusive MS' competences. The Court noted that the agreement lays down not a commitment but the possibility of applying a derogation. It was of the view that the clause in question 'does not encroach upon the competences of Member States regarding public order, public security and other public interests, but obliges Member States to exercise those competences in a manner that does not render trade commitments entered into by the European Union redundant'.[51]

[4] Factors to Be Considered

The Regulation also contains a list of factors that the MS and the European Commission may consider when assessing whether FDI impacts security or public order. The list of factors is non-exhaustive and the final decision rests with the MS and the European Commission. The factors reveal also sectors in which FDI may potentially affect security and public order. Since however the list is non-exhaustive, screening of FDI is not restricted to these sectors. Accordingly, Article 4(1) of the Regulation indicatively mentions the sectors of critical infrastructure, critical technologies and dual-use items, supply of critical inputs, access to sensitive information, such as personal data, as well as the freedom and pluralism of the press. Additional factors to be considered are mentioned in paragraph 2 of the same article and include any links the foreign investor might have to its government, prior track record relating to criminal activities or to activities affecting security or public order.

49. *See infra*, § 12.05.
50. Case 222/84, Marguerite *Johnston v. Chief Constable of the Royal Ulster Constabulary*, ECLI: EU:C:986:206, para. 26.
51. Opinion 2/15, *supra* n. 36, para. 103.

The list of factors to be considered during a CFIUS screening primarily relates to national defence, sales of military goods, equipment or technology, the US international technological leadership, critical infrastructure and critical technologies.[52] Comparing the list of factors and sectors in the review undertaken by CFIUS to the ones contained in the body of the EU Regulation, one can make a number of observations. First, both lists of factors are indicative, allowing a degree of leeway for the European Commission and the MS on the one hand, and the US President and CFIUS on the other hand, to consider other relevant factors in order to be able to protect the security and public order in the case of the EU Regulation, and national security in the case of CFIUS review. Second, the list of factors and sectors contained under FIRMMA is slightly longer and relate primarily to national security. Third, what both screening mechanisms share in common are the potential effects on critical infrastructure, critical technologies, as well as the consideration of whether the investor is foreign-government controlled.

Apart from the similarities, it is also worth mentioning some differences between the two texts in relation to the potential effects on specific sectors. Whereas both FIRMMA and the EU Regulation refer to critical infrastructure, critical inputs, data processing and critical technologies, as relevant sectors to consider when assessing national security or security and public order, there are some subtle differences in the terms employed.

One such difference relates to the content assigned to the term 'critical infrastructure'. Critical infrastructure under FIRRMA is defined more in the abstract as 'systems and assets, whether physical or virtual, so vital to the United States that the incapacity or destruction of such systems or assets would have a debilitating impact on national security'.[53] Whether something constitutes critical infrastructure (or not) is arguably exercising value judgment on whether the destruction would have a 'debilitating impact' on national security. The EU Regulation rather includes an open list of examples, such as 'energy, transport, water, health, communications, media, data processing or storage, aerospace, defence, electoral or financial infrastructure, and sensitive facilities, as well as land and real estate crucial for the use of such infrastructure'. Whereas, the US has opted for a more abstract definition to which new assets can be included, the EU has opted for a general definition including both physical and virtual infrastructure followed by an examples-based approach. The two approaches might not differ in terms of scope, but the one followed by the EU stands out easily as it catches a number of contemporaneous issues of pivotal importance to the EU, while drawing on actual events. One such area of EU importance is data processing.[54] Electoral infrastructure is quite topical given the recent cases and allegations on foreign countries meddling in internal (national) elections of other

52. For a detailed view of the factors, *see* 50 USC § 4565 (f), and James Mendenhall & Riana Terney, Ch. 10, in this book.
53. 50 USC § 4565(a)(5).
54. European Commission, *EU Data Protection Rules*, https://ec.europa.eu/commission/priorities/justice-and-fundamental-rights/data-protection/2018-reform-eu-data-protection-rules_en.

states.[55] The inclusion of land and real estate seems to echo the US Ralls case.[56] Under Ralls, a Delaware corporation owned by Chinese nationals acquired a windmill park project. Following a CFIUS review, the transaction was ultimately unwound, due to the proximity of the windmill park to US military facilities.

As concerns, the 'supply of critical inputs'[57] – yet another sector whose potential effects on security and public order should be considered in the investment screening process – explicitly includes food security. Food security was at the core of the Smithfield Foods, – Shanghui transaction in the US – that spurred an intense Congressional and public debate on including food security under CFIUS national security review.[58] Whereas the matter was never unequivocally resolved in the US, the European legislator clearly opted for including food security issues under an FDI screening.

The last point to be made relates to data processing and critical technologies, such as artificial intelligence (hereinafter 'AI'), robotics, cybersecurity and semiconductors. The EU Regulation explicitly considers these areas as sectors having the potential to impact on security and public order. FIRMMA on the other hand does not refer to these sectors directly, but only through inclusion under the term 'critical technologies'. Despite differences in details, both FIRRMA and the EU Regulation are largely concerned with the same or similar sectors. Hence, FIRRMA includes investments in companies dealing with personal data under the covered transactions that CFIUS in entitled to subject to investment screening. Real estate transactions also constitute covered transactions.[59] Hence, FIRMMA expanded CFIUS jurisdiction to cover real estate deals and non-controlling investments in critical infrastructure and critical technology companies, as well as companies that maintain or collect data of US citizens.[60] As concerns 'critical technologies', the term is defined under the FIRMMA, but not under the EU Regulation.[61] The US President is further under the obligation to set up an interagency process to identify 'emerging and foundational technologies' essential to national security. AI, robotics and semiconductors would fall under this category of emerging and foundational technologies.[62]

55. *See, e.g.*, Rebecca Staudenmaier, *EU Elections: Commissioner Warns of Russian Meddling*, DW (13 May 2019), https://www.dw.com/en/eu-elections-commissioner-warns-of-russian-meddling/a-48712195.
56. *Ralls Corp. v. Committee on Foreign Investment in the United States*, 758 F.3d 296 (D.C. Cir 2014).
57. Article 4(1)(c) of the Regulation, *supra* n. 3.
58. Steven M. Davidoff Solomon, *China's Pork Deal May Hinge on the Risk for an Uproar*, Dealbook N.Y. Times, (30 May 2013, 01:18 PM ET), http://dealbook.nytimes.com/2013/05/30/running-the-national-security-gantlet-in-a-pork-deal/?_r = 0; David Benoit, *Shuanghui-Smithfield: Is Bacon a National Security Issue*? WSJ Moneybeat (29 May 2013, 4:52 PM ET), http://blogs.wsj.com/moneybeat/2013/05/29/shuanghui-smithfield-is-bacon-a-national-security-issue/.
59. Under Art. 4(1)(a) of the Regulation, *supra* n. 3, land and real estate crucial for the use of infrastructure is included in the definition of 'critical infrastructure'.
60. 50 USC § 4565(a)(4)(B)(ii) and 50 USC § 4565(a)(4)(B)(iii)(III).
61. *See* 50 USC § 4565 (a)(6) and 31 C.F.R., § 800.209 (21 Nov. 2008), 70719, *supra* n. 45.
62. Laura Fraedrich, Justin T. Huff, Chase D. Kaniecki, Diego A. Ortega, Paul V. Lettow and D. Grayson Yeargin, *Insights: FIRMMA Broadens Scope of Foreign Investments Subject to CFIUS Review*, (Aug. 2018) https://www.jonesday.com/en/insights/2018/08/firrma-broadens-scope-of-foreign-investments-subje.

What can be concluded from the above, is that despite their different approach both the US CFIUS and the EU screening of FDI regimes seem to be in sync when it comes to sectors and factors to be considered in order to assess whether national security or security and public order have been affected.

[5] Undertakings of a Third Country

Pursuant to Article 2(2) of the Regulation, the term foreign investor covers equally natural persons, as well as legal persons, i.e., undertakings of a third country. The Regulation further defines undertaking of third country as 'an undertaking constituted or otherwise organised under the laws of a third country'.[63] These two provisions read in tandem with Recital 10 of the Preamble hint to the issue of foreign companies setting up subsidiaries in a MS, which does not maintain a screening review, in order to then set up subsidiaries in another MS so as to take advantage of the freedom of establishment provisions and hence circumvent MS FDI screening mechanisms. As interesting as the issue might be, we will not further address it here nor will we deal with the extent and the conditions under which such foreign held EU subsidiary is to be treated under the EU rules on right of establishment.[64] Suffice it to say that the possibility for a foreign undertaking to establish a subsidiary in a MS that does not screen FDI to circumvent the mechanism and a screening decision was of particular concern to the EU Parliament.[65] The matter is left to MS that have a screening mechanism in place: they are required to identify and prevent such circumvention.[66] The cooperation mechanism established by the Regulation aids MS and the Commission in communicating to each other such cases.

§12.04 THE COOPERATION MECHANISM AND MS' OBLIGATIONS

[A] The Cooperation Mechanism and Its Added Value

This mechanism is at the core of the Regulation, together with the screening by the European Commission in cases where the FDI may affect projects or programmes of Union interest. The importance assigned to the cooperation mechanism can be primarily found in the Preamble, i.e., to give legal certainty for MS' screening mechanisms. Its implied rationale lies however elsewhere. As has been pointed out, security or public order acquire in fact an increasingly EU dimension, as a result of the EU internal market and of the way societies and economies are interconnected, since a technological advance or infrastructure may be critical not only for a single MS but also

63. Article 2(7) of the Regulation, *supra* n. 3.
64. Jürgen Schwarze, Ulrich Becker, Armin Hatje and Johan Schoo (eds.), *EU Kommentar*, (Nomos 4th ed. 2018), 951–954.
65. Neergaard, Ch. 11, in this book.
66. Art. 3(6) of the Regulation, *supra* n. 3. This is an exception to the discretion of each MS to screen a particular FDI.

for a neighbouring one, and may be equally important for the whole EU.[67] A detailed analysis of the cooperation mechanism, as well as the screening powers of the European Commission for projects or programmes of Union interest, has been offered earlier in this book.[68] Following a brief presentation on the content of the cooperation mechanism, we focus our analysis on its added value.

The Regulation sets up a cooperation mechanism among MS and between MS and the European Commission, as detailed under Articles 6 and 7. The cooperation mechanism consists in essence of notifications originating either from the host MS (i.e., the MS where the FDI is taking place), or another MS, or the European Commission in relation to either FDI already undergoing screening or FDI which is not undergoing screening.

Accordingly, the Regulation envisages a triangular notification system ensuring that all stakeholders – the host MS, other MS that consider their security or public order to be at stake and the European Commission – remain informed at all times. Hence, MS conducting a screening are under the obligation to inform other MS and the European Commission and to provide them with information, pertaining to the investment, such as the ultimate ownership structure, the value of the investment, a list of MS affected by the proposed or completed investment, etc.[69] On the other hand, any MS other than the host MS may opt for providing comments to the host MS, when the MS considers that its own security/public order are at stake, or it simply has information on the FDI that is being screened at another MS. The MS providing the comments must also send these to the European Commission and the European Commission is under the obligation to inform the other MS it has received comments.[70] The European Commission, in turn, is obliged to issue an opinion when one-third of MS consider that their security or public order are likely affected by the FDI undergoing screening. The European Commission is merely entitled to issue an opinion, when the FDI potentially affects security or public order in multiple MS or the European Commission holds relevant information.[71]

Article 7 is similarly worded to Article 6 of the Regulation but sets out the notification mechanism in cases where the FDI does not undergo screening in the host MS.

The comments of the MS and the opinion of the European Commission are not binding on the host MS. The host MS is required however to afford the comments and/or the opinion due consideration, meaning that they need to be properly assessed prior to any decision.[72] The final decision of whether to allow or disallow an FDI from materialising rests with the host MS.

Logically then, one wonders what the added value of the cooperation mechanism is – and for this matter of the Regulation. The prescripts of the Regulation and the cooperation do not really attempt to harmonize investment screening legislation on

67. *See* M. Martin-Prat, Ch. 5, in this book.
68. *See* Neergaard, Ch. 11, in this book.
69. Art. 9(2) juncto Art. 6(1) of the Regulation, *supra* n. 3.
70. Art. 6(2) of the Regulation, *supra* n. 3.
71. Article 6(3) of the Regulation, *supra* n. 3.
72. Art. 6(8) and art. 7(8) of the Regulation, *supra* n. 3.

security and public order grounds across the EU. Had this been the case, the MS would not have been left with such a wide choice on multiple fronts, to maintain or adopt an investment screening mechanism, on grounds of security or public order, specifically taking (or not) into consideration the list of factors contained in Article 4 of the Regulation. Had harmonization actually served as the underlying goal of the Regulation, then one could also argue that the Regulation was one step closer to achieving the goal of providing certainty to foreign investors and to continue attracting FDI in the EU.

What the Regulation does contribute, is to provide at least two common grounds across MS and a list of factors to assess when deciding whether screening should (not) take place. The grounds are however not mandatory. Yet, should MS opt to take them up in their legislation, and should they also consider the stated factors, then there is a possibility to lay the groundwork for some clarity and certainty to foreign investors.

The added value of the Regulation might not lie in harmonization, but in raising awareness among MS that FDI can impact the larger EU area, along with the more restricted geographical confines of one MS. The Regulation thus creates a procedure where MS at least become aware of the possible effects of FDI in their own territory to the security or public order of other MS and are required to actually afford due consideration to concerns of other MS. The Regulation further paves the way for a discussion forum on policy developments in the area of FDI screening, as well as the implementation progress of the Regulation.[73] These tasks are assigned to the European Commission Expert Group on FDI screening, which was set up already in 2017.

Apart from the cooperation mechanism which is intra-EU focused, the Regulation also calls on the MS and the European Commission to cooperate with third countries on investment policies and practices. The aim of such cooperation with third countries is to strengthen the effectiveness of the framework set up by the Regulation.[74] This can be achieved through tackling issues related to EU inward FDI and its potential effects on security and public order already at the level of third countries, apart from the EU level. The Regulation further clarifies that this cooperation with third countries can either be carried out on a bilateral level or multilateral, and in particular through the work of the OECD on Investment policies related to national security and public order.[75]

[B] Some Obligations for MS

The application of EU law to the way in which MS make use of their reserved powers with respect to FDI has certain consequences.

First, there is case law to the effect that the screening of FDI grounds of public order and security may not be misapplied to serve ends other than public order and security, e.g., purely economic ends.[76]

Second, i.a., in the series of 'Golden Share' cases involving MS' measures derogating from freedom of capital movement applicable in intra-EU relations, the

73. Art. 12 of the Regulation and Recital 28 of the Preamble, *supra* n. 3.
74. Art. 13 of the Regulation and Recital 29 of the Preamble, *supra* n. 3.
75. Recital 3 of the Preamble of the Regulation, *supra* n. 3.
76. For example, Case C-54/99, *Association Église de Scientologie*, *supra* n. 48, para. 17.

Court held that the free movement of capital may be restricted only by national rules which are justified by reasons referred to in exceptions provided for in EU law, such as measures taken on grounds of public policy or public security.[77] Such measures must be proportionate, based on objective, non-discriminatory criteria, known in advance to the undertakings concerned and all persons affected must have a legal remedy available to them.[78]

The Regulation generally reflects these principles.

First, it imposes on MS' screening mechanisms a number of requirements: time frames for the screening, non-discrimination between third countries and transparent procedures setting out the circumstances triggering the screening, the grounds for screening and the applicable detailed procedural rules.[79] This is in line with the requirements of the case law referred to above.

Second, foreign investors must have the possibility to seek recourse against screening decisions.[80] Whether 'recourse' instead of 'judicial redress' – apparently at the insistence of some MS that did not want to change their internal rules – is consistent with EU law as it stands is doubtful. Pursuant to the Court's case law, when derogating from EU law on the basis of an exception, MS have to provide for effective judicial review.[81] Admittedly, the intensity of judicial review is left to the judge and depends on the case. A substantial review by the judge of the assessment by the government of the risk for public order and security is not very likely.

§12.05 COMPLIANCE WITH LONG-STANDING OECD INVESTMENT PRINCIPLES

In its Communication, the European Commission while delimiting the contours of its desired future EU international investment policy stated that it aims at 'a more activist approach... ensuring that EU investment relations with third partners constitute a "two-way street" ... ' pointing towards the need and MS requests for reciprocity in maintaining an open investment environment. To achieve this balance, the European Commission relies on building blocks laid down by the OECD and the United Nations Conference on Trade and Development. The text of the Regulation refers to international obligations undertaken by the Union under the OECD.

77. *See, e.g.*, Case C-503/99 *Commission of the European Communities v. Kingdom of Belgium (Distrigaz)*, ECLI:EU:C:2002:328; Case C-463/00 *Commission of the European Communities v Kingdom of Spain*, ECLI:EU:C:2003:272; Joined Cases C-282/04 and C-283/04 *Commission of the European Communities v. Kingdom of the Netherlands*, ECLI:EU:C:2005:712; Case C-112/05 *Commission of the European Communities v. Federal Republic of Germany (VWGesets), ECLI: EU:C:2007:623*.
78. Case C-463/00 *Commission v Spain*, *supra* n. 77, para. 69.
79. Art. 3(2) of the Regulation, *supra* n. 3.
80. Art. 3(5) of the Regulation, *supra* n. 3.
81. For example, in Case 222/84, *Johnston v. Chief Constable of the Royal Ulster Constabulary*, *supra* n. 50, para. 18, the Court held that: '[t]he requirement of judicial control ... reflects a general principle of law which underlies the constitutional traditions common to the Member States'; for further reading, Takis Tridimas, *Principles of EU Law* 443-476 (Oxford University Press 2d ed. 2006).

The work of the OECD has dealt before with the delicate balancing exercise of promoting investment to reap the benefits of FDI, while respecting concerns of the host countries linked to national security and public order. In this regard, the OECD published a set of guidelines for host countries, in search of such a balance.[82] These guidelines urge host countries to adhere to long-standing investment principles, such as non-discrimination, transparency of policies and predictability of outcomes, proportionality of measures and accountability of implementing authorities. This last section will review the provisions of the Regulation in relation to the principles of the OECD Guidelines.

Non-discrimination under the OECD Guidelines relates to treating similarly situated investors and investments in the same fashion. The Regulation does not contain any provisions targeting specific countries. To the contrary, it explicitly calls on MS to not discriminate between third countries.[83]

Transparency, as perceived under the OECD Guidelines, covers many facets. While protecting the confidentiality of sensitive information, transparency also relates to making regulatory objectives and practices known to foreign investors prior to the investment taking place. In this regard, host countries are encouraged to codify and publish any laws and regulations pertaining to investments, as well as making evaluation criteria easily available to the public. Host countries are further expected to notify any plans to change the investment environment to all interested parties, as well as to provide them with the opportunity to comment on these changes. Transparency however, also entails a procedural aspect. Hence, strict time limits should be established in relation to screening procedures. Lastly, as enhanced transparency is conducive to accountability, host states are urged to adequately disclose and assess their investment policies.

The Regulation touches upon all these facets of transparency, albeit to different degrees. MS are instructed to protect any confidential and commercially sensitive information they become privy to during the FDI screening process, according to both EU and national laws.[84] The Regulation entrusts the details of the protection to the MS and further demands that any information received shall be used merely for investment screening purposes on the grounds of security and public order.[85] The obligation to protect classified information is also extended to the European Commission.[86] Interestingly enough, Article 14 of the Regulation also requires the application of the GDPR provisions to any information collected under FDI screening processes that can also be classified as personal data. As concerns, codification and publication requirements, MS are expected to notify their existing screening mechanisms to the European Commission, which subsequently publishes them online. Any amendments thereto should also

82. OECD, *Guidelines for Recipient Country Investment Policies Relating to National Security: Recommendation adopted by the OECD Council on 25 May 2009*, http://www.oecd.org/daf/inv/investment-policy/43384486.pdf (hereinafter 'OECD Guidelines').
83. Article 3(2) of the Regulation, *supra* n. 3.
84. Art. 10(2) of the Regulation, *supra* n. 3.
85. Art. 10(1) of the Regulation, *supra* n. 3.
86. Article 10(3) of the Regulation, *supra* n. 3.

be conveyed to the European Commission.[87] The European Commission is to provide the MS with standardized forms so as to facilitate the comparison of the submitted information. Hence, the Regulation is in line with the OECD Guidelines, as it promotes and obliges MS to make their investment regimes known, at least at EU level. In relation to the procedural aspects of transparency, the Regulation does set strict time limits in relation to the exchange of information between the MS, and the European Commission.[88] Lastly, in order to facilitate accountability, the Regulation establishes reporting requirements on both the MS and the European Commission. Accordingly, MS are expected to submit annual reports to the European Commission containing aggregated data on FDI in their territories, as well as the application of their national screening mechanisms.[89] The European Commission is in turn obliged to submit an annual report to the European Parliament and the Council on the implementation of the Regulation.

The proportionality principle under the OECD Guidelines requires that any security concerns are self-judging and that any investment restrictions maintain a narrow focus and constitute merely a measure of last resort. As it is immediately apparent, proportionality considerations are more relevant in a national regulatory context that sets out in details a screening mechanism. As argued before, the Regulation does not establish such a screening mechanism, but merely a cooperation mechanism between MS and the European Commission. The proportionality principle is hence not as relevant in this context.

Accountability in the OECD context relates primarily to procedures internal to the legal and political order of host MS. Hence, the OECD Guidelines require, for example, that procedures for internal governmental oversight or parliamentary oversight and periodic impact assessments are in place. Such an examination is beyond the scope of this chapter, which focuses on the Regulation.

§12.06 A PIECE OF THE PUZZLE

[A] Other Tools

Apart from international agreements entered into by the EU on investments or containing clauses relating to investments, there are a number of EU rules dealing with public order and security and comparable aspects of FDI. The Explanatory Memorandum of the Commission proposal[90] identifies EU instruments along these lines. It

87. Recital 22 of the Regulation, *supra* n. 3.
88. Arts6(6), (7) and. 7(6) of the Regulation, *supra* n. 3.
89. Art.5 of the Regulation, *supra* n. 3.
90. European Commission, *Proposal for a Regulation of the European Parliament and of the Council Establishing a Framework for Screening of Foreign Direct Investments into the European Union*, SWD (2017) 297 final, COM (2017) 487 final, 2017/0224 (COD); *see also* European Commission, *Welcoming Foreign Direct Investment while Protecting Essential Interests*, Communication from the Commission to the European Parliament, the European Council, the Council, the European Economic and Social Committee and the Committee of the Regions, COM (2017) 494 final (13 Sep. 2017), 8–9.

qualifies them with a rich terminology as policies and initiatives which the Regulation 'complements', with which it is 'consistent' or which it does not 'affect'. It refers to *inter alia* legislation on energy, policies on cybersecurity and electronic communication, common rules for the operation of air services in the EU, legislation in the financial sector and the Merger Regulation, where specific rules subject FDI to restrictions or to prior authorization on the grounds of security and public order. The Merger Regulation permits MS to prohibit mergers that have been cleared by the Commission in order to protect public security, plurality of the media and prudential rules and any other public interest, provided such other interest has been recognized by the Commission.[91] The Commission decisions on such MS derogations from merger clearance are rare.[92]

[B] Economic Interests

Whether the EU should have a policy regarding the economic effects of FDI on EU companies has been debated on certain occasions *à propos* specific transactions and has reappeared in the context of an EU industrial policy advocated by France and Germany.[93] The political advisability of controlling FDI in view of its economic effects may be left aside here. Suffice it to recall certain arguments put forward in support of such policy and to explore whether the EU has the legal tools for such policy. There are basically four such arguments: state-ownership of and state influence over the company that carries out an FDI operation in the EU, lack of reciprocity, subsidization practices of certain home states and the promotion of 'European Champions'.

State-ownership and state influence have two potential consequences: they may lead to an acquisition of an EU company for strategic reasons rather than for purely commercial reasons; they may give the foreign company a competitive advantage over EU investors when competing for the acquisition of an EU company.[94]

The lack of reciprocity – and the argument is directed more often than not at China – protects less competitive companies in the home state from being acquired by more productive EU companies and could even allow these less productive foreign companies to acquire EU companies.[95]

---

91. *See* Art. 21(4) of the Council Regulation (EC) no. 139/2004 of 20 Jan. 2004 on the Control of Concentrations between Undertakings, OJ L24, 29 Jan. 2004, 1 (hereinafter the 'Merger Regulation').
92. Richard Whish and David Bailey, *Competition Law* 897-899(Oxford University Press 8th ed. 2015); *see* on public security case M.336 *IBM France/CGI* OJ C 151/05, 2 Jun. 1993 and case M.1858 *Thomson-CSF/Racal II,* 15 Jun. 2000; on free expression of opinion, *see*, case M.423 *Newspaper Publishing* OJ C 85/05, 22 Mar. 1994; *see also* case C-42/01 *Portuguese Republic v. Commission of the European Communities*, ECLI:EU:C:2004:379.
93. Bundesministerium für Wirtschaft und Energie & Ministère de l'Economie et des Finances, *A Franco-German Manifesto for European Industrial Policy fit for the 21st Century* (19 Feb. 2019).
94. Commission Staff Working Document on FDI in the EU, *supra* n. 14 at 61. It refers in particular to ChemChina's acquisitions of Syngenta, Pirelli, Klaus-Maffei, its acquisitions of Rhodia Global Silicon and Elkem, subsequently integrated in Elkem Silicones, which has become the world's leading silicone manufacturer.
95. *See* Hanemann and Huotari, *supra* n. 24.

Subsidization practices by the home state enhance the 'strike force' of foreign companies acquiring EU assets, increase the speed of their arrival on the EU market and give them a comparative advantage over EU companies.[96]

The promotion of 'European Champions' with the EU and MS encouraging mergers that create larger EU companies able to withstand competition on the EU and the world market has recently re-emerged as topic for debate, more specifically in relation to EU merger control.

As far as FDI by state-owned or state-influenced companies is concerned, current EU law does not provide some form of general oversight on economic policy grounds. The Merger Regulation deals with the parties to a merger as they are and does not distinguish between private companies and state-owned companies as such.[97] To the extent that EU foreign trade rules target operations by state-owned or state-influenced companies, they apply only to imports of goods into the EU. There are at present no EU rules in the framework of the CCP designed to offset a possible competitive advantage of such foreign companies in FDI transactions in the EU.

There is no apparent EU tool that could be relied upon to deal with a lack of reciprocity in investment relations. The Merger Regulation addresses the issue of reciprocity.[98] It does not, however, provide that lack of reciprocity should be taken into account for the purpose of assessing a merger. It refers to negotiations with the foreign country that does not grant reciprocal treatment. On the basis of available information lack of reciprocity has not led to, or has not been the main reason for, such negotiations. At present there are no other EU rules addressing in general the lack of reciprocity in investment relations with foreign countries. Rather than by possible unilateral measures, this issue should be addressed in bilateral negotiations, such as the ongoing China-EU negotiation on an investment protection agreement.

Neither is there at present an EU tool that could be relied upon to deal with FDI by foreign companies benefitting from subsidies in their home country. Again, the current Merger Regulation does not appear to take subsidization of a foreign company, party to a merger subject to this Regulation, into account for the purpose of clearing that merger.[99] In addition, the TFEU rules on state aid have no 'extraterritorial' effect, they apply to subsidies granted by EU MS, not to subsidies granted by a foreign country to one of its companies engaged in an EU transaction. Finally, there are EU rules dealing with subsidies granted by foreign countries. They apply to subsidies granted for the production and sale of goods and offset their effect by imposing countervailing duties imposed on the imported products. They do not provide for measures to offset the effect of subsidies on FDI by the foreign company.

96. Not referring specifically to FDI, *see* Anne Perrot, Victor Blonde, Axel Ropars, Serge Catoire, Hervé Mariton, *La Politique de la Concurrence et les Intérêts Stratégiques de l'UE* (Inspections Générales de Finance, Conseil Général de l' Economie, de l' Industrie, de l' Energie et des Technologies, Apr. 2019), 17–18; along the same lines, *see* Bundesministerium für Wirtschaft und Energie & Ministère de l'Economie et des Finances, *supra* n. 93, 3.
97. Another different issue is whether the fact that a potential foreign competitor is state-owned or state-influenced is to be taken into account when assessing a merger.
98. Art. 24(1) of the Merger Regulation, *supra* n. 91.
99. Again, another different issue is whether the potential competition by a foreign company where it is benefitting from subsidies ought to be taken into account when assessing a merger.

The promotion of 'European champions', a term studiously avoided in most official documents, has also been mentioned in relation to FDI. In February 2019, the Commission blocked the Alstom-Siemens merger on the ground that the remedies offered by the parties were insufficient to address the competition concerns to which the contemplated merger gave rise in the market for high-speed trains and in the market for train control system projects.[100] Critics are of the view that this merger should have been cleared allowing Alstom and Siemens to face up together to the competition of CRRC – manufacturing high-speed trains-and CRSC – manufacturing, *inter alia*, signalling systems – two Chinese companies. Their argument is that these two Chinese companies, even though only potential competitors on the EU market in the medium term, should have been taken into account when assessing the foreseeable impact of the contemplated Alstom-Siemens merger on competition within the EU.[101] Whether it would have been open to the Commission to clear the merger under the Merger Regulation or under the TFEU on these grounds is debatable to say the least. The Franco-German Manifesto recognizes implicitly that the current rules do not permit this. Whether they should be amended is a policy decision. At any rate, the link with regulating FDI is indirect to the extent that an FDI transaction, consisting of a merger of a foreign company with an EU company, would be blocked on account of the fact that such merger would prevent the emergence of a 'European champion'.

§12.07 CONCLUSION

The Regulation could have done a number of things, which in the end it does not do.

It could have addressed the issue of lack of reciprocity faced by EU investors abroad, and especially in China. It could have included a broader definition of investments, covering also PI. It could have eliminated the existing patchwork of national MS screening mechanisms by either directly establishing a Union-wide screening mechanism – comparable to national ones – or by (gradually) harmonizing the national MS screening mechanisms. Either way, it would have also dealt with the issue of third-country companies established in MS lacking screening mechanisms, so as to profit from the freedom of establishment provisions in order to resettle in another MS, thus circumventing the other national MS screening mechanisms.

Trying to maintain the delicate balance between the Union's and the MS' competences, while simultaneously respecting previous case law and the internal balance of primary EU law provisions, the Regulation leaves the possibility open for screening FDI on economic policy grounds.

100. Case M.8677 *Siemens/Alstom* OJ C 300/14, 5 Sep. 2019, paras 64 and 69.
101. For a short good description of the debate, *see* Konstantinos Efstathiou, *The Alstom-Siemens Merger and the Need for European Champions* Bruegel (11 Mar. 2019), https://bruegel.org/2019/03/the-alstom-siemens-merger-and-the-need-for-european-champions/. He recalls rightly that the Merger Regulation does not prevent the formation of European champions, provided that anti-competitive effects are outweighed by efficiency gains. *See also* Editorial Comments, Think Big? Think Twice! EU Competition Law in the Face of Calls for European Champions 56 CMLRev, 329 (April 2019).

The Regulation establishes a mechanism of cooperation between MS and the Commission, which performs a complementary function to that of MS screening mechanisms. In this setting, dialogue is fostered, promoting a common perception and reality that investments in one MS can have spill-over effects within other MS. Therefore, MS need to harken and consider the concerns of other MS.

Whereas MS can define themselves security and public order as grounds for investment review, the Regulation obliges them to maintain certain standards, abiding thus also with international standards, such as the OECD long-standing investment principles of accountability, transparency and proportionality. Accordingly, MS are required to maintain strict time limits and provide foreign investors with avenues of redress in the MS screening mechanisms.

The Regulation further contains a list of factors that MS should consider in their assessment of threats to security and public order. The list is non-exhaustive but contains sectors of imperative EU importance, such as data protection and infrastructure – such as the 5G network or electoral infrastructure. Consideration of these factors is not mandatory but should the MS follow these when interpreting the two screening grounds of security and public order, then clarity and predictability for both foreign investors and EU MS can be enhanced.

The Regulation is not the only piece of EU relevance dealing with security and public order. The terms are not unknown in the field of EU energy or even the Merger Regulation. The present Regulation constitutes therefore yet another piece of the ever increasingly complex regulatory puzzle on FDI within the EU.

APPENDIX

Regulation (EU) 2019/452 of the European Parliament and of the Council of 19 March 2019*

establishing a framework for the screening of foreign direct investments into the Union

THE EUROPEAN PARLIAMENT AND THE COUNCIL OF THE EUROPEAN UNION,
Having regard to the Treaty on the Functioning of the European Union, and in particular Article 207(2) thereof,
Having regard to the proposal from the European Commission,
After transmission of the draft legislative act to the national parliaments,
Having regard to the opinion of the European Economic and Social Committee ([1]),
Having regard to the opinion of the Committee of the Regions ([2]),
Acting in accordance with the ordinary legislative procedure ([3]),
Whereas:

(1) Foreign direct investment contributes to the Union's growth by enhancing its competitiveness, creating jobs and economies of scale, bringing in capital, technologies, innovation, expertise, and by opening new markets for the Union's exports. It supports the objectives of the Investment Plan for Europe and contributes to other Union projects and programmes.

(2) Article 3(5) of the Treaty on European Union (TEU) specifies that the Union, in its relations with the wider world, shall uphold and promote its values and interests and contribute to the protection of its citizens. Moreover, the Union

* *Source*: https://eur-lex.europa.eu/legal-content/EN/TXT/?uri=OJ:L:2019:079I:TOC.
1. OJ C 262, 25.7.2018, p. 94.
2. OJ C 247, 13.7.2018, p. 28.
3. Position of the European Parliament of 14 February 2019 (not yet published in the Official Journal) and decision of the Council of 5 March 2019.

and the Member States have an open investment environment, which is enshrined in the Treaty on the Functioning of the European Union (TFEU) and embedded in the international commitments of the Union and its Member States with respect to foreign direct investment.

(3) Pursuant to the international commitments undertaken in the World Trade Organization (WTO), in the Organisation for Economic Cooperation and Development, and in the trade and investment agreements concluded with third countries, it is possible for the Union and the Members States to adopt restrictive measures relating to foreign direct investment on the grounds of security or public order, subject to certain requirements. The framework established by this Regulation relates to foreign direct investments into the Union. Outward investment and access to third country markets are dealt with under other trade and investment policy instruments.

(4) This Regulation is without prejudice to the right of Member States to derogate from the free movement of capital as provided for in point (b) of Article 65(1) TFEU. Several Member States have put in place measures according to which they may restrict such movement on grounds of public policy or public security. Those measures reflect the objectives and concerns of Member States with respect to foreign direct investment, and might result in a number of mechanisms which are different in terms of scope and procedure. Member States wanting to put in place such mechanisms in the future could take into account the functioning, experiences and best practices of existing mechanisms.

(5) There is currently no comprehensive framework at Union level for the screening of foreign direct investments on the grounds of security or public order, while the major trading partners of the Union have already developed such frameworks.

(6) Foreign direct investment falls within the field of the common commercial policy. In accordance with point (e) of Article 3(1) TFEU, the Union has exclusive competence with respect to the common commercial policy.

(7) It is important to provide legal certainty for Member States' screening mechanisms on the grounds of security and public order, and to ensure Union-wide coordination and cooperation on the screening of foreign direct investments likely to affect security or public order. That common framework is without prejudice to sole responsibility of Member States for safeguarding their national security, as provided for in Article 4(2) TEU. It is also without prejudice to the protection of their essential security interests in accordance with Article 346 TFEU.

(8) The framework for the screening of foreign direct investments and for cooperation should provide Member States and the Commission with the means to address risks to security or public order in a comprehensive manner, and to adapt to changing circumstances, while maintaining the necessary flexibility for Member States to screen foreign direct investments on grounds of security and public order taking into account their individual situations and national specificities. The decision on whether to set up a screening

mechanism or to screen a particular foreign direct investment remains the sole responsibility of the Member State concerned.

(9) A broad range of investments which establish or maintain lasting and direct links between investors from third countries including State entities, and undertakings carrying out an economic activity in a Member State should be covered by this Regulation. It should, however, not cover portfolio investment.

(10) Member States that have a screening mechanism in place should provide for the necessary measures, in compliance with Union law, to prevent circumvention of their screening mechanisms and screening decisions. This should cover investments from within the Union by means of artificial arrangements that do not reflect economic reality and circumvent the screening mechanisms and screening decisions, where the investor is ultimately owned or controlled by a natural person or an undertaking of a third country. This is without prejudice to the freedom of establishment and the free movement of capital enshrined in the TFEU.

(11) It should be possible for Member States to assess risks to security or public order arising from significant changes to the ownership structure or key characteristics of a foreign investor.

(12) To guide Member States and the Commission in the application of this Regulation, it is appropriate to provide a list of factors that could be taken into consideration when determining whether a foreign direct investment is likely to affect security or public order. That list will also improve the transparency of Member States' screening mechanisms for investors considering making or having made foreign direct investments in the Union. The list of factors that might affect security or public order should remain non-exhaustive.

(13) In determining whether a foreign direct investment may affect security or public order, it should be possible for Member States and the Commission to consider all relevant factors, including the effects on critical infrastructure, technologies (including key enabling technologies) and inputs which are essential for security or the maintenance of public order, the disruption, failure, loss or destruction of which would have a significant impact in a Member State or in the Union. In that regard, it should also be possible for Member States and the Commission to take into account the context and circumstances of the foreign direct investment, in particular whether a foreign investor is controlled directly or indirectly, for example through significant funding, including subsidies, by the government of a third country or is pursuing State-led outward projects or programmes.

(14) Member States or the Commission, as appropriate, might consider relevant information received from economic operators, civil society organisations, or social partners such as trade unions, in relation to a foreign direct investment likely to affect security or public order.

(15) It is appropriate to lay down the essential elements of the framework for the screening of foreign direct investments by a Member State to allow

investors, the Commission and other Member States to understand how such investments are likely to be screened. Those elements should at least include timeframes for the screening and the possibility for foreign investors to seek recourse against screening decisions. Rules and procedures relating to screening mechanisms should be transparent and should not discriminate between third countries.

(16) A mechanism which enables Member States to cooperate and assist each other where a foreign direct investment in one Member State could affect security or public order in other Member States should be set up. It should be possible for Member States to provide comments to a Member State in which such investment is planned or has been completed, irrespective of whether that Member State has a screening mechanism in place, or such an investment is undergoing screening. Requests for information, replies and comments of Member States should also be forwarded to the Commission. It should be possible for the Commission, where appropriate, to issue an opinion within the meaning of Article 288 TFEU to the Member State in which the investment is planned or has been completed. It should also be possible for a Member State to request the Commission to issue an opinion or other Member States to provide comments on a foreign direct investment taking place in its territory.

(17) When a Member State receives comments from other Member States or an opinion from the Commission, it should give such comments or opinion due consideration through, where appropriate, measures available under its national law, or in its broader policy-making, in line with its duty of sincere cooperation laid down in Article 4(3) TEU.

The final decision in relation to any foreign direct investment undergoing screening or any measure taken in relation to a foreign direct investment not undergoing screening remains the sole responsibility of the Member State where the foreign direct investment is planned or completed.

(18) The cooperation mechanism should only be used for the purpose of protecting security or public order. For that reason, Member States should duly justify any request for information regarding a specific foreign direct investment in another Member State, as well as any comment they address to that Member State. The same requirements should apply when the Commission requests information on a particular foreign direct investment or issues an opinion to a Member State. Compliance with those requirements is also important in situations where an investor of a Member State competes with investors of third countries for making an investment in another Member State such as acquiring assets.

(19) Furthermore, it should be possible for the Commission to provide an opinion within the meaning of Article 288 TFEU with regard to foreign direct investments likely to affect projects and programmes of Union interest on grounds of security or public order. This would give the Commission a tool to protect projects and programmes which serve the Union as a whole and represent an important contribution to its economic

growth, jobs and competitiveness. This should include in particular projects and programmes involving substantial Union funding or established by Union law regarding critical infrastructure, critical technologies or critical inputs. Those projects or programmes of Union interest should be listed in this Regulation. An opinion which is addressed to a Member State should also be simultaneously sent to the other Member States.

The Member State should take utmost account of the opinion received from the Commission through, where appropriate, measures available under its national law, or in its broader policy-making, and provide an explanation to the Commission if it does not follow that opinion, in line with its duty of sincere cooperation under Article 4(3) TEU. The final decision in relation to any foreign direct investment undergoing screening or any measure taken in relation to a foreign direct investment not undergoing screening remains the sole responsibility of the Member State where the foreign direct investment is planned or completed.

(20) In order to take into account developments relating to projects and programmes of Union interest, the power to adopt acts in accordance with Article 290 TFEU should be delegated to the Commission to amend the list of projects and programmes of Union interest set out in the Annex to this Regulation. It is of particular importance that the Commission carry out appropriate consultations during its preparatory work, including at expert level, and that those consultations be conducted in accordance with the principles laid down in the Interinstitutional Agreement of 13 April 2016 on Better Law-Making ([4]). In particular, to ensure equal participation in the preparation of delegated acts, the European Parliament and the Council receive all documents at the same time as Member States' experts, and their experts systematically have access to meetings of Commission expert groups dealing with the preparation of delegated acts.

(21) In order to provide greater certainty for investors, Member States should have the possibility to make comments and the Commission should have the possibility to issue an opinion in relation to completed investments not undergoing screening for a period limited to 15 months after the completion of the foreign direct investment. The cooperation mechanism should not apply to foreign direct investments completed before 10 April 2019.

(22) Member States should notify their screening mechanisms and any amendment thereto to the Commission, and should report on the application of their screening mechanisms on an annual basis, including on decisions allowing, prohibiting or subjecting foreign direct investments to conditions or mitigating measures and on decisions regarding foreign direct investments likely to affect projects or programmes of Union interest. All Member States should report on the foreign direct investments that took place in their territory, on the basis of the information available to them. In order to

4. OJ L 123, 12.5.2016, p. 1.

improve the quality and comparability of information provided by Member States as well as to facilitate compliance with the notification and reporting obligations, the Commission should provide standardised forms considering, inter alia, relevant forms applied for the purpose of reporting to Eurostat, where appropriate.

(23) In order to ensure the effectiveness of the cooperation mechanism, it is also important to ensure a minimum level of information and coordination with regard to foreign direct investments falling under the scope of this Regulation in all Member States. That information should be made available by Member States for foreign direct investments undergoing screening as well as, upon request, for other foreign direct investments. Relevant information should include aspects such as the ownership structure of the foreign investor and the financing of the planned or completed investment, including, when available, information about subsidies granted by third countries. Member States should seek to provide accurate, comprehensive and reliable information.

(24) Upon request by a Member State where a foreign direct investment is planned or has been completed, the foreign investor or the undertaking concerned should provide the information requested. In exceptional circumstances, when, despite its best efforts, a Member State is unable to obtain such information, it should notify the Member States concerned or the Commission without delay. In such a case, it should be possible that any comment issued by another Member State or any opinion issued by the Commission in the framework of the cooperation mechanism be made on the basis of the information available to them.

(25) When making available the information requested, Member States are to comply with Union law and national law that complies with Union law.

(26) The communication and cooperation at Member State and Union level should be enhanced through the establishment of a contact point for the implementation of this Regulation in each Member State and the Commission.

(27) The contact points established by the Member States and the Commission should be appropriately placed within the respective administration, and should have the qualified staff and the powers necessary to perform their functions under the coordination mechanism and to ensure a proper handling of confidential information.

(28) The development and implementation of comprehensive and effective policies should be supported by the Commission group of experts on the screening of foreign direct investments into the European Union, set up by Commission Decision of 29 November 2017 ([5]), composed of representatives of the Member States. That group should discuss, in particular, issues

5. Commission Decision of 29 November 2017 setting up the group of experts on the screening of foreign direct investments into the European Union (not published in the Official Journal), C(2017) 7866 final.

related to the screening of foreign direct investments, share best practices and lessons learned and exchange views on trends and issues of common concern related to foreign direct investments. The Commission should consider seeking the advice of the group on systemic issues relating to the implementation of this Regulation. The Commission should consult the expert group on draft delegated acts in accordance with the principles laid down in the Interinstitutional Agreement of 13 April 2016 on Better Law-Making.

(29) Member States and the Commission should be encouraged to cooperate with the responsible authorities of like-minded third countries on issues related to screening of foreign direct investments likely to affect security or public order. Such administrative cooperation should aim to strengthen the effectiveness of the framework for screening of foreign direct investments by Member States and the cooperation between Member States and the Commission pursuant to this Regulation. It should also be possible for the Commission to monitor developments with regard to screening mechanisms in third countries.

(30) Member States and the Commission should take all necessary measures to ensure the protection of confidential information in compliance with, in particular, Commission Decision (EU, Euratom) 2015/443 ([6]), Commission Decision (EU, Euratom) 2015/444 ([7]) and the Agreement between the Member States of the European Union, meeting within the Council, regarding the protection of classified information exchanged in the interests of the European Union ([8]). This includes, in particular, the obligation not to downgrade or declassify classified information without the prior written consent of the originator ([9]). Any non-classified sensitive information or information which is provided on a confidential basis should be handled as such by the authorities.

(31) Any processing of personal data pursuant to this Regulation should comply with the applicable rules on the protection of personal data. Processing of personal data by the contact points and other entities within Member States should be carried out in accordance with Regulation (EU) 2016/679 of the European Parliament and of the Council ([10]). Processing of personal data

6. Commission Decision (EU, Euratom) 2015/443 of 13 March 2015 on security in the Commission (OJ L 72, 17.3.2015, p. 41).
7. Commission Decision (EU, Euratom) 2015/444 of 13 March 2015 on the security rules for protecting EU classified information (OJ L 72, 17.3.2015, p. 53).
8. OJ C 202, 8.7.2011, p. 13.
9. Point (a) of Article 4(1) of the Agreement between the Member States of the European Union, meeting within the Council, regarding the protection of classified information exchanged in the interests of the European Union and Article 4(2) of Decision (EU, Euratom) 2015/444.
10. Regulation (EU) 2016/679 of the European Parliament and of the Council of 27 April 2016 on the protection of natural persons with regard to the processing of personal data and on the free movement of such data, and repealing Directive 95/46/EC (General Data Protection Regulation) (OJ L 119, 4.5.2016, p. 1).

by the Commission should be carried out in accordance with Regulation (EU) 2018/1725 of the European Parliament and of the Council ([11]).

(32) On the basis of, inter alia, the annual reports submitted by all Member States, and with due respect to the confidential nature of certain information included in those reports, the Commission should draw up an annual report on the implementation of this Regulation and submit it to the European Parliament and to the Council. For greater transparency, the report should be made public.

(33) The European Parliament should have the possibility to invite the Commission to a meeting of its committee responsible to present and explain systemic issues related to the implementation of this Regulation.

(34) By 12 October 2023 and every five years thereafter, the Commission should evaluate the functioning and effectiveness of this Regulation and present a report to the European Parliament and to the Council. That report should include an assessment of whether or not this Regulation requires an amendment. Where the report proposes amending this Regulation, it may be accompanied by a legislative proposal.

(35) The implementation of this Regulation by the Union and the Member States should comply with the relevant requirements for the imposition of restrictive measures on grounds of security and public order in the WTO agreements, including, in particular, Article XIV(a) and Article XIV bis of the General Agreement on Trade in Services ([12]) (GATS). It should also comply with Union law and be consistent with commitments made under other trade and investment agreements to which the Union or Member States are parties and trade and investment arrangements to which the Union or Member States are adherents.

(36) When a foreign direct investment constitutes a concentration falling within the scope of Council Regulation (EC) No 139/2004 ([13]), the application of this Regulation should be without prejudice to the application of Article 21(4) of Regulation (EC) No 139/2004. This Regulation and Article 21(4) of Regulation (EC) No 139/2004 should be applied in a consistent manner. To the extent that the respective scope of application of those two regulations overlap, the grounds for screening set out in Article 1 of this Regulation and the notion of legitimate interests within the meaning of the third paragraph of Article 21(4) of Regulation (EC) No 139/2004 should be interpreted in a coherent manner, without prejudice to the assessment of the compatibility of the national measures aimed at protecting those interests with the general principles and other provisions of Union law.

11. Regulation (EU) 2018/1725 of the European Parliament and of the Council of 23 October 2018 on the protection of natural persons with regard to the processing of personal data by the Union institutions, bodies, offices and agencies and on the free movement of such data, and repealing Regulation (EC) No 45/2001 and Decision No 1247/2002/EC (OJ L 295, 21.11.2018, p. 39).
12. OJ L 336, 23.12.1994, p. 191.
13. Council Regulation (EC) No 139/2004 of 20 January 2004 on the control of concentrations between undertakings (OJ L 24, 29.1.2004, p. 1).

(37) This Regulation does not affect Union rules for the prudential assessment of acquisitions of qualifying holdings in the financial sector, which is a distinct procedure with a specific objective ([14]).

(38) This Regulation is consistent with and without prejudice to other notification and screening procedures set out in sectoral Union law,

HAVE ADOPTED THIS REGULATION:

Article 1

Subject matter and scope

1. This Regulation establishes a framework for the screening by Member States of foreign direct investments into the Union on the grounds of security or public order and for a mechanism for cooperation between Member States, and between Member States and the Commission, with regard to foreign direct investments likely to affect security or public order. It includes the possibility for the Commission to issue opinions on such investments.
2. This Regulation is without prejudice to each Member State having sole responsibility for its national security, as provided for in Article 4(2) TEU, and to the right of each Member State to protect its essential security interests in accordance with Article 346 TFEU.
3. Nothing in this Regulation shall limit the right of each Member State to decide whether or not to screen a particular foreign direct investment within the framework of this Regulation.

Article 2

Definitions

For the purposes of this Regulation, the following definitions apply:

(1) 'foreign direct investment' means an investment of any kind by a foreign investor aiming to establish or to maintain lasting and direct links between the foreign investor and the entrepreneur to whom or the undertaking to which the capital is made available in order to carry on an economic activity in a Member State, including investments which enable effective participation

14. As introduced by Directive 2013/36/EU of the European Parliament and of the Council of 26 June 2013 on access to the activity of credit institutions and the prudential supervision of credit institutions and investment firms, amending Directive 2002/87/EC and repealing Directives 2006/48/EC and 2006/49/EC (OJ L 176, 27.6.2013, p. 338); Directive 2009/138/EC of the European Parliament and of the Council of 25 November 2009 on the taking-up and pursuit of the business of Insurance and Reinsurance (Solvency II) (OJ L 335, 17.12.2009, p. 1); Directive 2014/65/EU of the European Parliament and of the Council of 15 May 2014 on markets in financial instruments and amending Directive 2002/92/EC and Directive 2011/61/EU (OJ L 173, 12.6.2014, p. 349).

in the management or control of a company carrying out an economic activity;

(2) 'foreign investor' means a natural person of a third country or an undertaking of a third country, intending to make or having made a foreign direct investment;

(3) 'screening' means a procedure allowing to assess, investigate, authorise, condition, prohibit or unwind foreign direct investments;

(4) 'screening mechanism' means an instrument of general application, such as a law or regulation, and accompanying administrative requirements, implementing rules or guidelines, setting out the terms, conditions and procedures to assess, investigate, authorise, condition, prohibit or unwind foreign direct investments on grounds of security or public order;

(5) 'foreign direct investment undergoing screening' means a foreign direct investment undergoing a formal assessment or investigation pursuant to a screening mechanism;

(6) 'screening decision' means a measure adopted in application of a screening mechanism;

(7) 'undertaking of a third country' means an undertaking constituted or otherwise organised under the laws of a third country.

Article 3

Screening mechanisms of Member States

1. In accordance with this Regulation, Member States may maintain, amend or adopt mechanisms to screen foreign direct investments in their territory on the grounds of security or public order.
2. Rules and procedures related to screening mechanisms, including relevant timeframes, shall be transparent and not discriminate between third countries. In particular, Member States shall set out the circumstances triggering the screening, the grounds for screening and the applicable detailed procedural rules.
3. Member States shall apply timeframes under their screening mechanisms. The screening mechanisms shall allow Member States to take into account the comments of other Member States referred to in Article 6 and 7 and the opinions of the Commission referred to in Articles 6, 7 and 8.
4. Confidential information, including commercially-sensitive information, made available to the Member State undertaking the screening shall be protected.
5. Foreign investors and the undertakings concerned shall have the possibility to seek recourse against screening decisions of the national authorities.
6. Member States which have a screening mechanism in place shall maintain, amend or adopt measures necessary to identify and prevent circumvention of the screening mechanisms and screening decisions.
7. Member States shall notify the Commission of their existing screening mechanisms by 10 May 2019. Member States shall notify the Commission of any

newly adopted screening mechanism or any amendment to an existing screening mechanism within 30 days of the entry into force of the newly adopted screening mechanism or of any amendment to an existing screening mechanism.

8. No later than three months after having received the notifications referred to in paragraph 7, the Commission shall make publicly available a list of Member States' screening mechanisms. The Commission shall keep that list up to date.

Article 4

Factors that may be taken into consideration by Member States or the Commission

1. In determining whether a foreign direct investment is likely to affect security or public order, Member States and the Commission may consider its potential effects on, inter alia:
   (a) critical infrastructure, whether physical or virtual, including energy, transport, water, health, communications, media, data processing or storage, aerospace, defence, electoral or financial infrastructure, and sensitive facilities, as well as land and real estate crucial for the use of such infrastructure;
   (b) critical technologies and dual use items as defined in point 1 of Article 2 of Council Regulation (EC) No 428/2009 ([15]), including artificial intelligence, robotics, semiconductors, cybersecurity, aerospace, defence, energy storage, quantum and nuclear technologies as well as nanotechnologies and biotechnologies;
   (c) supply of critical inputs, including energy or raw materials, as well as food security;
   (d) access to sensitive information, including personal data, or the ability to control such information; or
   (e) the freedom and pluralism of the media.
2. In determining whether a foreign direct investment is likely to affect security or public order, Member States and the Commission may also take into account, in particular:
   (a) whether the foreign investor is directly or indirectly controlled by the government, including state bodies or armed forces, of a third country, including through ownership structure or significant funding;
   (b) whether the foreign investor has already been involved in activities affecting security or public order in a Member State; or
   (c) whether there is a serious risk that the foreign investor engages in illegal or criminal activities.

15. Council Regulation (EC) No 428/2009 of 5 May 2009 setting up a Community regime for the control of exports, transfer, brokering and transit of dual-use items (OJ L 134, 29.5.2009, p. 1).

Article 5

Annual reporting

1. By 31 March of each year, Member States shall submit to the Commission an annual report covering the preceding calendar year, which shall include aggregated information on foreign direct investments that took place in their territory, on the basis of information available to them, as well as aggregated information on the requests received from other Member States pursuant to Articles 6(6) and 7(5).
2. For each reporting period, Member States that maintain screening mechanisms shall, in addition to the information referred to in paragraph 1, provide aggregated information on the application of their screening mechanisms.
3. The Commission shall provide an annual report on the implementation of this Regulation to the European Parliament and to the Council. That report shall be made public.
4. The European Parliament may invite the Commission to a meeting of its committee responsible to present and explain systemic issues related to the implementation of this Regulation.

Article 6

Cooperation mechanism in relation to foreign direct investments undergoing screening

1. Member States shall notify the Commission and the other Member States of any foreign direct investment in their territory that is undergoing screening by providing the information referred to in Article 9(2) of this Regulation as soon as possible. The notification may include a list of Member States whose security or public order is deemed likely to be affected. As part of the notification, and where applicable, the Member State undertaking the screening shall endeavour to indicate whether it considers that the foreign direct investment undergoing screening is likely to fall within the scope of Regulation (EC) No 139/2004.
2. Where a Member State considers that a foreign direct investment undergoing screening in another Member State is likely to affect its security or public order, or has information relevant for such screening, it may provide comments to the Member State undertaking the screening. The Member State providing comments shall send those comments to the Commission simultaneously.

   The Commission shall notify the other Member States that comments were provided.
3. Where the Commission considers that a foreign direct investment undergoing screening is likely to affect security or public order in more than one Member State, or has relevant information in relation to that foreign direct investment, it may issue an opinion addressed to the Member State undertaking the

screening. The Commission may issue an opinion irrespective of whether other Member States have provided comments. The Commission may issue an opinion following comments from other Member States. The Commission shall issue such opinion where justified, after at least one third of Member States consider that a foreign direct investment is likely to affect their security or public order.

The Commission shall notify the other Member States that an opinion was issued.

4. A Member State which duly considers that a foreign direct investment in its territory is likely to affect its security or public order may request the Commission to issue an opinion or other Member States to provide comments.
5. The comments referred to in paragraph 2 and the opinions referred to in paragraph 3 shall be duly justified.
6. No later than 15 calendar days following the receipt of the information referred to in paragraph 1, other Member States and the Commission shall notify the Member State undertaking the screening of their intention to provide comments pursuant to paragraph 2 or an opinion pursuant to paragraph 3. The notification may include a request for additional information to the information referred to in paragraph 1.

   Any request for additional information shall be duly justified, limited to information necessary to provide comments pursuant to paragraph 2 or to issue an opinion pursuant to paragraph 3, proportionate to the purpose of the request and not unduly burdensome for the Member State undertaking the screening. Requests for information and replies provided by Member States shall be sent to the Commission simultaneously.
7. Comments referred to in paragraph 2 or opinions referred to in paragraph 3 shall be addressed to the Member State undertaking the screening and shall be sent to it within a reasonable period of time, and in any case no later than 35 calendar days following receipt of the information referred to in paragraph 1.

   Notwithstanding the first subparagraph, if additional information was requested pursuant to paragraph 6, such comments or opinions shall be issued no later than 20 calendar days following receipt of the additional information or the notification pursuant to Article 9(5).

   Notwithstanding paragraph 6, the Commission may issue an opinion following comments from other Member States where possible within the deadlines referred to in this paragraph, and in any case no later than five calendar days after those deadlines have expired.
8. In the exceptional case where the Member State undertaking the screening considers that its security or public order requires immediate action, it shall notify the other Member States and the Commission of its intention to issue a screening decision before the timeframes referred to in paragraph 7 and duly justify the need for immediate action. The other Member States and the Commission shall endeavour to provide comments or to issue an opinion expeditiously.

9. The Member State undertaking the screening shall give due consideration to the comments of the other Member States referred to in paragraph 2 and to the opinion of the Commission referred to in paragraph 3. The final screening decision shall be taken by the Member State undertaking the screening.
10. Cooperation pursuant to this Article shall take place through the contact points established in accordance with Article 11.

Article 7

Cooperation mechanism in relation to foreign direct investments not undergoing screening

1. Where a Member State considers that a foreign direct investment planned or completed in another Member State which is not undergoing screening in that Member State is likely to affect its security or public order, or has relevant information in relation to that foreign direct investment, it may provide comments to that other Member State. The Member State providing comments shall send those comments to the Commission simultaneously.

   The Commission shall notify the other Member States that comments were provided.
2. Where the Commission considers that a foreign direct investment planned or completed in a Member State which is not undergoing screening in that Member State is likely to affect security or public order in more than one Member State, or has relevant information in relation to that foreign direct investment, it may issue an opinion addressed to the Member State in which the foreign direct investment is planned or has been completed. The Commission may issue an opinion irrespective of whether other Member States have provided comments. The Commission may issue an opinion following comments from other Member States. The Commission shall issue such opinion where justified, after at least one third of Member States consider that a foreign direct investment is likely to affect their security or public order.

   The Commission shall notify the other Member States that an opinion was issued.
3. A Member State which duly considers that a foreign direct investment in its territory is likely to affect its security or public order may request the Commission to issue an opinion, or other Member States to provide comments.
4. The comments referred to in paragraph 1 and the opinions referred to in paragraph 2 shall be duly justified.
5. Where a Member State or the Commission considers that a foreign direct investment which is not undergoing screening is likely to affect security or public order as referred to in paragraph 1 or 2, it may request from the Member State where the foreign direct investment is planned or has been completed the information referred to in Article 9.

Any request for information shall be duly justified, limited to information necessary to provide comments pursuant to paragraph 1, or to issue an opinion pursuant to paragraph 2, proportionate to the purpose of the request and not unduly burdensome for the Member State where the foreign direct investment is planned or has been completed.

Requests for information and replies provided by Member States shall be sent to the Commission simultaneously.

6. Comments pursuant to paragraph 1 or opinions pursuant to paragraph 2 shall be addressed to the Member State where the foreign direct investment is planned or has been completed and shall be sent to it within a reasonable period of time, and in any case no later than 35 calendar days following receipt of the information referred to in paragraph 5 or of the notification pursuant to Article 9(5). In cases where the opinion of the Commission follows comments from other Member States, the Commission shall have 15 additional calendar days for issuing that opinion.
7. A Member State where a foreign direct investment is planned or has been completed shall give due consideration to the comments of the other Member States and to the opinion of the Commission.
8. Member States may provide comments pursuant to paragraph 1 and the Commission may provide an opinion pursuant to paragraph 2 no later than 15 months after the foreign direct investment has been completed.
9. Cooperation pursuant to this Article shall take place through the contact points established in accordance with Article 11.
10. This Article shall not apply to foreign direct investments completed before 10 April 2019.

Article 8

Foreign direct investments likely to affect projects or programmes of Union interest

1. Where the Commission considers that a foreign direct investment is likely to affect projects or programmes of Union interest on grounds of security or public order, the Commission may issue an opinion addressed to the Member State where the foreign direct investment is planned or has been completed.
2. The procedures set out in Articles 6 and 7 shall apply *mutatis mutandis*, subject to the following modifications:
   (a) as part of the notification referred to in Article 6(1) or the comments referred to in Articles 6(2) and 7(1), a Member State may indicate whether it considers that a foreign direct investment is likely to affect projects and programmes of Union interest;
   (b) the opinion of the Commission shall be sent to the other Member States;
   (c) the Member State where the foreign direct investment is planned or has been completed shall take utmost account of the Commission's opinion and provide an explanation to the Commission if its opinion is not followed.

3. For the purpose of this Article, projects or programmes of Union interest shall include those projects and programmes which involve a substantial amount or a significant share of Union funding, or which are covered by Union law regarding critical infrastructure, critical technologies or critical inputs which are essential for security or public order. The list of projects or programmes of Union interest is set out in the Annex.
4. The Commission shall adopt delegated acts in accordance with Article 16 to amend the list of projects and programmes of Union interest.

Article 9

Information requirements

1. Member States shall ensure that the information notified pursuant to Article 6(1) or requested by the Commission and other Member States pursuant to Articles 6(6) and 7(5) is made available to the Commission and the requesting Member States without undue delay.
2. The information referred to in paragraph 1 shall include:
   (a) the ownership structure of the foreign investor and of the undertaking in which the foreign direct investment is planned or has been completed, including information on the ultimate investor and participation in the capital;
   (b) the approximate value of the foreign direct investment;
   (c) the products, services and business operations of the foreign investor and of the undertaking in which the foreign direct investment is planned or has been completed;
   (d) the Member States in which the foreign investor and the undertaking in which the foreign direct investment is planned or has been completed conduct relevant business operations;
   (e) the funding of the investment and its source, on the basis of the best information available to the Member State;
   (f) the date when the foreign direct investment is planned to be completed or has been completed.
3. Member States shall endeavour to provide any information additional to that referred to in paragraphs 1 and 2, if available, to requesting Member States and to the Commission without undue delay.
4. The Member State where the foreign direct investment is planned or has been completed may request the foreign investor or the undertaking in which the foreign direct investment is planned or has been completed to provide the information referred to in paragraph 2. The foreign investor or the undertaking concerned shall provide the information requested without undue delay.
5. A Member State shall notify the Commission and the other Member States concerned without delay, if, in exceptional circumstances, it is unable, despite its best efforts, to obtain the information referred to in paragraph 1. In the notification, that Member State shall duly justify the reasons for not providing

such information and explain the best efforts undertaken to obtain the information requested, including a request pursuant to paragraph 4.

If no information is provided, any comment issued by another Member State or any opinion issued by the Commission may be based on the information available to them.

Article 10

Confidentiality of information transmitted

1. Information received as a result of the application of this Regulation shall be used only for the purpose for which it was requested.
2. Member States and the Commission shall ensure the protection of confidential information acquired in application of this Regulation in accordance with Union and the respective national law.
3. Member States and the Commission shall ensure that classified information provided or exchanged under this Regulation is not downgraded or declassified without the prior written consent of the originator.

Article 11

Contact points

1. Each Member State and the Commission shall establish a contact point for the implementation of this Regulation. Member States and the Commission shall involve those contact points on all issues relating to the implementation of this Regulation.
2. A secure and encrypted system shall be provided by the Commission to support direct cooperation and exchange of information between the contact points.

Article 12

Group of experts on the screening of foreign direct investments into the European Union

The group of experts on the screening of foreign direct investments into the European Union providing advice and expertise to the Commission shall continue to discuss issues relating to the screening of foreign direct investments, share best practices and lessons learned, and exchange views on trends and issues of common concern relating to foreign direct investments. The Commission shall also consider seeking the advice of that group on systemic issues relating to the implementation of this Regulation.

The discussions in that group shall be kept confidential.

Article 13

International Cooperation

Member States and the Commission may cooperate with the responsible authorities of third countries on issues relating to the screening of foreign direct investments on grounds of security and public order.

Article 14

Processing of personal data

1. Any processing of personal data pursuant to this Regulation shall be carried out in accordance with Regulation (EU) 2016/679 and Regulation (EU) 2018/1725 and only in so far as it is necessary for the screening of foreign direct investments by Member States and for ensuring the effectiveness of the cooperation provided for in this Regulation.
2. Personal data related to the implementation of this Regulation shall be kept only for the time necessary to achieve the purposes for which they were collected.

Article 15

Evaluation

1. By 12 October 2023 and every five years thereafter, the Commission shall evaluate the functioning and effectiveness of this Regulation and present a report to the European Parliament and to the Council. Member States shall be involved in this exercise and if necessary provide the Commission with additional information for the preparation of that report.
2. Where the report recommends amendments to this Regulation, it may be accompanied by an appropriate legislative proposal.

Article 16

Exercise of the delegation

1. The power to adopt delegated acts is conferred on the Commission subject to the conditions laid down in this Article.
2. The power to adopt delegated acts referred to in Article 8(4) shall be conferred on the Commission for an indeterminate period of time from 10 April 2019.
3. The delegation of power referred to in Article 8(4) may be revoked at any time by the European Parliament or by the Council. A decision to revoke shall put an end to the delegation of the power specified in that decision. It shall take effect the day following the publication of the decision in the *Official Journal of the European Union* or at a later date specified therein. It shall not affect the validity of any delegated acts already in force.

4. Before adopting a delegated act, the Commission shall consult experts designated by each Member State in accordance with the principles laid down in the Interinstitutional Agreement of 13 April 2016 on Better Law-Making.
5. As soon as it adopts a delegated act, the Commission shall notify it simultaneously to the European Parliament and to the Council.
6. A delegated act adopted pursuant to Article 8(4) shall enter into force only if no objection has been expressed either by the European Parliament or the Council within a period of two months of notification of that act to the European Parliament and the Council or if, before the expiry of that period, the European Parliament and the Council have both informed the Commission that they will not object. That period shall be extended by two months at the initiative of the European Parliament or of the Council.

Article 17

Entry into force

This Regulation shall enter into force on the twentieth day following that of its publication in the *Official Journal of the European Union*.

This Regulation shall apply from 11 October 2020.

This Regulation shall be binding in its entirety and directly applicable in all Member States.

Done at Brussels, 19 March 2019.

For the European Parliament
The President
A. TAJANI
For the Council
The President
G. CIAMBA

ANNEX

List of projects or programmes of Union interest referred to in Article 8(3)

1. European GNSS programmes (Galileo & EGNOS):

Regulation (EU) No 1285/2013 of the European Parliament and of the Council of 11 December 2013 on the implementation and exploitation of the European satellite navigation systems and repealing the Council Regulation (EC) No 876/2002 and Regulation (EC) No 683/2008 of the European Parliament and of the Council (OJ L 347, 20.12.2013, p. 1).

2. Copernicus:

Regulation (EU) No 377/2014 of the European Parliament and of the Council of 3 April 2014 establishing the Copernicus Programme and repealing Regulation (EU) No 911/2010 (OJ L 122, 24.4.2014, p. 44).

3. Horizon 2020:

Regulation (EU) No 1291/2013 of the European Parliament and of the Council of 11 December 2013 establishing Horizon 2020 – the Framework Programme for Research and Innovation (2014-2020) and repealing Decision No 1982/2006/EC (OJ L 347, 20.12.2013, p. 104), including actions therein relating to Key Enabling Technologies such as artificial intelligence, robotics, semiconductors and cybersecurity.

4. Trans-European Networks for Transport (TEN-T):

Regulation (EU) No 1315/2013 of the European Parliament and of the Council of 11 December 2013 on Union guidelines for the development of the trans-European transport network and repealing Decision No 661/2010/EU (OJ L 348, 20.12.2013, p. 1).

5. Trans-European Networks for Energy (TEN-E):

Regulation (EU) No 347/2013 of the European Parliament and of the Council of 17 April 2013 on guidelines for trans-European energy infrastructure and repealing Decision No 1364/2006/EC and amending Regulations (EC) No 713/2009, (EC) No 714/2009 and (EC) No 715/2009 (OJ L 115, 25.4.2013, p. 39).

6. Trans-European Networks for Telecommunications:

Regulation (EU) No 283/2014 of the European Parliament and of the Council of 11 March 2014 on guidelines for trans-European networks in the area of telecommunications infrastructure and repealing Decision No 1336/97/EC (OJ L 86, 21.3.2014, p. 14).

7. European Defence Industrial Development Programme:

Regulation (EU) 2018/1092 of the European Parliament and of the Council of 18 July 2018 establishing the European Defence Industrial Development Programme aiming at supporting the competitiveness and innovation capacity of the Union's defence industry (OJ L 200, 7.8.2018, p. 30).

8. Permanent structured cooperation (PESCO):

Council Decision (CFSP) 2018/340 of 6 March 2018 establishing the list of projects to be developed under PESCO (OJ L 65, 8.3.2018, p. 24).

Commission statement

Following the request of the European Parliament, the European Commission undertakes to:

- share with the European Parliament the standardised forms which the European Commission will prepare to facilitate compliance of Member States with the annual reporting obligations under Article 5 of the Regulation once they are finalised, and
- share with the European Parliament such standardised forms each year, in parallel to presenting the annual report to the European Parliament and to the Council, in accordance with Article 5(3) of the Regulation.

Index

EUROPEAN MONOGRAPH SERIES

1. Lammy Betten (ed.), *The Future of European Social Policy,* 1991 (ISBN 90-654-4585-4).
2. Annemarie Loman, Kamiel Mortelmans, Harry H.G. Post & Stewart Watson, *Culture and Common Law: Before and After Maastricht,* 1992 (ISBN 90-654-4638-9).
3. John A.E. Vervaele, *Fraud against the Community: The Need for European Fraud Legislation,* 1994 (ISBN 90-654-4634-6).
4. Philip Raworth, *The Legislative Process in the European Community,* 1993 (ISBN 90-654-4690-7).
5. Jules Stuyck, *Financial and Monetary Integration in the European Economic Community,* 1993 (ISBN 90-654-4718-0).
6. Jules Stuyck & A.J. Vossestein (eds), *State Entrepreneurship, National Monopolies and European Community Law,* 1993 (ISBN 90-654-4773-3).
7. Jules Stuyck & A. Looijestijn-Clearie (eds), *The European Economic Area EC-EFTA,* 1994 (ISBN 90-654-4815-2).
8. Rosita B. Bouterse, *Competition and Integration: What Goals Count?,* 1995 (ISBN 90-654-4816-0).
9. René Barents, *The Agricultural Law of the EC: An Inquiry into the Administrative Law,* 1994 (ISBN 90-654-4867-5).
10. Nicholas Emiliou, *Principles of Proportionality in European Law: A Comparative Study,* 1996 (ISBN 90-411-0866-1).
11. Eivind Smith, *National Parliaments as Cornerstones of European Integration,* 1996 (ISBN 90-411-0898-X).
12. Jan H. Jans, *European Environmental Law,* 1996 (ISBN 90-411-0877-7).
13. Síofra O'Leary, *The Evolving Concept of Community Citizenship: From the Free Movement of Persons to Union Citizenship,* 1997 (ISBN 90-411-0878-5).
14. Laurence W. Gormley (ed.), *Current and Future Perspectives on EC Competition Law,* 1983 (ISBN 90-411-0691-X).
15. Simone White, *Protection of the Financial Interests of the European Communities: The Fight against Fraud and Corruption,* 1998 (ISBN 90-411-9647-1).
16. Morten P. Broberg, *Broberg on the European Commission's Jurisdiction to Scrutinise Mergers,* 4th Edition, 2013 (ISBN 978-90-411-3339-7).
17. Doris Hildebrand, *The Role of Economic Analysis in the EC Competition Rules: The European School,* 2nd Edition, 2002 (ISBN 90-411-1706-7).
18. Christof R.A. Swaak, *European Community Law and the Automobile Industry,* 1999 (ISBN 90-411-1140-9).

19. Dorthe Dahlgaard Dingel, *Public Procurement: A Harmonization of the National Judicial Review of the Application of European Community Law,* 1999 (ISBN 90-411-1161-1).
20. John A.E. Vervaele (ed.), *Compliance and Enforcement of European Community Law,* 1999 (ISBN 90-411-1151-4).
21. Martin Trybus, *European Defence Procurement Law: International and National Procurement Systems as Models for a Liberalized Defence Procurement Market in Europe,* 1999 (ISBN 90-411-1167-0).
22. Helen Staples, *The Legal Status of Third Country Nationals Resident in the European Union,* 1999 (ISBN 90-411-1277-4).
23. Damien Geradin (ed.), *The Liberalization of State Monopolies in the European Union and Beyond,* 1999 (ISBN 90-411-1264-2).
24. Katja Heede, *European Ombudsman: Redress and Control at Union Level,* 2000 (ISBN 90-411-1413-0).
25. Ulf Bernitz & Joakim Nergelius (eds), *General Principles of European Community Law,* 2000 (ISBN 90-411-1402-5).
26. Michaela Drahos, *Convergence of Competition Laws and Policies in the European Community,* 2002 (ISBN 90-411-1562-5).
27. Damien Geradin (ed.), *The Liberalization of Electricity and Natural Gas in the European Union,* 2001 (ISBN 90-411-1560-9).
28. Gisella Gori, *Towards an EU Right to Education,* 2001 (ISBN 90-411-1670-2).
29. Brendan P.G. Smith, *Constitution Building in the European Union,* 2001 (ISBN 90-411-1695-8).
30. Friedl Weiss & Frank Wooldridge, *Free Movement of Persons within the European Community,* 2nd Edition, 2007 (ISBN 978-90-411-2545-3).
31. Ingrid Boccardi, *Europe and Refugees: Towards an EU Asylum Policy,* 2002 (ISBN 90-411-1709-1).
32. John A.E. Vervaele & André Klip (eds), *European Cooperation Between Tax, Customs and Judicial Authorities,* 2001 (ISBN 90-411-1747-4).
33. Wouter P.J. Wils, *The Optimal Enforcement of EC Antitrust Law: Essays in Law and Economics,* 2002 (ISBN 90-411-1757-1).
34. Damien Geradin (ed.), *The Liberalization of Postal Services in the European Union,* 2002 (ISBN 90-411-1780-6).
35. Nick Bernard, *Multilevel Governance in the European Union,* 2002 (ISBN 90-411-1812-8).
36. Jill Wakefield, *Judicial Protection through the Use of Article 288(2) EC,* 2002 (ISBN 90-411-1823-3).
37. Sebastiaan Princen, *EU Regulation and Transatlantic Trade,* 2002 (ISBN 90-411-1871-3).
38. Amaryllis Verhoeven, *The European Union in Search of a Democratic and Constitutional Theory,* 2002 (ISBN 90-411-1872-1).
39. Paul L.C. Torremans, *Cross Border Insolvencies in EU, English and Belgian Law,* 2002 (ISBN 90-411-1888-8).

40. Malcolm Anderson & Joanna Apap (eds), *Police and Justice Cooperation and the New European Borders,* 2002 (ISBN 90-411-1893-4).
41. Christin M. Forstinger, *Takeover Law in EU and USA: A Comparative Analysis,* 2002 (ISBN 90-411-1919-1).
42. Antonio Bavasso, *Communications in EU Antitrust Law: Market Power and Public Interest,* 2003 (ISBN 90-411-1974-4).
43. Fiona G. Wishlade, *Regional State Aid and Competition Policy in the European Union,* 2003 (ISBN 90-411-1975-2).
44. Gareth Davies, *Nationality Discrimination in the European Internal Market,* 2003 (ISBN 90-411-1998-1).
45. René Barents, *The Autonomy of Community Law,* 2003 (ISBN 90-411-2251-6).
46. Gerhard Dannecker & Oswald Jansen (eds), *Competition Law Sanctioning in the European Union,* 2004 (ISBN 90-411-2100-5).
47. Nauta Dutilh (ed.), *Dealing with Dominance: The Experience of National Competition Authorities,* 2004 (ISBN 90-411-2211-7).
48. Stefaan van den Bogaert, *Practical Regulation of the Mobility of Sportsmen in the EU Post Bosman,* 2005 (ISBN 90-411-2327-X).
49. Katalin Judit Cseres, *Competition Law and Consumer Protection,* 2005 (ISBN 90-411-2380-6).
50. Philipp Kiiver, *The National Parliaments in the European Union: A Critical View on EU Constitution Building,* 2006 (ISBN 978-90-411-2452-4).
51. Alexander Turk, *The Concept of Legislation in European Community Law,* 2006 (ISBN 978-90-411-2472-2).
52. Dimitrios Sinaniotis, *The Interim Protection of Individuals before the European and National Courts,* 2006 (ISBN 978-90-411-2498-2).
53. M. Holoubek & D. Damjanovic, M. Traimer (eds), *Regulating Content: The European Regulatory Framework for the Media and Related Creative Sectors,* 2006 (ISBN 978-90-411-2597-2).
54. Anneli Albi & Jacques Ziller (eds), *The European Constitution and National Constitutions: Ratification and Beyond,* 2006 (ISBN 978-90-411-2524-8).
55. Gustavo E. Luengo, *Regulation of Subsidies and State Aids in WTO and EC Law: Conflicts in International Trade Law,* 2007 (ISBN 978-90-411-2547-7).
56. Eniko Horvath, *Mandating Identity: Citizenship, Kinship Laws and Plural Nationality in the European Union,* 2007 (ISBN 978-90-411-2662-7).
57. Rass Holdgaard, *External Relations Law of the European Community: Legal Reasoning and Legal Discourses,* 2007 (ISBN 978-90-411-2604-7).
58. Jill Wakefield, *The Right to Good Administration,* 2007 (ISBN 978-90-411-2697-9).
59. Dimitry Kochenov, *EU Enlargement and the Failure of Conditionality: Pre- accession Conditionality in the Fields of Democracy and the Rule of Law,* 2008 (ISBN 978-90-411-2696-2).
60. Despina Mavromati, *The Law of Payment Services in the EU: The EC Directive on Payment Services in the Internal Market,* 2008 (ISBN 978-90-411-2700-6).

61. Anne Meuwese, *Impact Assessment in EU Lawmaking,* 2008 (ISBN 978-90-411-2720-4).
62. Ulf Bernitz, Joakim Nergelius & Cecilia Cardner (eds), *General Principles of EC Law in a Process of Development,* 2008 (ISBN 978-90-411-2705-1).
63. Johan van de Gronden (ed.), *The EU and WTO Law on Services: Limits to the Realisation of General Interest Policies within the Services Markets?,* 2008 (ISBN 978-90-411-2809-6).
64. Alina Tryfonidou, *Reverse Discrimination in EC Law,* 2009 (ISBN 978-90-411-2751-8).
65. Mikael Berglund, *Cross-Border Enforcement of Claims in the EU: History Present Time and Future,* 2014 (ISBN 978-90-411-4564-2).
66. Theodore Konstadinides, *Division of Powers in European Union Law: The Delimitation of Internal Competence between the EU and the Member States,* 2009 (ISBN 978-90-411-2615-3).
67. Mattias Derlén, *Multilingual Interpretation of European Union Law,* 2009 (ISBN 978-90-411-2853-9).
68. René Barents, *Directory of EU Case Law on the Preliminary Ruling Procedure,* 2009 (ISBN 978-90-411-3150-8).
69. Yan Luo, *Anti-dumping in the WTO, the EU and China: The Rise of Legalization in the Trade Regime and Its Consequences,* 2010 (ISBN 978-90-411-3207-9).
70. Patrick Birkinshaw & Mike Varney (eds), *The European Union Legal Order after Lisbon,* 2010 (ISBN 978-90-411-3152-2).
71. Thomas Gr. Papadopoulos, *EU Law and Harmonization of Takeovers in the Internal Market,* 2010 (ISBN 978-90-411-3340-3).
72. Bas van Bockel, *The* Ne Bis In Idem *Principle in EU Law,* 2010 (ISBN 978-90-411-3156-0).
73. Veljko Milutinović, *The 'Right to Damages' under EU Competition Law: From* Courage v. Crehan *to the White Paper and Beyond,* 2010 (ISBN 978-90-411-3235-2).
74. Amandine Garde, *EU Law and Obesity Prevention,* 2010 (ISBN 978-90-411-2706-8).
75. Leonard Besselink, Frans Pennings & Sacha Prechal (eds), *The Eclipse of the Legality Principle in the European Union,* 2011 (ISBN 978-90-411-3262-8).
76. Sacha Garben, *EU Higher Education Law: The Bologna Process and Harmonization by Stealth,* 2011 (ISBN 978-90-411-3365-6).
77. Dimitry Kochenov (ed.), *EU Law of the Overseas: Outermost Regions, Associated Overseas Countries and Territories, Territories Sui Generis,* 2011 (ISBN 978-90-411-3445-5).
78. Pablo Ibáñez Colomo, *European Communications Law and Technological Convergence: Deregulation, Re-regulation and Regulatory Convergence in Television and Telecommunications,* 2012 (ISBN 978-90-411-3829-3).
79. Elise Muir, *EU Regulation of Access to Labour Markets: A Case Study of EU Constraints on Member State Competences,* 2012 (ISBN 978-90-411-3823-1).
80. Tim Corthaut, *EU Ordre Public,* 2012 (ISBN 978-90-411-3232-1).

81. Oana Ştefan, *Soft Law in Court: Competition Law, State Aid and the Court of Justice of the European Union*, 2013 (ISBN 978-90-411-3997-9).
82. Francesco Rossi dal Pozzo, *Citizenship Rights and Freedom of Movement in the European Union*, 2013 (ISBN 978-90-411-4660-1).
83. Jens Hartig Danielsen, *EU Agricultural Law*, 2013 (ISBN 978-90-411-3280-2).
84. Ulf Bernitz, Xavier Groussot & Felix Schulyok (eds), *General Principles of EU Law and European Private Law*, 2013 (ISBN 978-90-411-4683-0).
85. Michelle Everson, Cosimo Monda & Ellen Vos (eds), *European Agencies in between Institutions and Member States*, 2014 (ISBN 978-90-411-2843-0).
86. Stefan Leible & Matthias Lehmann (eds), *European Contract Law and German Law*, 2014 (ISBN 978-90-411-2588-0).
87. Piero Leanza & Ondrej Pridal, *The Right to a Fair Trial: Article 6 of the European Convention on Human Rights*, 2014 (ISBN 978-90-411-4855-1).
88. Patrick J. Birkinshaw, *European Public Law: The Achievement and the Challenge*, 2014 (ISBN 978-90-411-4744-8).
89. George Cumming, *Expert Evidence Deficiencies in the Judgments of the Courts of the European Union and the European Court of Human Rights*, 2014 (ISBN 978-90-411-4123-1).
90. Vesna Rijavec, Tomaž Keresteš & Tjaša Ivanc (eds), *Simplification of Debt Collection in the EU*, 2014 (ISBN 978-90-411-4854-4).
91. Nina Półtorak, *European Union Rights in National Courts*, 2015 (ISBN 978-90-411-5863-5).
92. Kyriaki-Korina Raptopoulou, *EU Law and Healthcare Services: Normative Approaches to Public Health Systems*, 2015 (ISBN 978-90-411-5013-4).
93. Torsten Frank Koschinka & Piero Leanza, *Preliminary Injunctions: Germany, England/Wales, Italy and France*, 2015 (ISBN 978-90-411-5833-8).
94. Vesna Rijavec, Tomaž Keresteš & Tjaša Ivanc (eds), *Dimensions of Evidence in European Civil Procedure*, 2016 (ISBN 978-90-411-6662-3).
95. Stefan Leible (ed.), *General Principles of European Private International Law*, 2016 (ISBN 978-90-411-5955-7).
96. Patrick J. Birkinshaw & Andrea Biondi (eds), *Britain Alone!: The Implications and Consequences of United Kingdom Exit from the EU*, 2016 (ISBN 978-90-411-5832-1).
97. René Barents, *Remedies and Procedures before the EU Courts*, 2016 (ISBN 978-90-411-6614-2).
98. Luca Prete, *Infringement Proceedings in EU Law*, 2017 (ISBN 978-90-411-6900-6).
99. Robert van den Hoven van Genderen, *Privacy Limitation Clauses: Trojan Horses under the Disguise of Democracy*, 2017 (ISBN 978-90-411-8599-0).
100. Mariusz Krzysztofek, *Post-Reform Personal Data Protection in the European Union: General Data Protection Regulation (EU) 2016/679*, 2017 (ISBN 978-90-411-6237-3).
101. Gianni Lo Schiavo, *The Role of Financial Stability in EU Law and Policy*, 2017 (ISBN 978-90-411-8230-2).

102. Emmanuel Guinchard & Marie-Pierre Granger (eds), *The New EU Judiciary: An Analysis of Current Judicial Reforms*, 2017 (ISBN 978-90-411-6834-4).
103. Kirsten Henckel, *Cross-Border Transfers of Undertakings: A European Perspective,* 2017 (ISBN 978-90-411-9227-1).
104. Vesna Rijavec, Wendy Kennett, Tomaž Keresteš & Tjaša Ivanc, *Remedies Concerning Enforcement of Foreign Judgements: Brussels I Recast,* 2018 (ISBN 978-90-411-9416-9).
105. Albert Sanchez-Graells & Constant De Koninck, *Shaping EU Public Procurement Law: A Critical Analysis of the CJEU Case Law 2015–2017*, 2018 (ISBN 978-94-035-0160-4).
106. Andrea Biondi, Patrick J. Birkinshaw & Maria Kendrick, *Brexit: The Legal Implications*, 2019 (ISBN 978-90-411-9540-1).
107. Mariusz Krzysztofek, *GDPR: General Data Protection Regulation (EU) 2016/679: Post-Reform Personal Data Protection in the European Union*, 2019 (ISBN 978-94-035-0594-7).
108. Giovanni Bassani, *The Legal Framework Applicable to the Single Supervisory Mechanism: Tapestry or Patchwork?,* 2019 (ISBN 978-94-035-0872-6).
109. Piotr Staszczyk, *A Legal Analysis of NGOs and European Civil Society*, 2019 (ISBN 978-94-035-1251-8).
110. Patrizio Messina, *Finance for SMEs: European Regulation and Capital Markets Union – Focus on Securitization and Alternative Finance Tools*, 2019 (ISBN 978-94-035-0161-1).
111. Jacques H.J. Bourgeois (ed.), *EU Framework for Foreign Direct Investment Control,* 2020 (ISBN 978-94-035-1883-1).

www.ingramcontent.com/pod-product-compliance
Ingram Content Group UK Ltd.
Pitfield, Milton Keynes, MK11 3LW, UK
UKHW020257051026
15470UKWH00020B/964

9 789403 518831